I0008586

A LIFE TIME
IN SOUTH AFRICA

BEING THE RECOLLECTIONS OF
THE FIRST PREMIER OF NATAL

BY THE HONOURABLE

SIR JOHN ROBINSON, K.C.M.G.

AUTHOR OF

"GEORGE LINTON," "THE COLONIES AND THE CENTURY," ETC

LONDON

SMITH, ELDER, & CO., 15 WATERLOO PLACE

1900

PREFATORY NOTE

THE pages which follow are not intended in any way
to deal exhaustively with what is known as "The
South African Problem" They claim to be nothing
more than a series of cameos of the past, extending
back over a period of fifty years, and covering the life
and growth of a British Colony from its birth to the
developments of to-day.

It is hoped that these sketches (some of which have
already appeared in the pages of *Cornhill Magazine*)
may serve to show not only how the Empire of Great
Britain has been and is being extended in the wild
places of the earth, but how valid and unassailable is
the title by which that Empire holds its position of
paramountcy in South Africa

J. R

October 1900.

CONTENTS

CHAPTER VII

CHAPTER VIII

CHAPTER IX

CHAPTER X

CHAPTER XI

CHAPTER XII

INTRODUCTORY RETROSPECT

LOOKING back after a half-century's lapse to the years of my boyhood, when as a child of eleven years, and as one of a large family, I first made acquaintance with South Africa, I am keenly conscious of two dominating deprivations—the lack of regular school-training and the absence of youthful companionship. In 1850 there were no proper schools of a higher class in Natal, and lads of my own age and tastes were almost entirely out of reach. Shortly after our arrival it had been my father's hope to send me as a pupil to Capetown, where good schools existed, but want of means—at that time the prevailing colonial disability —blocked the way. I had at once to take my part in the active struggle for subsistence, and for such education as I acquired I had to depend upon my own studies, carried on during leisure moments, under the stimulating direction of cultured parents. It was a desultory and fitful experience, devoid altogether of academical training or order, but I daresay it sufficed to equip me as usefully for the battle of life, as might have done a costly and conventional school course at establishments of world-wide renown. I read at all times, when not otherwise engaged in work or relaxation—for "play" properly so called there were few opportunities. Books were not very plentiful in those days—the modest collection of standard volumes we took out with us included, however, a good many classics, and the original issue of all the Waverley Novels—we had to borrow and to lend; but I read anything I could get hold of—tales, textbooks, histories, manuals. In Maritzburg and in Durban there was a small public library of volumes lent or given by generous contributors, and I levied constant toll upon their shelves Bohn's libraries were a great resource, and to them I was indebted for much of whatever knowledge I picked up In fiction, the green shilling volumes of the Railway Library—forerunner of all the multitudinous tribe of yellow-backs—were a continuous diversion, the mild romances of G. P. R. James being read with an avidity that is now a constant astonishment to me. As years went on, and as cheap reprints multiplied, enterprising storekeepers would now and then receive consignments of those paper-clad publications, and great would be the demand therefor. During many years an English book-dealer, named Lumley, sent out assortments of second-hand books, made up into small parcels, and accompanied by yellow catalogues. These were sold by auction, and the sales, lasting two or three days, were eagerly anticipated events My first appropriation of pocket-

money—carefully saved up through many months—
was represented by a small selection of standard books,
specially imported through a friendly watchmaker,
consisting, so far as I can recollect, of Alison's History
of Europe (5 volumes), Prescott's Histories of Peru
and Mexico, Bancroft's History of the United States,
Shakespeare, Longfellow, Byron, a tale or two, and
some Latin class-books. The case containing these
treasures went down in a sailing-ship which foundered
near the line, and the order had to be repeated; so
nearly eighteen months elapsed before it was actually
executed, and the foundations of my future library
were laid.

Though circumstances made it necessary, even before I entered my teens, that I should be a working
member of the household, it happened that with the
exception of the first nine months, spent rather fruit-
lessly in a commercial office, the whole of my boyhood
and youth was passed in association with my father,
who found in the pursuit of journalism a congenial
field for his talents and energies. In November 1852,
in conjunction with the proprietor of a local printing-
office, he started the *Natal Mercury*. Two years later
he became the sole proprietor of that newspaper,
and from the first I helped him in his work. It was
a little weekly sheet, containing twenty short columns
of matter, the preparation of which at the time seemed
to absorb as much time and thought as does to-day
the daily broadsheet of many pages. For years the

cost of printing absorbed nearly the whole of the very
modest incomings, while there was little left for the
support of the proprietor and editor, and nothing
whatever available for the payment of outside assistants.   My father's health, moreover, never strong,
gradually declined, and more and more of the routine
work of the business fell on my shoulders.   For many
years I was reporter, proof corrector, accountant, and
collector, and as the fifties advanced towards their
close, much of the editorial work was superadded.   In
March 1860 the state of his health compelled my
father to hand over to his son, then just of age, the
full control of the business as a responsible partner;
and six months later he retired altogether from direct
connection with it.   A valued friend of much commercial experience joined me as partner in the establishment of the firm that has been for forty years
connected with my name.   Much to my relief and
satisfaction, he took entire charge of the financial and
business departments of the newspaper, and continued
to do so up to the day of his lamented death in 1886,
after an unbroken and perfectly harmonious association
of more than a quarter of a century.

It will thus be seen that throughout my life, up to
the time when I finally relinquished editorial work on
taking office in 1893, I was engaged in journalism, and
have been actually my own master.   The two facts
have undoubtedly co-operated to shape and influence
my career: the first focussed my mind and interests

at a very early age on public life and current events, while the last accustomed me to think and to act under a sense of responsibility that was not ordinarily an accompaniment of my years. In both cases circumstances rather than choice have controlled destiny; nor, let me gratefully add, do I in any way regret the kindly compulsion.

Though journalism became alike my profession and my pursuit, I was not as a youth without leanings in other directions. When about sixteen or seventeen, mission work amongst the natives had strong attractions for me, and my father was in actual correspondence with members of the American mission to receive me as an assistant. If I remember rightly, lack of years was the chief impediment. For nearly a whole year, however, I devoted every night of the week to attendance at a Church of England native school, where, for at least two hours, I did my best to teach such native men as could be induced to come the rudiments of knowledge in the shape of pothooks and letters. When I think now of the clamour of barbarous tongues, and the reek of barbarian exhalations which assailed the senses throughout these spontaneous ministrations, the sacrifice of time and energy in the work seems distinctly heroic; but it meant a change in the dull routine of early colonial life, and it indicated the extreme paucity of other means of juvenile diversion. The school flourished as long as its novelty lasted, and it was kept going by one or two feasts and magic-lantern entertainments. It fell to my lot on one of these occasions to act as executioner to an aged bullock that had been provided for purposes of refreshment. I shot the poor animal through the head with an ancient musket, and two hours later it had been devoured by an eager crowd. These, however, were costly methods of attraction, and had to be relinquished, whereupon the attendance rapidly declined. Slates and blackboards ceased to lure, and before a year was over the school perished from inanition. This experience quenched any enthusiasm I had cherished for mission work, and although the Bishop (Dr. Colenso) offered to facilitate as far as he canonically could my admission to Holy Orders, the Church failed to draw me further within its fold. After that the Law proved seductive. I nibbled at proposals made by friendly local practitioners, and I went so far as to enter into correspondence with an eminent firm of London solicitors, with a view to qualifying as an English barrister. Oxford and Cambridge being inaccessible, my idea was to graduate at King's College, London, and thus to gratify a morbid longing to visit the old world, and to breathe life in the great metropolis. But other considerations intervened. My father's failing strength made it more and more incumbent on me to help him in his work, and the visions of professional activity in other spheres had to be abandoned. A journalist I had become, and a journalist I had to remain.

Nor did I grieve over the fact. The calling of a journalist seemed then—and indeed has seemed ever since—full of honourable possibilities. There was the further satisfaction of feeling that I was in a way—though but a small way—associated with the sphere of letters. A passion for writing beset me from a very early time. At the mature age of thirteen I amused myself by composing a descriptive account of the Colony of which I had then been two years a resident. This crude performance covered some sheets of foolscap, and was sent by fond parents to my grandfather in England Those were days when postage rates were counted by shillings, not by pence, and I rather fear that my juvenile essay cost more than it was worth. Two or three years later I yearned for the distinction of print, but mistrusting the impartiality of the paternal judgment on my verdant performances, I determined to write my production in a feigned hand and to transmit it anonymously to the editor. Church controversies were beginning to rage furiously at the time. An eminent dignitary had affronted a certain religious community by saying that he did not think the erection of their new place of worship would conduce to the well-being of the Church of God, and I felt moved to enter the lists as a champion of religious equality and tolerance. The letter fell in with my father's views on the question, and I had the satisfaction not only of seeing my heated protestations appear in the *Mercury*, but of hearing

b

the probabilities of their authorship gravely discussed in the family circle

Encouraged by this success, I followed it up by
other anonymous contributions on public topics
They included a series of five letters on " Immigration," at that time an urgent need of the Colony
Another long production discussed a proposal—most
fortunately nipped in the bud—to bring convicts to
Natal for the execution of public works At last,
through some accident or suggestion, my father got
on the track of his anonymous contributor, and appended to the last of my letters a footnote of decidedly
snubbing tendency. I never spoke to him on the
subject, but confined myself henceforward to such
composition as came in the way of ordinary duty.
Looking, however, further afield, to quarters where my
age and personality might be unknown, I sent contributions to the *South African Commercial Advertiser*,
at Capetown, at that time under the conduct of Mr.
John Fairbairn, long recognised as the ablest writer
and most statesmanlike politician in South Africa—
outside the public service. The first of these com-
munications, which continued for some years, was on
the question of Confederation, so that as far back as
1856 that absorbing theme had engaged my thoughts
and pen. In 1857 the *Cape Monthly Magazine* first
appeared. One of the editors was my good friend of
later years Professor Noble. To him I sent some lines
on " A Zulu Massacre." and also a paper on " Colonisa-

tion." Both promptly appeared, and elicited kindly and appreciative letters from the Professor, with whom up to the time of his death, more than twenty years afterwards, I maintained a constant and most agreeable correspondence. I became a regular contributor to the *Magazine*, in verse, in fiction, and in descriptive essay. Whether the time thus spent might not have been more usefully employed in graver studies is, I must now admit, more than probable, but the enjoyment I derived from these efforts can only be understood by other young aspirants in the literary field.

It was one of my ambitions to establish a monthly magazine in the Colony itself, but successive efforts in that direction bore no result. The time was far from ripe for any such venture. A quarterly periodical called the *Natal Review* was issued for a time under the auspices of Bishop Colenso, but it failed to command adequate support. Some verses I published in it, entitled "A Zulu Mother," were pleasantly noticed. A very modest literary development was started on my own initiative in 1859 in the form of a "Christmas Supplement" to the *Natal Mercury*. I was the sole contributor to the first issue, which consisted in the main of a would-be humorous sketch headed "Mrs. Miffins's Experiences." It also contained some patriotic stanzas entitled "The Home Land a Colonist's Song." This was the forerunner of an annual series which continued for several years. It was not until 1868 that I gained entry into any Home periodical, and it was in the hospitable pages of the *Cornhill Magazine* that I first met the British reader. "A South African Watering-Place" was the theme; and its novelty probably won me ingress into that famous monthly, to which from the first issue I had been a subscriber. Two or three other contributions thereto followed at intervals, to the great satisfaction of the writer. I shall never forget the surprise and exultation I felt when, in November 1868, I chanced to take up from the counter of a London bookseller the October number and found in it two articles from my pen. I had only a week or two before arrived in England, and during the voyage had amused myself by preparing a long and rather elaborate account of "The South African Gold Discoveries," then in their earliest infancy. This article was accepted by the *Cornhill* and put into type. I had corrected the proof-sheets before leaving for Italy, and looked forward to the appearance of the essay in the January number. Imagine therefore my disappointment on receiving in Rome a note from the editor, regretting that the receipt of contradictory tidings from South Africa had made it inexpedient to publish the contribution. It was quite true that the first discoveries of gold in Matabeleland had been discredited by premature and sinister denials, but subsequent events have not only borne out the accuracy of the narrative, but have shown how immeasurably below the mark the predictions of that time were. I may add that in the years which immediately followed, the *Westminster Review*, *Fraser's Magazine*, and *All the Year Round* found room for contributions on such topics as "South Africa," "The Pilgrim Fathers," "The Future of the British Empire," and "A Voice from the Colonies on the Colonial Question." At that time apathy, ignorance, and pessimism were the prevailing notes on all Imperial and colonial questions, and it seemed a duty to do what one could to propagate a truer and more inspiriting faith.

Any tendency I may have had towards literary work was confirmed and strengthened by a success which closely identified my name with the first official handbook on the Colony. In 1856, when I was seventeen years of age, the Government offered three prizes, of £50, £25, and £15 respectively, for the three best essays upon Natal as a field for immigration. Encouraged by my father, I determined to compete for one or other of these distinctions, and proceeded very carefully with the work. Gathering information from all quarters, and reducing to manuscript the impressions of boyish years, I covered 150 foolscap pages with a discursive, though not unmethodical, survey of the land which had been our home for the past six years, and confidently despatched it to the three scholarly gentlemen who had been chosen as judges of the rival essays. The remark casually made to me by one of the arbiters, to the effect that mine was a long way ahead of its competitors in amplitude and information,

led me confidently to await the result; and I was not
a little disappointed when it appeared to find that the
first prize had been jointly awarded to two of the
essayists, myself and another, and that the residue of
the funds was to be applied to the compilation from
both our manuscripts of a separate and expanded
monograph from the facile pen of Dr. Mann, who had
recently come to the Colony in quest of health and
rest. My share in the authorship of this volume was
duly acknowledged in the preface, and I had the satisfaction of finding that a large proportion of the pages
was practically a reproduction of my own matter,
revised or paraphrased by the gifted compiler. The
association thus established with Dr. Mann, who for
several years acted as the first Superintendent of Education in Natal, and was subsequently Natal Emigration
Agent in London, was the source of much subsequent
benefit and pleasure.

Meanwhile, as time went on, editorial cares and
duties multiplied, and political responsibilities accumu-
lated. Both left little leisure for purely literary diver-
sions. The *Natal Mercury* gradually developed from a
weekly issue into a bi-weekly, a tri-weekly, and finally,
in 1877, into a daily publication. With the exception
of those periods of absence which were spent in visits
to the old world, I kept practically the whole of the
leader-writing in my own hands; primarily because I
liked the work, and partly because it was extremely
difficult to find any one who could be trusted to say

exactly what one wished to say on any given subject.
In a small colonial community the personality of an
editor counts for much. He is directly responsible in
the eyes of the public for the opinions and utterances
of his journal. He is known to everybody, and this
is particularly the case where and when he happens to
be also an active representative politician. The difficulty of detaching or dissociating the editorial critic
from the responsible legislator has always been a
cause of solicitude and anxiety. Looking back over
the past, I am surprised that it has not been attended
by greater complication and trouble. No doubt much
unnecessary strain might have been saved had I been
content to depend more upon the help of others.
Seven years have elapsed since I relinquished active
connection with editorial work, and it is comforting to
find how successfully and well that work is done by
others.

In 1861 occurred the greatest event of my earlier
life. For years I had yearned with a mighty longing
to see a little of the vast outer world—to breathe the
air of an older civilisation—to come into touch with
the past—to realise by sense what books had impressed upon mind and imagination. The acquisition
of an active and zealous colleague enabled me, a few
months after my father's passing, to gratify this desire.
A friend—much older than myself—wanted to travel
homeward by way of Mauritius and the Red Sea, then
an unattempted route. He wished for a companion, and

one morning he spent all his powers of persuasion in
urging me to accompany him. At first it seemed a
wild and preposterous idea, on the score of expense,
and in view of my own ordinary engagements. But the
idea being planted, grew with astounding rapidity. It
possessed and overpowered me. It converted a craving
into a passion. That night I got no sleep, thinking of
my friend's arguments, and consumed by my own desires. The next day I communicated with my partner
on the subject, and he lent a sympathetic ear. He
saw difficulties, however, and so did others, but as the
event proved they were not insuperable. At any rate
they disappeared under the stress of my eagerness.
One after another they were disposed of. Through
the kindness of friends I was able to borrow the necessary funds. Other friends offered their help as writers
for the *Mercury* during my absence. They all recognised the educational value of the proposed expedition.
Three weeks after the proposal had been mooted, I
stood on the deck of the *Village Pride*, a cranky little
brig of 160 tons, with 100 sovereigns stitched by
loving hands into a belt that I wore next my skin,
with a letter of credit for £200 in my pocket-book,
and with a heart as full of enthusiasm and expectation
as ever throbbed in a youthful pilgrim eager for novelty
and experience.

Never were time and money better spent than on
this journey. It gave life and fixity to all the desultory reading of previous years, and stored the mind

with impressions and recollections that have never
been effaced. They are as vivid to-day as they were
at the moment. During the year of my wanderings,
the panorama of history seemed to unfold itself under
my eyes. Egypt, Palestine, Syria, Asia Minor, the
Isles of Greece, Athens, Sicily, Calabria, Naples, Rome,
and Paris were all touched and trodden, and London,
the final goal where the second, and last, Great International British Exhibition was that year held, closed
the pilgrimage. How well do I remember the early
morning in late winter when, followed by a boy bearing
my bag, I exultantly trudged from London Bridge
Station, across the river and past St. Paul's, to the
quiet little inn in Norfolk Street, where I had decided
to take up my first quarters! I piloted myself along
the much-conned route without an error, and thought
the murky air of the mighty metropolis more enchant-
ing than the divinest ether of the Orient or the South.
The five months which followed were another period
of experience and revelation. Though London was, as
it has ever been, the centre and focus of interest
and activity, both England and Scotland were visited
from end to end. The introductions I bore with me
opened, when delivered, hospitable doors. Kind friends
everywhere —though never seen before— offered cordial
welcome, and the old country, indeed, proved itself to
be " Home." A short summer trip to the Continent,
with three South African companions, gave me pleasant glimpses of Belgium, Holland, Rhineland and of

Paris again, while the whole expedition was closed by a
voyage back to South Africa in a noble "frigate-built"
sailing-ship, the *St. Lawrence*, Indiaman.

Since then I have travelled northward many times,
and have paid five visits to Italy; but the memory
of that first trip (I do not count the original voyage
out, as a child, in the category) is fresh as ever, as my
friends know, perhaps, to their cost. It was the
turning-point of my life, and enabled me to see events
and things in their true proportions. It gave me
standards of estimate and comparison apart from those
that came within the narrow sphere of merely local
observation. The world outside and the world of the
past became concrete realities, not abstract expressions.
The passionate cravings of the poet in "Locksley Hall"
had rung in my ears ever since I chanced to read
them, and—

> "   Heard my days before me, and the tumult of my life ;
> Yearning for the large excitement that the coming years would
>   yield,
> Eager-hearted as a boy when first he leaves his father's field,
> And at night along the dusky highway near and nearer drawn
> Sees in heaven the light of London flaring like a dreary dawn ;
> And his spirit leaps within him to be gone before him then
> Underneath the light he looks at in among the throngs of men."

Yet let me also add, with infinite thankfulness, that
the joy of travel amidst old-world scenes and surroundings has only abated in so far as the ardour
of youth has been moderated by the sobriety of age,

and that an added and a purer zest has been found in those experiences when shared with the cherished companions of my life.

It was during this first visitation northward that I made my debût as a public lecturer. The friend with whom I had travelled homeward persuaded me to give a lecture on "Natal" before a small provincial audience in the quiet little town of Woodbridge, in Suffolk. It was a daring venture, as I had been in the dentist's hands, and a swollen face was not conducive to a favourable effect. As every one present, except my friend, was absolutely a stranger, considerations of vanity were overborne by his importunity; and I daresay that the temporary disfigurement was regarded as normal by my bucolic auditors. I subsequently delivered the same lecture before much larger and more critical gatherings—and under less painful physical conditions—in Aberdeen and Glasgow; and as listeners seemed appreciative, I suppose the effort was not unsuccessful. It was published subsequently by Street & Co. as a sixpenny guide to the Colony. That was the first venture in book form for which I was individually responsible. After my return to Natal, having felt my feet on the rostrum, I lectured—always by request and without fee—on many subjects and occasions. It was very difficult in those days to find persons ready and willing to take the platform in such a capacity, and having once broken the ice it was no easy matter to withstand the appeals that were made on behalf of the many public institutions that sprang up all over the country for " the improvement of the mind ", though I was ever conscious of being but inadequately equipped as a public teacher.   I think that the lecture which gave its author the keenest enjoyment was one on " Charles Dickens," accompanied by illustrative readings   The genius of that marvellous writer never failed to evoke the enthusiasm of the appreciative colonists, who, often in remote localities, responded with laughter, or with tears, to the magic of his unmatched creations.

Of this, and other lectures delivered in out-of-the-way country places, many anecdotes might be told did space permit.   I can truly say that as much pleasure was derived from addressing a handful of pleased and grateful auditors under the unceiled thatch roof of some rural shanty, as in appearing before a crowded and fashionable assembly in one or other of the towns.   Sometimes the lecturer would have to spend the night as the guest of a friendly neighbour.   At others he would have to ride back by moonlight along lonely bush-paths, or in the dark, with a lantern-bearer, possibly, to guide him.   Once, when camping out, he returned to his tent to find it robbed of the morrow's provender by a prowling dog.   I may here add, that whatever my own performances as a lecturer may have been—or may not have been— they were far outstript by those of my old associate and later colleague, Mr. Escombe, whose discourses on astronomical subjects held his audiences spellbound. Lasting for an hour and a half, replete with elaborate figures and calculations, and delivered without a note or a break, they were marvels of fluency and exposition.

Though there were no schools of elocution in Natal opportunities for practice in that art were not wanting. The first time I ever spoke in public was at a library meeting in a little village, and the agonies of nervousness I then endured were but the prelude of many a similar experience. Though circumstances have often forced me to speak without premeditation, I prefer, if possible, to have more or less time for preparation. Yet to this day it is a moot question with me whether it is best to prepare elaborately or not at all. Everything depends upon the occasion, the subject, and the physical condition of the moment. Most true it is that "out of the fulness of the heart the mouth speaketh"— best and most effectively, but the body must also be in tune, and the tongue will be not the less persuasive if memory has had opportunity to equip it with some suitable phrases. The longest speeches are certainly not the most successful from a rhetorical point of view, though they may be unavoidable. Five minutes' earnest speaking will often produce better effect than hours of laboured exposition, and there cannot be a doubt that with the multitude delivery is a greater factor than language in the achievement of platform success.

This reference to work as a public speaker, associated as it has been with my labours as a journalist, naturally leads to that other aspect of my life which may be said to have been the direct result of both, namely, political and parliamentary activity. It was inevitable, under the circumstances I have named, that politics should become something more than an interest or a pastime. They soon became the absorbing pursuit of life. As in the sphere of physical development the fruits of men's toil and energy are more immediately manifest in younger than in older lands, so in the field of public or legislative work are the results of individual effort more quickly perceptible in a colony than in a parent country. In other words, a colonial politician has, I think, a greater sense of direct immediate power than he would, or could, have ordinarily in an older community. The stimulus to public service and effort is therefore all the more effective. Apart from the committee work of local institutions, or business connected with Church movements, two openings for representative aspirations presented themselves in Natal. One was in connection with municipal work, which never had any special attraction for me, and the other was in the direction of legislative action. It was the latter which from the first claimed and commanded all my sympathy and attention.

At the age of nineteen, having taught myself
the rudiments of shorthand (though never techni-
cally proficient as a stenographer), I went to Maritzburg to report the proceedings of the Legislative
Council, then in the second session of its existence.
That duty I discharged for four years, until the
trip to Europe interrupted the work. Practically,
therefore, I became associated with the parliamentary
life of the Colony from the threshold of its existence, and, in spite of my years, was on a footing
of personal intimacy with the non-official members
and, as far as as a non-member could be, was one
of themselves. I shared the same quarters with
most of them, first at the old Crown Hotel (which
still stands), and later at the Victoria Club, of which
I was one of the earliest members. Admitted to
their full confidence and often participating in their
private consultations, I was frequently able to be of
use in the drafting of resolutions and reports, and may
be said, therefore, to have served a practical apprentice-
ship to the calling of a Colonial Legislator.

Six months after my return from Europe (in March
1863), when I was just twenty-four, one of the two members for Durban announced in my hearing his intention
to resign, and a very few days afterwards a well-known
and active townsman of electioneering proclivities
suggested to me that I might fill the vacant place
I did not deny that the proposal was agreeable, but
submitted that the electors might probably desire

an older candidate. That, he said, would be their business, not mine, and the end of it was that before many days had passed I was the recipient of a requisition headed by the mayor of the borough, and signed by a number of voters so large and influential that I felt justified in at once accepting it. The retiring member, however, vigorously opposed the candidature of one so young and inexperienced, "a slip of a boy," who ought rather to be learning his lessons than aspiring to a seat in the legislature. A good many others, and especially men who supported the existing official régime, followed his lead. They put forward as an opposing candidate an estimable retired officer of the East Indian Service, a gentleman of independent means, but of no special political experience. He and I maintained the most cordial relations all through the contest which followed. At a meeting called to hear us address the electors he excused himself from much speaking on the ground that he was a soldier, "not a scribbler," and that his weapon had been the sword, not the pen.

That meeting was a momentous occasion to me, as I had done no political speaking so far, and was quite in the dark as to my ability to face a heated or hostile audience. Warmly encouraged by sympathetic friends, however, I got through the ordeal without discredit. Public opinion was perceptibly on the side of the "young horse," and not the less so because he was "agin the Government"

in a general way.   After speaking for half-an-hour
there was a good deal of heckling, in which I did
not seem to come off second best.   A little chaff
goes a long way on such occasions, and the meeting
broke up in high good-humour.   It was a lively
but not embittered contest.   I made a house-to-house
canvass of the constituency, and met my committee
every night of the week, when each vote was carefully classified and discussed.   Never had a youngster
a more enthusiastic or devoted body of supporters.
Placards, skits, colours, favours, and banners were the
vogue of the day.   In those days "treating" was not
unpermissible, and I fear that a good deal of money
was squandered in that way by both sides.

When the two polling-days arrived the whole place
was given up to the excitement of the struggle.   There
were less than 300 votes to be registered, and each
had a solid and obvious value.   The sandy roads did
not permit of wheel traffic, so carriages were not in
evidence, but horses were in great request.   I do not
think that the actual result was ever doubtful, but
the struggle continued keen to the end, when a
majority of about two to one placed me at the top
of the poll.   After the declaration had been made
I was carried round the town in a chair on the
shoulders of cheering electors, whose ardour and excitement sometimes threatened to plunge me in the
sand.   It was distinctly one of the perilous periods
of my life, but it fortunately ended without disaster.

Not that the election was finally over. When the next session of the Council opened, the Governor declined to swear me in on the ground of a formal irregularity, but that incident will be found recorded elsewhere.

Thus began a legislative career which has lasted, with one or two intervals of rest, up to the present time. This record of thirty-seven years is, I think, in point of length at this moment almost, if not quite, without parallel in South Africa. It not only covers nearly the whole of my own active life, but it covers also nearly the whole parliamentary life of Natal. To attempt any narrative of it would be to review the political history of the Colony throughout the period, a task which is altogether beyond my present scope or purpose. Succeeding chapters embody the more salient aspects of my experience as a representative, and all that I need add here is a brief statement of the chief aims that have engrossed me—of the principles that have governed my action—of the main objects for which I have striven, and of the more memorable incidents that have marked my experience of public service

Looking back to that far-off time when I first entered the legislative arena, I think that I may without any arrogation of superior rectitude, say that my aim was from the start to be useful and independent. Taught from a child to detest prescription, intolerance, and subserviency; confirmed by study in love of freedom and admiration of patriotic service; taught by observation to appreciate the necessity of expansion and progress, I merely trod the only path that seemed to stretch in front. Nor, in fact, had I any incentive to do otherwise. Time-serving or self-seeking found little favour in those days from any class of colonist. In small and isolated communities public representatives speak and act in the white light and under the searching scrutiny of keen and constant observation. Woe to any lapse of faith or conduct on the part of a chosen and trusted recipient of public confidence! I can truly say that under such conditions the better part is also the easier part to play, and that singleness of purpose, incorruptibility of action, and fidelity to duty are in the long run and at all times their only great and exceeding reward.

It would be quite impossible to refer, no matter how generally, to the various questions and measures that have at different times engaged my attention. I took the position and duties of a legislator—even in the limited area of a small South African colony—very seriously. Natal was a new country, with all its future to be made and shaped. Natal was a part of South Africa, and South Africa was a part of the Empire. Those were elementary thoughts, never absent from my mind. They probably led to the recognition, at a very early stage, of three great cardinal lines of policy, which should dominate all others. Railway Extension, Responsible Government,

and South African Union represented this trinity of
political aspirations. The one would develop and
enrich the Colony, and link it with its neighbours.
The next would give it freedom, dignity, and self-
rule. The last would merge the narrower provincial
life into the larger and nobler national existence, and
help on the evolution and consolidation of the then
formless and embryo empire.

It has been my good fortune to witness and assist
in the realisation of the first two of these policies,
while the last seems nearer its fulfilment than it has
ever been. In one of the chapters which follow I
sketch the progress of railway extension in Natal from
the time when, just forty years ago, the first line
opened for traffic in South Africa began work at
Durban, to the day when it fell to my lot, as Prime
Minister, to link the final rails connecting the Natal
system at Heidelberg, in the Transvaal, with the rest
of the railway systems of South Africa. In another
chapter I recount the steps and struggles which led
up to the establishment of responsible government in
1893, and in a third I endeavour to trace the action
and attitude of Natal in connection with her neighbours.

So far as railways and responsible government are
concerned, I see no cause for regret in the retrospect,
nor do I believe that the coming federalisation of
South Africa will prove in any degree less conducive
to the welfare of all who may be affected, now or

hereafter, by its achievement. I may add here that
the cause of Confederation engaged my thoughts long
before I became a responsible politician.   How it
came to attract my fancy as a boyish dreamer, I
cannot now explain or recollect, but it did so.   In
1857 I published in Capetown articles dealing (1)
with the whole question of Colonisation from historical,
Anglo-Saxon, and colonial standpoints, and (2) with
Confederation as a goal of South African policy.   In
addition to speeches and writings in the Colony
during subsequent years, in 1869 I treated the same
subjects in papers read before the Society of Arts and
the Royal Colonial Institute, and subsequently in contributions to Home periodicals.   In 1876 the Legislative Council appointed me one of its three delegates to
the South African Conference held that year in London
under Lord Carnarvon's presidency, and in 1887 the
same body chose me as its sole representative at the
first Imperial Conference, held in London just before
the Queen's first Jubilee.   A year later I was again
one of three delegates at the first South African
Customs Conference, that was the precursor of the
Conference which, ten years later (after my retirement
from office), brought Natal for the first time into the
pale of the Customs Union.

It was a cause of profound disappointment to me
that I was debarred by the collapse of my health
from accepting the invitation which Mr. Chamberlain
addressed to the Premiers of the self-governing

colonies, with their wives, to take part in the celebration of her Majesty's Diamond Jubilee in 1897.
It was the receipt of that invitation which determined me, under medical advice, to retire from both
official and public life, and seek that rest which was
imperatively enjoined as an absolute condition of
the case.   As it was manifestly necessary that
Natal should be represented on so unique and historical an occasion, and being physically incapable,
for the time being, of taking part in the proceedings, I
deemed it my duty to make way for a more fortunate
successor, and in the person of my old associate and
colleague, the late Mr. Harry Escombe, the Colony had
a worthy and most successful representative in that
marvellous demonstration of an Empire's loyalty and
enthusiasm.

Of the many experiences in my life that have
seemed to me at the time to be memorable—the one
which stands out most prominently—is the occasion
when, on May 5, 1887, together with all the other
delegates at the Colonial Conference of that year, I
was received by her Majesty at Windsor, and placed
in her hands the casket which contained the address
of congratulation from the town of Durban on the
attainment of her Jubilee.   It was the realisation of
long hopes and dreams, cherished in remote South
Africa, amidst wild colonial conditions and naked
savage races, to whom the Great White Queen, though
far off and unseen, was yet a presence and a power.

From my mother's lips in a northern home I had first heard of that Queen, and all my life up the idea of her personality had been a very vivid and ever present association.   To see her and to hear her in the ancient home of her ancestors, and to do this as one of the spokesmen, gathered from all parts of her world-wide Empire, was a privilege that I had never looked for. All the circumstances of the reception—its stately yet simple ceremony, its gracious cordiality, its restriction to the delegates themselves, above all, the pathos and dignity that invested the central figure—were in harmony with one's expectations and with the occasion The calm and quiet which pervaded the Castle and its precincts well befitted the august position of its mistress,

> " Queen of innumerable realms,"

to whom

> " The envoys of her Empire '

thus bore the collective and the individual tributes of their love and homage.   At least eleven out of those twenty-five colonial representatives have since passed to their account, but to each one of them the memory of that day must have remained a precious possession to the last.

A LIFE TIME
IN SOUTH AFRICA

CHAPTER I

THE OUTGOERS

SOME twenty-three years ago a visitor from South
Africa called upon an eminent firm of publishers in
London to make inquiry concerning a certain manuscript that had been left with them many months
before. It was the work of a busy man who had been
relegated to private life by his constituents in consequence of political differences which, for the time being,
had placed him on the unpopular side. In other words,
having been released at a recent election from legislative
duties, I had occupied my unwonted hours of leisure by
the production of a novel. Mr. Lamprey, who then
filled the position of Librarian to the Royal Geographical Society, a post held by him to the time of his death,
was primarily responsible for the genesis of that work.
We had both lamented the lack of interest and appreciation which then prevailed in regard to British colonisation, and he had suggested that a work of fiction setting

A

forth as simply as might be the early experiences of
British colonists in the southern world might prove
useful and popular On my return to South Africa,
being, for the reason I have named, in command of the
time required for such a literary diversion, I set to work
and wrote "George Linton; or, the First Years of an
English Colony." Confided to the care of a friend in
London—whose younger brother was himself a very
eminent novelist—the manuscript had been submitted
to different publishers and readers, without having as
yet found acceptance. The theme was not then as
fashionable as it has since become For some time past
I had heard nothing of the venture. Being in England
on official business, and armed with a letter of introduction from a mutual friend, I called upon the firm
with whom the package had last been left The genial
head of the publishing house, when the matter had
been named, gave an exclamation of relief and pleased
surprise. "Was it in a little case about this size ?" he
eagerly asked. I replied in the affirmative. "Then it
is not dynamite," he rejoined, with obvious satisfaction.
That the humble and inoffensive offspring of my brain
should be capable of such a classification was too astounding a proposition to need denial. Nor did the
effect it subsequently produced upon the public mind
in any way justify such an imputation of explosive
quality. I could not help feeling, however, that the
relief engendered by the discovery that the little case
did *not* contain either dynamite or any other "infernal"

compound or contrivance contributed to the favourable
reception accorded by the publishers to the contents
It appeared that somehow the case had been left without address or explanation. It was a time when dynamite "scares" were rife, when "outrages" were not
infrequent. The mysterious little package, of sinister
size and aspect, with neither owner nor sponsor, had
been, not unnaturally, regarded as "suspect," and had
been suffered to remain in the cellar, untouched and
unmolested, until such time as circumstances might lead
to its identification.

So "George Linton" appeared in the autumn of
1876. Though the edition was, I believe, sold out, the
book was hardly to be regarded as a success. Owing
perhaps, to its own defects, and also to the prevailing
indifference at that time to colonial subjects, the reception given to the book was only lukewarm. The writer
had striven to be realistic, but as the reality itself
excited neither interest nor enthusiasm, the effort was
necessarily a failure. One journal, it is true, and the
one whose good opinion I valued most, gave it the distinction of a long and even flattering review. The
Spectator closed that kindly notice by asking "for
more." I had originally intended to follow up "George
Linton" by other recitals of experience and adventure,
but more pressing duties and labours supervened, and
both impulse and opportunity were lacking.

I have been told that "George Linton" failed in not
being either one thing or the other. It was not suffi-

ciently either all fact or all fiction. I now propose,
without any drafts upon imagination, to recall from the
recollections of fifty years' life as a colonist certain reminiscences that may serve to illustrate the birth and
the growth of a British colony during the last half of
the present century. Of all the decades covered by the
history of Anglo-Saxon colonisation, the "fifties" of the
nineteenth century were in a social sense the most pro-
lific and significant. They were in a peculiar sense a
period of fertilisation and seed-time. It was then that
to Australasia and South Africa the stream of outgoing
population flowed forth from the parent shores. In the
first case gold discoveries were the magnetic power that
drew men southward. California had already, during
the closing years of the previous decade, been the goal
of a similar migration. In South Africa the golden lure
was not to operate until the century should near its
close. As far back as 1820 a body of British settlers
had emigrated to the eastern province of the Cape
Colony, there to be the pioneers of a thriving community. They were succeeded by no others until a
speculative Irishman—one Joseph Charles Byrne—organised a scheme of emigration to Natal. He had obtained from the young Government there certain grants
of land, upon which he proposed to plant English
settlers, who for a payment of £10 each were to receive,
per head, a free passage out and twenty acres of ground
in the colony. Both bait and grant were ridiculously
small—at that time the normal area of a South African

"farm" was 6000 acres—but they sufficed to tempt forth
the class which of all others was perhaps the least fitted
for the life that lay ahead. Society at that time was
suffering from the effects of speculative madness. The
great railway gamble, in which George Hudson was the
dominant figure, had blasted many fortunes and ruined
many households. People of all classes, but especially
middle-class folk, had been smitten hard. Persons
accustomed to more or less comfort, if not affluence, had
risked all their possessions, only to find themselves and
their families—had they any—stripped and destitute.
With little, if any, prospect of speedy retrieval in the
old country, the lure of golden opportunities in unknown lands beyond the sea to men in such plight was
irresistible. They were the easy prey of the wily specu-
lator. Reckless of their own inexperience and ignorance,
they accepted the terms offered them with a confident
optimism that took no heed of warnings or of facts.
They were told that the African land to which they
were being beguiled was fair and goodly, with a soil of
marvellous fecundity and a climate of rare excellence.
"Port Natal" was in their eyes a Land of Promise,
where two crops, at least, could be reaped yearly, and
life was free from the hard conditions that beset it in
the old world. So in dozens, in scores, and in hundreds,
they took their passages and packed up their traps, and
set sail in one or other of "Byrne's ships," to begin from
the moment of their setting foot on board a piteous and
inexorable process of disenchantment.

Half a century has passed since those days, but my
recollections of that first voyage are as vivid as ever
The experiences of childhood are sometimes more deeply
graven on mind and memory than are those of a much
later age.   One or two of them may be worth recalling,
as there are none such nowadays, when gigantic steam-
ships—those "mighty shuttles of empire"—carry men
to and fro across the ocean with a speed and comfort of
which passengers fifty years ago had no conception   In
1850 hardly one steamship had yet crossed the Equator.
The vessels which bore the emigrants were sailors,
mostly, though not always, of an inferior class.   Badly
found, poorly manned, horribly provisioned, they were
abodes of misery to most of the wayfarers in them.
The space between decks, where the latter herded, had
been hastily fitted up in the coarsest fashion.   The
intermediate or second-class passengers had rough
pens, miscalled "cabins," assigned to them, run up on
either side, with a rough plank table and backless
benches dividing them.   The steerage passengers, whether
married or single, occupied sleeping-berths opening end-
wise direct upon the common feeding-space, with such
curtains veiling them as, for decency's sake, the inmates
might themselves provide.   Admission to these dark
and stifling depths was obtained by ladders fixed to
common hatchways, down which the only light available
found scanty ingress.

Feeding arrangements were equally primitive   Once
a week the stores, provided according to a dietary scale,

were served out to both classes; the recipients had to
do the rest. The rough old "salt" dignified by the
style of "cook" had charge of the "galley" on deck
—an open stove, where he boiled or baked, in the order
of their coming, the contents of the nets, cloths, or
pans, promiscuously shoved into oven or boiler, as
prepared by the owners below. Of the quality of the
stores thus dealt with the less said the better. Bought
in the cheapest market, subject to no inspection, in
too many instances foul, rotten, weevily, such as in
these days would be condemned as unfit for human
food, it is marvellous that the stuff so consumed did
not breed pestilence amongst those who had perforce
to subsist upon it or to starve. That it failed to do so
can only be ascribed to the counteracting effects of
pure sea air. It is bad enough for hardy and seasoned
seamen to live for months on impenetrable "biscuit"
and leathery junk, but it is infinitely harder for women
of softer fibre and gentler lives to have to do so—as
did, with strangely little murmuring, Byrne's emigrants
to Natal at that time.

But, in truth, these experiences are best forgotten.
There is no satisfaction in recalling their squalid aspects.
I was a child then, and thought less of them than I
should at a later age. Those upon whom the brunt
of them fell—the mothers and the grown-up women—
God bless their sweet and ennobling memories !—have
mostly passed to their rest, full of all the honour due
to bravely-borne trials and patient toil. It is well,

however, that a later and more happily endowed generation should know what sort of life the earlier outgoers
of Greater Britain had to face and to endure in days
that are not yet venerable.

The ship in which I first sailed to South Africa was
117 days on the voyage from London to Natal, and
98 days from Plymouth to Durban. During that period
she sighted land only once before the shore of South-
east Africa rose in view. In the middle of the great
South Atlantic, about half-way between Cape Horn and
the Cape of Good Hope, three small islands rise out
of the ocean. Of all the islets of the sea they are
perhaps the most lonely. Tristan d'Acunha is the
largest and the only inhabited one of the group Its
companions, Gough Island and Inaccessible Island,
regard it bleakly from a distance. Stern and forbidding
as is the aspect of the first-named, it nevertheless was
a very welcome spectacle to the weary emigrants aboard.
Live stock, poultry, and vegetables had long vanished
from the gaze of the few favoured people in the cuddy,
and when, the morning after we first sighted the island,
Corporal or "Governor" Glass came on board with his
crew of skin-clad islanders, and with a modest store
of flesh, fowls, and sheep, he was welcomed as heartily
as though he had been a gold-laced representative of
the Queen he served. Some of our passengers rowed
ashore at the back of the island in one of the ship's
boats and never returned; for the next morning a dead
calm fell, and our ship—there being no safe anchorage

—drifted in shore and got entangled in long masses of
trailing seaweed. So closely were we drifting in towards
the breaker-crested rocks that much alarm was felt as
to the issue, and all the remaining boats were let down
to do what their crews could to drag the ship's head off
shore. It was an anxious time, and fears were freely
expressed until, as afternoon drew on, a blessed breeze
sprang up from the island and bore us merrily on
our way.

It would profit nothing in these days to recite the
repulsive details of life in a mid-century emigrant ship.
In the case of old and seasoned voyagers there might
be some mitigation, but as most of the hapless passengers
had never crossed the sea before, experience was seldom
available. Tin pannikins and platters mostly formed
the table equipage. Floors and tables were seldom if
ever scrubbed Scraped they were, as the voyage advanced, at long intervals, the dirt of weeks being thus
removed. Of the atmosphere 'tween decks the less
said the better. For months or even years afterwards,
the "smell of the ship" haunted the nostrils of the
emigrants with a sense of loathing that no words can
describe. Long before shore was neared the water
supply ran short, and the foul contents of the wooden
butts that did duty for tanks were doled out in pints
and half-pints for the relief of palates parched by the
sun of a southern summer. Occasional sips of lime-
juice were more precious than nectar ever was. But
why continue the dismal record? I recall it now only

by way of encouraging a spirit of contentment with the
happier conditions of the present time. Let those who
grumble, as some do, at the food and accommodation
enjoyed (and I use that word in its literal sense) on
board the great ocean liners of to-day, think of the
experiences which befell their forerunners, and be
abashed by the contrast.

And yet there are redeeming touches in the retrospect.
The expansive influences of the sea as seen from deck,
combined with the bitter lessons that were being learnt
below, helped to train and fit the pioneers for the work
before them The majestic and ever-changing aspects
of the encircling ocean must always have a tonic and
bracing, if not an elevating, effect upon the human
mind, while the hardships and privations of the new life
schooled the sufferers for the business that awaited
them ashore. As distance grew between the old world
and the new, as the southern stars displaced the familiar
constellations of the north, the emigrants became inured
to novelty, and nerved to face with equanimity whatever surprises or disappointments might be in store.
There is much pathos in the vision of these slow and
shabby little sailing-ships following each other across
the mysterious ocean, each with its company of helpless, ignorant, trustful people, wandering to a wild and
unknown country on the shores of savage Africa, in
quest of a new home and a new life, amidst scenes and
surroundings utterly alien to all past experience, and
absolutely without any personal knowledge of the con-

ditions they had to encounter. Had any of them been
questioned as to their expectations in setting forth, the
answer would probably have been largely tinged by
recollections of "Swiss Family Robinson" or "Master-
man Ready," or by the romantic stories of imaginative
travellers and adventurous missionaries.

But the voyage, with all its unsavoury associations,
was soon forgotten when the emigrant—or "immigrant" as he then became—was once ashore.   How
passing fair the coast of Africa seemed on that Sunday
morning in March when first we saw it closely !   For a
month our ship had beaten up and down the seaboard,
vainly trying to make the roadstead of " Port Natal."
Again and again foul winds had driven her out of her
course and sent her southward , but at last fate was
kindly, and a light breeze off the land found us running
cheerfully to the north-eastward, within full view of as
soft and sweet a coast-line as ocean's surges lap.   The
shore of Natal is neither mountainous and frowning
like that of the Cape of Good Hope, nor . flat and
marshy like that of Delagoa Bay.   It is hilly, sylvan,
and singularly attractive.   Every few miles, streams
that have passed down wooded valleys run into the
sea   From the strip of dazzling sand-beach below,
upon which the breakers pound or croon incessantly,
hills of modest height rise more or less abruptly.
They are skirted with thick bush, over which the
plumes of the dwarf palm or strelitzia droop grace-
fully, while their grassy brows are dappled with patches

of woodland. Beyond, the land rises rapidly to higher altitudes, seamed by deep gorges, but keeping a level continuity of outline until the far western horizon closes the pleasant prospect. The outlook from the sea reveals a luxuriant and attractive land, with a manifest capacity for tilth, depasturage, and home-making ; a wilderness, as we knew it to be at that time, but a wilderness, nevertheless, of bounty and of beauty.

Africa as seen from the sea seemed an idyll Africa as it proved to be ashore was disenchantment. Natal, when I first landed there, had only seven years been a British dependency. But eight years had passed since the Boer trek farmers fought with British troops for the possession of Durban. Ten years before that the country had been devastated by the trained hordes of Chaka. Though so young in the eyes of civilisation, the land had already a history, and a bloodstained one. Somehow, none of us thought anything about that as we drifted over the harbour bar in a flat-bottomed surf-boat. It was a fine day, and the sea was smooth, and the bush-clad bluff which guards the all but land-locked bay looked as beautiful as Ellen's Isle as we passed along it. Nimble and naked figures bounding along the sand-dunes opposite were taken to be baboons or monkeys, but we were told that they were " Kaffirs." That was our first introduction to the baffling savage. Not long had we to wait for a closer acquaintance, as the women and children of the party were borne ashore on the backs of laughing barbarians

Then began our first experience of the Dark Continent. On a sand-mound above the landing-place stood the little block-house, with its garrison of a dozen redcoats, who then sufficed to uphold the majesty of British rule at that remote outpost of the Empire. Two or three old carronades of a type now extinct peeped harmlessly out of the undergrowth. Three or four small thatched cottages, with a more solid brick building in their midst—the Custom-house—represented commerce and civilisation on the threshold of the colony. A winding track, deep in sand, led for two miles through a jungly thicket mantled with sheets of gorgeous convolvuli to what was supposed to be the "town." Durban then consisted only of about a score or so of thatched shanties with walls of "wattle and dab," scattered about a trackless waste of blown sand, with clumps and patches of "bush" to redeem it from desolation. It was no uncommon thing for new arrivals to wander from end to end of the place without knowing that they were there. The immigrants were mostly encamped in tents pitched on the outskirts of the bush, the rough wooden "barrack" provided for their accommodation being wholly inadequate for their needs. Some of them, who might have a little money in their pockets, were fortunate enough to secure tenancy of such small hovels (for to English eyes they were nothing better) as might have been erected and left by predecessors. Rougher or humbler abodes could hardly be imagined, and yet to women of gentle nurture

they seemed havens of rest and comfort after the ships
they had left. Nothing by way of domicile could be
more crude. The floors were of mud smoothed over
with cow-dung. Walls might or might not be whitewashed. Doors and window-places might or might
not be filled in with planks, calico, or matting. Ceil-
ings were not. The little enclosure outside, which did
duty for "cook-house," might or might not be roofed
in, but it was certainly without grate or stove. Fires
were lit upon the ground, and bits of stone held up
the frying-pan, pot, or kettle which sufficed for culinary
purposes. As for food, that was as it might be. Happy
they who could manage to make and bake a loaf that
was not leaden, or a "scone" that could be masticated.
If firewood were not gathered amidst the surrounding
bushes, it could be bought for twopence or threepence
a bundle from the natives, who were also ready to sell
fowls at threepence or sixpence each, and pumpkins,
calabashes, or water melons at like prices. They also
brought maize in baskets, with wild fruits, and eggs of
doubtful age; milk in bottles, too often half churned
in transit, and with a flavour, alas! all its own. Mats
and baskets, reeds and brooms, of native workmanship
also helped, at trifling prices, to equip the simple
households of the pioneers.

It is astonishing, when reduced to rudimentary conditions, with how few of the accessories of life civilised
men can get along. Though it was the fashion in
those days to lament the conveniences and luxuries

that had been left behind, I do not know, on looking
back, that people were actually much the less happy
because they had to do without so much and to be
content with so little. With very few exceptions they
were all in the same case, though those that had been
used to least came off the best in the experience of
privation. Yet not wholly so. It is worthy of note—
it ought never to be forgotten—that the gentler bred
of these outgoers faced their privations, in most cases,
with a brave disdain of circumstance and a cheerful
acceptance of their lot that might well be called heroic.
Coarse and humble though their surroundings might
be, they never forgot what they had been, and never
ceased to be what they were. In those days casual
travellers would often be surprised on reaching some
distant homestead, and after begging there a night's
lodgment—the common and necessary practice—to find
within its rough walls and amidst its slender resources
the unmistakable evidences of personal culture and
refinement—the tell-tale accent, the stray books, the
treasured print or picture, the manner, the allusion,
and the mien, that betokened a different past. As an
old colonist I love to think and am proud to write of
these scattered households, veritable oases of gentle
life in the wilderness, reproducing in savage Africa the
best qualities of our race, and sending forth sons and
daughters to perpetuate those qualities through other
generations amidst the changeful conditions of a new
land.

Yet let me not be mistaken. I have no desire to imply that mere grade of birth or class secures any superior capacity for the work of civilisation. My only aim is to show that gentleness of birth or breeding was not in itself any disqualification for the rough-and-tumble business of pioneering. It is not less pleasant to be able to say that to people of humbler upbringing the colonist's life almost invariably proves a ladder that leads upward and onward. It means social advancement and mental expansion. Even to the original settler himself—possibly the home labourer, or artisan, or the cottage farmer—the life has a mellowing and broadening tendency. It is proverbial that possession of property develops the conservative instinct, and most effectively converts the restless agitator into the steadfast supporter of law and order. This truth is being constantly exemplified in the colonies. As his acres multiply and his wealth increases, the man who lands an eager and clamorous agitator or Socialist soon changes into a cautious and circumspect citizen, by no means anxious to upset existing systems or institutions, and always bent upon knowing the reason why. The less education he may have had himself, the more anxious he is that his children should have advantages denied to him. While, as regards himself, it is astonishing in many instances how soon the prosperous colonist of humble origin acquires a certain fitness for public duties and social responsibilities which would seldom have been open to him in older spheres.

At that time, however, the sphere of public activity in Natal was as contracted as it could be; at any rate in Durban, the seaport The little inland town of Pieter-maritzburg was the seat of government and the centre of official authority, but on the coast signs of admini-strative activity were almost imperceptible. The collector of customs acted as magistrate, and he was supported by a badly-paid person in plain (and very shabby) clothes, known, politely, as a policeman. At first there was no place of confinement for prisoners, but ere long a tiny cottage was secured as a jail Its walls were built of clay and twigs, and could easily be broken through by the hands of an enterprising inmate; but the rigours of existence there were slight and escapes were rare Unruly captives were clapped into the stocks, or handcuffed, while the certainty of a flogging if caught again acted as an effective deterrent upon efforts for liberty. Municipalities and juries were all unknown. Postal facilities came first as acts of grace on the part of the worthy old Baron, who was good enough to receive and to dispense the corre-spondence of the community. Commerce was trans-acted in an easy and dignified fashion which mocked any thought of vulgar competition. Storekeepers—there were no "shops" then—were gentlemanly and friendly persons, who did not disdain to exchange for coin or kind anything that their motley stocks might include, whether food, hardware, or dress. Wrapping-paper and twine being as yet superfluities, purchases

B

were carried away in canisters, baskets, or bags by
the grateful buyers. Civilisation in its rudimentary
stages implies unconstrained equality, artless confidence,
and cheerful content. It is sad to think how soon
these qualities disappear as the community advances,
never to exist again. It is something, fifty years later,
to feel that one has witnessed life under such primitive,
if not Arcadian conditions, and to know from actual
experience that it is possible for European men to
live, not unhappily, with so little to help, to guide,
to serve, or to equip them in the struggle of existence.
One's faith in human nature is strengthened, one's
disdain of mere conventionalism is quickened, by the
memories of those early days.

Byrne's earlier emigrants were not long ashore before
they discovered that the conditions under which they
had been decoyed across the sea were delusive and
visionary. The lands promised them were unsurveyed
and unsuitable. A twenty-acre lot was a ridiculously
inadequate area under any circumstances as a means
of subsistence. The cotton plantations of which they
had heard existed only in imagination. It was still
an open question whether cotton could be grown with
success or not. As a rule the emigrants knew nothing
whatever of agriculture, while those who had been
accustomed to farm life in the mother country found
their knowledge and experience all at fault in South
Africa. Of cotton cultivation the whole were equally
ignorant. Not many weeks sped before meetings were

held, committees appointed, and memorials signed for
the purpose of securing better terms. Unfortunately,
the first Governor of the colony died early in his
administration. His successor (Mr. Pine) had yet to
arrive, and relief had to await his advent. When he
landed in April 1850, from the little gun-brig employed to convey him to his scene of duty, he found
a band of Englishmen ready to meet him with a list
of grievances worthy of their nationality; and it is
but right to say that he at once perceived the hardships of their case, the justice of their claims, and
the necessity of redress. So the twenty-acre lots
became forty-five-acre grants, and other concessions
were authorised. It is pleasant to know that some
of the grantees personally occupied their allotments
and left their mark in several localities of the colony.
The story of their struggles would be an honourable
record, and would suffice clearly enough to show
how it is that the Anglo-Saxon has proved mankind's best coloniser. Failures did not daunt nor
disappointment outweary them. "The drawbacks of
agriculture" became a common phrase of sinister significance. But still the pioneers strove and struggled
on, and still the fair wilderness continued to blossom
under their labours, while stubborn Nature wrestled
with them for the produce of their hands. But
this is a theme to which I shall return in a later
chapter.

My desire in these pages is to depict as briefly

as 1 can from my own experiences and recollections the evolution of a British colony, and if in doing so the recital should be somewhat grim, fidelity to truth compels me to make it so. With later developments brighter aspects may reveal themselves.

CHAPTER II

THE GOVERNORS

WITH Governor Pine's advent in Natal in 1850 there came to the infant settlement an era of change and progress. What ministries are under responsible government, that governorships are under Crown rule. They mark periods and indicate stages of development. Sometimes they make or mar reputations. It may be of interest to gather up here certain recollections of some of the governors I have known during the last fifty years. Two or three of them bore names that have since become famous. All of them were faithful even though in certain instances misdirected, servants of their country.

The position of governor in a colony which is still under the rule of the Colonial Office has no exact counterpart. If invested with the dignity of sovereignty it is also weighted by all the cares of administration. Though in no sense responsible to the people of the land he rules, the governor is directly and personally responsible to the Ministers of the Crown he represents, who in their turn are responsible to the lectorate of the mother country. His ultimate responsibility is therefore to a power which knows little or nothing

of the affairs he is called upon to deal with. The
anomalies and difficulties besetting such a position are
apparent. To a conscientious and high-minded man,
sincerely anxious to do his duty to the people under
him on the one hand, and to his chiefs in Downing
Street on the other, these conflicting conditions are
often intractable. Many a governor has succumbed
to misfortune, not because he failed in duty or in
purpose, but because he found it impossible to reconcile
duty with obligation.

In Governor Pine's days the position was made more
onerous by the difficulties of communication There
were no telegraphs either by land or sea For a year
or two he was directly subordinate to the Governor of
the Cape Colony; but correspondence with Capetown
was often a matter of months The need of immediate
action sometimes made it impossible to await instructions A few months after Mr. Pine's arrival the
"Kafir War" of 1850–54 broke out, and he was confronted by a critical situation of the most acute kind
Though the scene of outbreak was four hundred miles
distant, the intervening country was occupied by kindred
tribes, and the native population of Natal outnumbered
by twelve to one the white inhabitants. Immediately
beyond the northern border lived the Zulu people—the
race of warriors who, less than twenty years before, had
carried death and devastation to the confines of the
older colony. Then, and for many years later, the only
garrison in Natal was a small force of Imperial infantry,

about 400 strong. The European settlers were unarmed
and unorganised. Except at Maritzburg, forts and
rallying-places were unknown. In such circumstances
panic was inevitable, and panic is too often the parent
of disaster.

To understand aright the alarm begotten in such a
community by sudden outbreaks of "native" rebellion
or disorder, or by rumours of native invasion, one
must have lived amid the prevailing conditions.
The massacres which followed the great Boer "trek"
into Natal were still vivid and ghastly memories. So
lately as 1838, more than 600 men, women, and children
had been surprised and slaughtered on Natal soil by
the hordes of Dingaan. A few weeks later the handful
of British settlers on the coast had been slain in combat
by the exultant Zulu hordes, and all that remained of
them at the port which is now known as Durban had
been forced to take refuge on a small island in the bay.
Not five years before these events settlers on the Cape
frontier had been slain and their homesteads destroyed
by insurgent Kafirs. Tales were rife of atrocities
committed upon helpless women and children by savage
assailants. The older settlers told the raw immigrants
of their own tragical experiences in language whose
vividness did not suffer by repetition. Those experiences might, it seemed, be at any time the lot of the
later arrivals. The naked Kafirs, who mixed continuously in their daily lives, were a constant reminder
of these possibilities. At that time there were no rules

or regulations in force to restrain the actions of anybody. The natives roamed the so-called roads or footpaths in unbridled freedom, shaking their assegais, shouting their war songs, or brandishing their clubs and sticks as they stalked along, the embodiment of bloodthirsty barbarism. Far into the night they would chant their eerie songs, which blended with the dreams or disturbed the slumbers of their white neighbours and kept alive the day's alarms.

It was no easy matter to pacify the minds or appease the clamour of people suffering under such excitements, and demanding protection or news. Governor Pine was a sympathetic, impulsive man, anxious to do something, but hampered by want of a free hand. One of his first projects was to organise a native force and march through Kafirland to the succour of the imperilled garrisons and settlers on the Cape frontier, but the proposal was vetoed as too precarious. Some doubt existed as to the absolute loyalty of the natives within the colony, and still more uncertainty prevailed as to the possible attitude of the Zulus beyond the northern border. Though the Zulu king, M'Pande, was a nominee and professed ally of the English Government, he might prove as treacherous as his brother and predecessor Dingaan, who fell upon and slew the Dutch pioneers while they were in the very act of negotiating a treaty with them. Then, and for many years afterwards, the ' Zulu war cloud" brooded over the little colony, until in 1879 it was dissipated amid disaster and bloodshed by Sir Bartle Frere.

As a matter of fact the colonists were at that time, and for long after, at the mercy of the natives around them. Had the latter chosen to combine and fall upon the settlers, they might have swept the country. Only their own intertribal differences, a salutary dread of the Boers, and the mighty though mysterious name of England availed to keep the peace which for fifty years, with but two interruptions, was the happy fate of Natal. Governor Pine knew how to make the most of all three influences. He kept the chiefs and tribes divided. He fostered and flattered Boer sensibilities. He invited deputies from Zululand to see the little garrison of redcoats at Maritzburg parading, to hear the voices of the small cannon at the fort there, and to watch rockets exploding. Insignificant though the demonstration was in point of magnitude, it sufficed to impress the un-tutored minds of the shrewd savages who witnessed it with a due sense of the resources of English war-power. They went back to their king and told him of the spectacle with natural embellishments of descrip-tive speech. The Governor was supported in his action by the counsel and co-operation of the head of the Native Department, Mr Theophilus Shepstone, whose name has been so closely and prominently identified with the native affairs of South-east Africa during forty years. Not that the two were by any means at one in questions of native policy. It was no secret that they differed widely on many points, but between them they managed to keep the natives in hand and the colonists in security while war was raging in the Cape Colony and Basutoland.

An instance of the alarms that were frequent during this period may be cited. One winter evening a simple-minded, not to say silly, European arrived in Maritzburg with a sensational story. On the hills overlooking the town he had seen two large "impis" of armed natives evidently advancing on the town. That was all he had to tell, but it sufficed to spread the alarm from end to end of the scattered township. Everything in the shape of a gun was loaded; windows were barricaded, and people went about the brook-skirted streets eagerly asking for news. Mr. Shepstone had the good sense to ride through the town in person, visiting each house and carefully advising the inmates to keep indoors, so as to avoid panic, but by no means to disregard preparedness or to ignore contingencies. The consequence was that all kept calm through that dark night, though none went to bed, while ears kept on the alert listening for the long drone—half hum half roar—with which Zulus beguile the war-path. That ominous sound, however, did not arise, and with the morning's light came the explanation. The alarmist had mistaken in the dimness of evening two droves of cattle for native impis!

A similar false alarm visited a country settlement on the high-road from Durban. The white inhabitants all

mustered together and spent the night in throwing
up an enclosure, or laager, of sods and branches, within
which they meant to hold their own, with their families, against the expected foe. The attack never came,
but "Fort Funk," as it was derisively christened, remained a memorial of troubled times for many a day.
The hastily-reared "bastion" is now a bushy mound,
crowned by a summer-house !

Governor Pine's great abilities were unfortunately
marred by personal eccentricities, which too often
gave occasion to the reviler. In small communities,
where people know each other's private affairs far too
intimately, the memory of high and abiding public
service is too often crushed out by personal animosities or envenomed criticisms. Governor Pine gave
Natal a magisterial system, municipal institutions,
popular district control, trial by jury, administrative
independence; he did what he could to make roads
and provide harbour improvement; he settled the land
claims of the Dutch farmers, and thereby did away
with their chief grievance; he encouraged the volunteer system before it was established in Great Britain,
and urged upon the Imperial authorities the necessity
of legislative representation. He recognised the importance of keeping on good terms with the Dutch
communities of the interior, and steadfastly discouraged
race animosities or jealousies. All this and much more
may be entered to his credit, yet his individual idiosyn-
crasies won for him obloquy on the part of opponents

and distrust on the part of his chiefs. Though the colonists at large generally recognised the value of his services, his erratic actions in minor or more personal directions too often obscured the value of his work Had he been more humdrum, his career might have been less embittered

Mr Pine left Natal in 1855 to return as Sir Benjamin Pine in 1873. During the interval many of his former adversaries had disappeared, but the remembrance of his work was fresh in the minds of most of the older colonists, and he met with a warm welcome. Four months later he was called upon to cope with the only serious native rising that has taken place in Natal. The story of the Langalibalele rebellion is a long business, and has been told in many books I shall have occasion later on to refer to that strenuous controversy. I only mention it here to show that Governor Pine retained to the end his old qualities of clear insight and statesmanlike impulse. The nettle of danger was there, and he did not hesitate to grasp it. Again sustained by the Secretary for Native Affairs, Mr. Shepstone, and by the sympathy of the whole colony, he took prompt and decisive measures to put down the insurrection and to punish the offenders. Those measures were completely successful, and they did not cost the mother country a penny. But in carrying out these measures incidents occurred which excited the ire and indignation of Bishop Colenso, and led him to champion the cause of the rebels with an ardour which fed itself.

It is not my purpose here to re-enter that troubled field of contention. A quarter of a century has passed since the contest raged, but I see no reason to change the opinion which I held then, and lost no opportunity of expressing, namely, that both the Government and colonists were right in the course pursued, just as Sir Bartle Frere and the colonists were right in regard to the affairs of Zululand. Piles of blue-books and dozens of volumes have been printed on both questions, but convictions on either side probably remain unchanged. No one desires to dispute the sincerity of the motives which inspired the Bishop and his English allies in their crusade against the local authorities, but not less sincere were the latter in their aim and purpose—the maintenance of British supremacy and the guardianship of peace and civilisation

Though the term of Sir Benjamin Pine's second administration was short, it cannot be described as merry. It was embittered throughout by the Langalibalele affair and its consequent complications. In 1874 Mr. Froude, the historian, visited Natal and formed erroneous impressions on many points. He saw the country at its worst, parched by drought, blackened by grass fires, and generally upset by the late rebellion. These impressions, reproduced in his own fascinating style, created a prejudice which time has hardly yet outworn. That they greatly influenced the mind of the late Lord Carnarvon, whose unofficial emissary in a sense Mr. Froude was understood to

have been, is not denied. They led to the injudicious
attempt to force on confederation, to Sir Garnet
Wolseley's special mission to Natal, and to the abortive
London Conference in 1876. Though that meeting
bore no direct fruit, it was followed by the return of
Sir Theophilus Shepstone to South Africa armed with
the commission under which he subsequently annexed
the Transvaal. What that meant we did not know
then, but all the world knows to-day.

A few days before the British flag was hoisted in Pretoria, Sir Bartle Frere reached Capetown with larger
powers than had ever before been confided to any Governor of the Cape Colony, and with a splendid conception of the work that lay before him. A year later the
last Kafir war broke out on the Cape frontier, to be
followed in a few months by the invasion of Zululand.
Once again Sir Garnet Wolseley was despatched to
Natal, to supersede Sir Bartle Frere in his functions
as High Commissioner, so far as South-east Africa
was concerned. Twelve months subsequently the last-
named servant of the Crown and Empire left Capetown
discredited and recalled, another victim to circumstance
and misconception. Then followed in quick succession
Sir George Colley's appointment as High Commissioner
for South-east Africa; the war of independence, Laing's
Nek, Majuba, and retrocession. What has happened
since need not be set down here, but it is worthy of
note that this long chain of varied and stirring events
began with Governor Pine's successful repression of

Langalibalele's rebellion in November 1873. All that
he, poor man, gained by his action was obloquy outside
the colony and humiliation within it. Sir Garnet
Wolseley's first proceeding on his arrival in 1875 was
to send for Sir Benjamin and to let him understand
that his early departure from the colony would be
conducive to Imperial interests. How bitterly this
summary treatment rankled in the Governor's mind
no one knows better than myself. Unfortunately he
had, against the advice of friends, lingered on at his
post until after the arrival of the Special Commissioner.
Procrastination was in certain cases a weakness with
him. It was a sad termination, however, to a useful,
though chequered, career. Not often have England's
African proconsuls borne homeward with them the full
sheaves of their labours in that Dark Continent.

Governor Scott succeeded Mr. Pine in his first term
of office, and his experiences deserve more attention
than can be given here. Charged with the inaugura-
tion of a liberal though limited or "hybrid" constitution, he might confidently have looked forward
to a popular and brilliant career, but he soon drifted
into antagonism with the representative legislature,
which it was his first duty to establish. He allowed
himself to become imbued with the belief that the
white colonists were hostile to the natives, he came
too readily under the influence of the existing official
clique, and he failed to give large and sympathetic
effect to the spirit of the charter he had been called

upon to administer. No good end can be served at
this distance of time by recalling incidents that are
best forgotten. They were a natural outcrop of Crown
government, now happily a fast diminishing quantity
in British colonies. It is pleasant to remember, however, that Mr Scott remained long enough at his post
to secure the recognition by the colonists at large of
his many sterling qualities of head and heart, and that
when he left after eight years of rule he bore with him
abundant evidences of respect and regard.

One little instance may serve to indicate the causes
of Governor Scott's unpopularity. It had been my
misfortune, as a very young man, to incur his Excellency's displeasure by criticisms in the press, which
were, perhaps, more forcible than polite. I have little
doubt now that they seemed to older men flippant
and improper—youth is prone to excess. Unhappily
the hostility thus engendered extended itself to other
spheres of action. In 1863 I first entered the Legislative Council as one of the members for the seaport,
and it was no secret that my appearance in that arena
was regarded with disfavour at Government House.
Among the many wants of the young colony at that
time European immigration was regarded as one of
the foremost. Governor Scott, whose general policy
pointed to his conviction that Natal belonged rather
to the natives than the white man, did not share that
view, nor did he hide his opinions. One of my earliest
legislative efforts was to move and carry a resolution

asking that a sum of £5000 might be appropriated to
purposes of immigration. That proposal was seconded
by the oldest member—as I was the youngest—of the
Council, and in accordance with custom it became our
duty to present it in person as a "Respectful Address"
to the Governor. To the viceregal presence, therefore,
we betook ourselves one morning. In due course we
were ushered into his Excellency's sanctum, and for
the first and only time I had audience with him. The
object of the address was briefly explained, and the
document handed over. With angry mien and im-
patient gesture the Governor received it, and ejaculated
in wrathful tones: "Childish nonsense! childish nonsense!" Possibly, had the object of this thrust been
a few years older, the words would not have seemed so
aggressive, but they sufficed to cut short the interview.
"It may be that, your Excellency," was the rejoinder,
"but it is, at any rate, the proposal of the Legislature
of the colony." And bowing our adieux we left.

Our next Governor, Colonel MacLean, had the rare
distinction of being able to read his own obituary. An
invalid to start with, he had soon to return to his old
home in British Kafraria in quest of health. Thence
issued one day the announcement of his death. A
special Gazette was published containing the black-edged
notification of the sad event. The local newspapers
contained long and fortunately appreciative notices
of the deceased's character and career. A day later
came the authoritative contradiction of a report which

c

was, however, only an anticipation of what actually
happened a few weeks later.

Poor Governor Keate's name and fate may be mentioned as a melancholy instance of an empire's hard
treatment of its servants. It fell to his lot to administer
the government during a period of extreme depression.
Trade collapsed and revenue dwindled. Finances had
to be readjusted. The Legislature and the colonists
insisted upon the equilibrium being restored by re-
trenchment, and especially by the abolition of offices
and the reduction of salaries. The Governor opposed
this policy as an injustice to the service and as a breach
of faith. He preferred rather to effect the process by
the stoppage of public works and the increase of taxation   A long and bitter struggle ensued, and in the end
the Governor was rewarded—for persisting in a policy
approved, if not prescribed, by his chiefs in Downing
Street—by being "promoted" to the governorship of
the Gold Coast colonies. His status there as a governor-
in-chief was titularly higher, and his stipend was £4000
a year instead of £2500. But—the climate! He had to
exchange a healthy place of abode for the least healthy
in the Empire. Necessity left him no alternative but
to accept, and he went out, despite enfeebled health,
to undertake his duties on those pestilential shores.
Rumour said that he had, in doing so, to sacrifice his
insurance policies. The inevitable happened, and in a
few weeks another name was added to the list of England's faithful but sacrificed proconsuls.

Apart from the political differences which clouded his administration, Governor Keate's term of office was marked by many pleasant aspects. It improved and elevated the social tone. Government House for the first time became a centre of gracious and impartial hospitality, and no one impugned the conscientious sense of duty which guided alike the policy and the conduct of her Majesty's representative.

Sir Garnet Wolseley's special administration in 1875 offered many points of interest. It was, as I have indicated, the outcome of misunderstandings connected with the rebellion of Langalibalele, and the attitude of the Government and settlers of the colony towards the natives. It was headed by a man who was described by one of his own lieutenants in the local legislature as "the strong arm of the British Army and the long arm of the British Empire." Lord Carnarvon selected the most brilliant soldier and most successful general in that army to remodel the constitution and reorganise the administration of the little South African colony. In undertaking this rather incongruous task, the gallant commissioner was responsible for the boldest exploit of his life. He had to win success not by arms, but by the arts of peace. He had to persuade an unwilling colonial community to part with its legislative independence. He had to induce a colonial legislature voluntarily to efface itself. The existing Legislative Council of Natal consisted of five members nominated by the Crown, and fifteen members elected by the colonists. The Bill

which was at once submitted to the colony after Sir
Garnet Wolseley's arrival, proposed to substitute a body
in which fifteen members would be appointed by the
Crown, and only fourteen would be elected by the people,
so that in the last resort the Crown would always be
able to secure the passing of a measure, however unpopular or unpalatable it might be.

The colonists of Natal have always plumed them
selves upon being "English" in origin as well as in
instincts and characteristics, and it was altogether
improbable that they would part with their privileges
—such as they were—without a struggle. Yet their
loyalty was beyond question. Sir Garnet equipped
himself for the work before him. He took out with
him from England a "brilliant" staff of carefully
chosen and specially qualified officers, who after arrival
were all gazetted to positions of high local responsibility. Mr. Napier Broome was translated from the
staff of the *Times* to the post of Colonial Secretary. Colonel Colley became Colonial Treasurer. Major
Butler, who had acquired literary fame as author of
"The Great Lone Land," was appointed "Immigration
Agent." All these three had seats as official members
in the Legislative Council. Major Henry Brackenbury
acted as Private Secretary. Lord Gifford, with his lately-
won Victoria Cross, was A D C. Never before had a
representative of the Crown come to South Africa
attended by such a galaxy of able and famous men.
Arms, diplomacy, administration, literature, and pluck

were all notably represented. Her Majesty's flagship *Raleigh* took the illustrious party on from Capetown to Durban. There were no cables in those days, and the first news we had in Natal of Sir Garnet's appointment and mission was followed by his arrival two days later.

I was up-country at the time, and hurried down to Durban in complete ignorance of this latest move on the part of Imperial statesmanship. While sitting on the box of the post-cart, a few miles from the seaport, a "special extra" of the local journal was handed me by a passing traveller, giving particulars of the Administrator's advent. An hour or two later I heard from the lips of poor Governor Pine that he had already been asked to leave the colony at the earliest opportunity. He was bewildered, as we all were, if not stunned, by the sudden and startling stroke of policy thus swiftly decided upon and carried out. Next morning I had an interview with the genial Administrator, and subsequently with Mr. Napier Broome, whose duty it was to have the objects and policy of her Majesty's Government fully explained to the colonists. In the evening some of us dined with Sir Garnet at the first of those little functions which were subsequently said by a certain witty judge to have "drowned the independence of the colony in sherry and champagne." As I voted against the proposed constitution, I can repeat this caustic saying without confusion. As a matter of fact, it not inaptly described the campaign upon which Sir Garnet then entered. Persuasion, not coercion, was his motto. Better instruments for such a process could not have been chosen. Famous, gallant, gay, masterful, yet accessible and courteous, the brilliant general and his lieutenants did their best to disarm hostility and over-bear opposition by hospitality and personal charm.

Space would fail me to describe the many amusing incidents that marked the Wolseley mission. One of graver import may, however, be given. It has already been referred to in print by Sir William Butler and Sir Henry Brackenbury. Theirs, of course, was the strictly Imperial point of view. Mine was that of the colonist—one of the colonists whose rights were being shorn. The new constitution, considerably modified already in compliance with local protests and repre-sentations, was to be considered in special session by the doomed Legislature. The hall occupied by the Assembly was crowded with eager spectators. Members sat in their cane-bottomed armchairs round a horse-shoe table. The Speaker, oddly clad in tail-coat and tartan trousers under his silken gown, was in his place. The galleries overhead were packed. The judges' bench behind was filled with gaily-dressed ladies. Every spare foot of room was occupied. "The Bill" had been called on for second reading. One or two less important introductory speeches had been delivered. Then came Colonel Colley's turn. As chief of the staff he would, it had been understood, deliver the principal speech in support of the measure. Alike popular and respected, he was the cynosure of every eye. If not sympathetic his audience was manifestly appreciative, and his leading opponents greeted his rising with cordial cheers. He was carefully prepared with copious notes for his undertaking. No one doubted that he would do his best, by argument and moderation, to make his chief's mission a success.

Amid profound attention he began his speech. In calm and measured tones the reputed strategist and accomplished soldier opened up his theme. For three or four minutes all went well, and then he hesitated, paused, looked at his notes and then at his auditors with that look of deprecation which in a public speaker means so much. A friendly and encouraging note of applause went round the tables. Again the gallant officer seemed to pursue his thoughts vainly through the air. Again he rubbed his brow as though to dispel the mist that had obscured his memory, and then, murmuring gently, "Mr. Speaker, excuse me, I cannot proceed," he sat down, and, with his head resting on his hands, remained in gloomy silence as the debate proceeded. Members cheered as warmly as though the arrested speech had closed with a well-rounded peroration, but there was in the mind of every listener the keenest sense of regret and sympathy. I thought at the time, and still think, that Colonel Colley's collapse of memory and effort on that occasion was due to the distaste with which he, a high-minded Irishman, had undertaken a duty so repugnant to his instincts, and probably to his convictions.

This misadventure on his part only served, I think, to
enhance the respect and esteem in which he was held
in Natal. He did much good work in connection with
administrative inquiry and reform, and when five years
later he returned to fill the high position of Governor
as well as High Commissioner for South-east Africa, he
was welcomed with open arms by all classes of the
community. Nor was there anywhere throughout the
Empire deeper lamentation or more acute distress than
prevailed in Natal when the terrible tragedy of Majuba
was added to the thrilling episodes of those eventful
years.

If Colonel Colley had been beset by any misgiv-
ings as to the wisdom or justice of the constitutional
experiment attempted by Sir Garnet Wolseley, it was
fully borne out by the result. The measure finally
agreed upon by a bare majority of the Legislature left
the nominative and elective elements in the new body
almost evenly balanced, with the inevitable result that
they only served to thwart and paralyse each other.
Fortunately the measure was given but five years of
life, and on Sir Garnet's own suggestion no effort was
made to continue it when it had run its course. It
simply lapsed by effluxion of time, and the old constitution came into force again, to be gradually amended
and liberalised, until in 1893 what was practically a
new charter, establishing responsible government in its
full form, was adopted and approved. It was not the
fault of Imperial statesmen that Natal did not earlier

acquire her enfranchisement. In 1882 Lord Kimberley, through the hands of that able and popular Governor, Sir Henry Bulwer, offered the colony that boon, but the electors refused it by a substantial majority. The dread of unknown consequences, more especially as regards the natives, deterred the colonists from taking what to many of them seemed a perilous plunge. Eleven years were spent in further agitation and discussion before the advocates of a progressive policy succeeded in their crusade.

Whatever other results may have followed the Wolseley administration, it certainly lifted the politics of Natal to a higher and broader plane. It extended the political outlook of the colonists, and made them feel that they belonged to an empire as well as to a small bit of South Africa. It was an assurance to them that their interests were not wholly disregarded by the mother country. Though it left them, nominally, more of a "Crown Colony" than they were before, it gave them an expressed hope of rising to a better state hereafter. The mission may be said, I think, to have marked the birth of the new era of "Imperialism." If the present Commander-in-Chief of Her Majesty's forces ever looks back to that episode in his brilliant career, he must perceive that it was coincident with the first ripple of the refluent tide. It was a demonstration of awakening feeling on the part of the Home Government and the home people. After forty years of apathy and indifference, both seemed at last aroused to a conscious-

ness of Imperial interests and obligations. From that
time onward there has been a quickening of Imperial
vitality and a growing recognition of Imperial duties.
To South Africa Sir Garnet Wolseley's errand proved
the preface of a whole volume of eventful history.
Wars, expeditions, controversies, negotiations, all representing Imperial action and intervention, crowd the
records of the last quarter of a century, and as I write
these words [1] the most tremendous crisis that has yet
menaced the country is impending, and a struggle
fraught with incalculable issues to the continent and
the Empire seems inevitable.

[1] October 1899.

CHAPTER III

THE VOERTREKKERS

THE time was a summer night in January 1851. The place was the stony brow of a long table-topped hill or plateau, overlooking the broad sweep of the Natalian coastlands, a wilderness of grassy slope and bush-clad valley, stretching to where, ten miles away, and fifteen hundred feet below, the dazzling Indian Sea closed the outlook. At that hour, however, only the stars and the dim outlines of adjacent hills were visible. No dwelling-place was in view, but a roughly tented African waggon, scotched from rolling backward by blocks of stone under the hinder wheels, representing the resting-place of its inmates. They were three, a young English girl and her brother, a boy of twelve, travelling from Durban to Maritzburg in the care of a rough English-speaking colonist, who both owned and drove the waggon, and who had graciously consented, on payment of a few shillings, to carry them by what was then the only means of conveyance between the seaport and the capital. Horses they had none. Light though the load was, the " span " of fourteen oxen had failed to drag the cumbrous vehicle over the stones which encumbered the steep and rutty track, and, as darkness fell, the easy-minded proprietor decided to remain perched up on the hill crest for the night. The situation was, or seemed, somewhat precarious, for had the stones under the wheels given way, the waggon must have rolled backward and downward to destruction; but South African life in those days was rich in such risks and possibilities, and the young travellers, rolled in their blankets inside the waggon, slept not less soundly than did their hardy guardian underneath it. There were no sounds to disturb their rest except the occasional bark of a prowling hyena, or the drone of a native chant from some distant kraal.

That night's experience was the counterpart of several others during the week's journey that ensued. For, after the murmuring oxen, refreshed by their rest and goaded by the merciless lashes of the driver, had managed to drag the waggon on to a safer halting-place, by the side of a friendly clump of brushwood, they in their turn disappeared amongst the neighbouring gorges, only to be recovered after a two days' search. Then came rain, which made the rough roads—falsely so called—impassable for three days more. Time dragged very wearily during these compulsory delays. Books there were none. An old newspaper found in the "waggon chest" had been read more than once from the first line to the last. The uncouth but good-hearted driver, however, sought to enliven his young companions by stories from the past, his own past, which in its way had been as fruitful in stirring incident as any

novel of Scott or Fenimore Cooper. It was there, from
his lips, that I first heard of the experiences of the
Voertrekkers.

John Tosen was an Africander of mixed birth. His
father had been English—an old soldier, I fancy—his
mother Dutch. His accent was that of a cockney he
had read one book in his life, and was ever quoting it,
"The Wicar," as he pronounced it, "of Wakefield."
Short, hirsute, and insignificant, he was not lacking in
either pluck or independence. He deemed himself
socially the equal of anybody, and spoke with bitter
disdain of the lofty pretensions and affectations of " them
emigrants," the poor folk who were then pouring into
the country. He " couldn't abide those stuck-up snobs
who turned up their noses at men who were their
betters," albeit dressed in moleskin and veldschoens
"Reel ladies" put on no airs, and he cited with high
commendation the wife and sister of an eminent Government official who had lately travelled to Durban with
him. It was from him that I learnt, while crouching
out of the rain, the story of the Bushman's River
massacres, which were then an episode only twelve
years old. It seemed ancient history to my boyish
mind, though some of the survivors of the tragedy were
still little more than children. The story, as yet, had
not been told in England, and to this day its ghastly
incidents are little known outside South Africa. There,
however, they are household legends in many a Boer
family, and they shed a lurid light upon subsequent

and now pending events. John Tosen's tale as told me
at that time has been confirmed in all its main details
by officially authenticated documents, and a moving
narrative it is

Much has been written and printed concerning the
expatriation of the Cape Boer farmers in the years
1835 37, but the genesis of that movement cannot, I
think, be better described than it was by Mrs. Anna
Elizabeth Steenekamp in the quaint and artless record
that was published in the *Cape Monthly Magazine*
for September 1876. The writer was a niece of the
great and gallant Boer leader, Piet Retief.

"The reasons for which we abandoned our lands
and homesteads, our country and kindred, were the
following :—

"1 The continual depredations and robberies of the
Kafirs, and their arrogance and overbearing conduct,
and the fact that in spite of the fine promises made to
us by our Government we nevertheless received no compensation for the property of which we were despoiled.

"2. The shameful and unjust proceedings with
reference to the freedom of our slaves; and yet it is
not so much their freedom that drove us to such
lengths, as their being placed on an equal footing with
Christians, contrary to the laws of God and the natural
distinction of race and religion, so that it was intolerable
for any decent Christian to bow down beneath such a
yoke; wherefore we rather withdrew in order thus to
preserve our doctrines in purity"

These simple but honest admissions on the part of the pious-minded old Dutch lady who made them, suffice to show how irreconcilable are the two stand-points · that of the British statesman and the British citizen, to whom the mere thought of slavery in any form is abhorrent, and that of the South African trek Boer, to whom a black skin was the badge of bondage, and the inferiority of the black man a canon of religious belief. The whole history of South Africa during sixty years has been moulded by this difference. The Boers not only regarded the blacks as an inferior race, but they treated them as such, not with the atrocious cruelty falsely imputed to them by censorious philan-thropists, but with a parental stringency which too often gave colour to the slanders of their traducers These calumnies, accepted by British Governors and repeated in official documents, added bitterness to the more substantial wrongs of which Mrs. Steenckamp complained. Unable to obtain redress for the losses suffered through native depredations, debarred from exacting retributive and substantial reparation in their own way, cheated, as they considered, out of adequate compensation for the liberated slaves, continually feeling the pressure of new restrictions and obligations, they lent a ready ear to the stories that reached them of vast pasturelands and rich wildernesses in the north, where they might find new homes and fuller freedom, and rule themselves—and the natives round them—under their own laws and in their own way

Of the adventures which befell the emigrants in their quest of freedom, a properly pictorial account has yet to be written. Their experiences embody all the materials of an epic. No one who reads the published records of them can doubt the courage, the simple faith, or the natural resourcefulness of the pious and sturdy pioneers. That these qualities were tempered by an innate distrust of the black man was, under the circumstances, not unnatural. Though the perils of the wilderness they had to encounter were such as to test their endurance to the uttermost, their chief and constant cause of anxiety was the treacherous savage. Though their avowed wish in setting out was to remain at peace with the tribes around them, the hostility they aroused soon put an end to any hope of peaceful advance through the territories traversed. Their original purpose was to settle in the neighbourhood of Delagoa Bay, but the accounts which reached them of the deadly climate in that country, led them to turn their faces towards the nearer and more attractive region to the southward, now known as Natal. A small colony of Englishmen, some fifty in number, had for years been located at the port, but the country inland, devastated and depopulated by the Zulu tyrant, Chaka, was unoccupied, and the emigrants determined to pitch their tents and establish themselves permanently there.

I cannot pretend here to review the circumstances, that attended the earliest settlement of Natal by both Boers and British. It must suffice to say that after all sorts of sufferings and adventures, the emigrants, early in 1838, passed down the eastern slopes of the Drakensberg to the meadowy hills below, and encamped along the banks of the Tugela River and its affluents, between the present—and now historically famous—townships of Colenso and Estcourt. The country, as first seen by them, offered a refreshing contrast to the bare and arid plains of the interior. Its widespread basking hills were clothed with long or crisp grass, and the many watercourses winding between them were dotted about with the fragrant mimosa, which there grows to a greater height than elsewhere. Along the beds of the streams thicker vegetation nestles. The southern and western outlooks—free and open— were closed by the distant ramparts of the great mountain range that bisects East Africa from end to end. The view of this region as you approach it from the coast, whether suffused with the dreamy haze-glow of evening, or clarified by the sparkling atmosphere of morning, reminds you of a picture by Claude or Turner, and may well have captivated the fancy and appeased the longings of the weary wanderers in their search for a new home. To them this, indeed, seemed a Promised Land, an abode of peace and contentment, where, unvexed by tyrannic governments, they might live literally under their own vines and fig-trees, as the patriarchs did of yore.

Not long, however, was Arcadia to be enjoyed. One of the first steps taken by the emigrants was to secure,

D

as far as they could do so, a possessory title to the
country. They commissioned one of their leaders, Piet
Retief, a man of singular capacity and character, to
visit Dingaan, Chaka's successor in the sovereignty of
the Zulus, rightly styled a "monster," with all the
ferocity of his predecessor, but with none of his savage
kingliness, and to establish with him relations of amity
and concord. Taking with him an armed and mounted
party, Retief approached the king, and after much
parley he gave the wily savage the most effective
guarantee of his good faith by rescuing from the
clutches of a neighbouring chieftain about 7000 head
of cattle, of which he, the king, had been despoiled.

A few weeks later, having during the interval visited
and propitiated the English settlement at the seaport,
Retief, with an escort of about sixty followers, returned
to Dingaan's great kraal and obtained from him, in
return for the service he had rendered, a document
ceding to him and his countrymen "the place called
Port Natal, together with all the land annexed, that is
to say, from Tugela to the Umzimvubu River westward, and from the sea to the north, as far as the land
may be useful and in my possession." This document,
which is dated February 4, 1838, is now in the archives
at Pretoria. Its practical value, however, as an act of
cession, was destroyed by the immediate sequel. Three
days later the king invited his visitors to see him in
his kraal, where he assured them of his desire that
the farmers should "come and possess the land he had

given them " He wished them a pleasant journey, and
he asked them to sit down and drink native beer as a
parting cup Unversed as yet in the arts of Zulu
treachery, the farmers accepted the invitation. We
are told that "after drinking some beer together,
Dingaan ordered his troops to amuse the farmers by
dancing and singing, which they immediately commenced doing. The farmers had not been sitting
longer than a quarter of an hour when Dingaan called
out, 'Seize them!' upon which an overwhelming rush
was made upon the party before they could get on
their feet. They were then 'dragged with their feet
trailing on the ground, each man being held by as
many Zulus as could get at him, from the presence of
Dingaan, who still continued sitting and calling out
'Bulala amatakati!' (Kill the witches). He then said,
'Take the liver and the heart of the king of the
farmers and place them in the road of the farmers,'
who were then all clubbed to death, Retief being held
and forced to witness the deaths of his comrades before
they despatched him "

It is for jurists to determine what validity could
attach to a deed of cession signed under such circumstances. That it in no sense expressed the wish or will
of the grantor was proved by the bloody act of cancella-
tion. So far from being desirous to encourage the
settlement of the farmers, or even to tolerate their
existence, within two hours of the massacre Dingaan
gave orders to his *impi* to set off and destroy the wives

and children of the murdered farmers left behind on
the Tugela. And shouting out, "We will go and kill
the white dogs!" the bloodthirsty warriors rushed off on
their cowardly mission. And thoroughly they accomplished it. With the same noiseless celerity which
marked, forty years later, so many swift attacks on
British camps or garrisons, the Zulus swept across the
broad uplands of the Buffalo and through the broken
defiles of the Tugela Valley, to the unsuspecting
bivouacs of the Boers. Heedless of treachery and
danger, they had broken up into detached parties, and
were camped out in sylvan nooks and resting-places,
confidently awaiting the return of their representatives.
Let one of them tell the tale as it is recorded in Bird's
"Annals of Natal":—

"We had remained behind with the women and
children under the Drakensberg, along the Blaauwkrantz and Bushman's River—not in a camp (laager),
but in little bivouacs of three or four waggons each,
every family separately, all along the course of
the Blaauwkrantz downwards. We were in tranquil
security, for there was peace; and as Retief had recovered the cattle belonging to Dingaan's people, we
could hardly imagine that matters would not all go
right. This Dingaan knew, and, in order to come upon
us unawares, immediately after the murder of Retief
and his sixty men, he sent a Zulu commando to fall
upon us by night. Blaauwkrantz is between Klip River
and Weenen, towards the sea.

"The first assault of the Zulus was on Barend Johannes Liebenberg's bivouac, the second on that of Wynand Frederick Bezuidenhout (my father). Each stood with its cattle separately, no camp

"Of the Liebenbergs, four sons came forward, who, together with young Biggar, went to meet the Kafirs. All the other Liebenbergs were murdered. Young Biggar was an English bastard from Port Natal He and the Zulus understood each other: and he must have acted treacherously, for he went among the Zulus without receiving any molestation from them. When Van Vooren, who was Liebenberg's son-in-law, and was 'n his bivouac, saw this, he shot at Biggar, breaking his arm. Upon this Biggar said, 'Uncle, you have shot off my arm!' Van Vooren said, 'What, then, are you seeking among the Kafirs?' And then he shot Biggar, and killed him Liebenberg's bivouac was the lowest down along the Blaauwkrantz Kloof, and was thus first attacked.

"The second attack was on Adriaan Js. Rossouw, who was murdered with his wife and four children. We found two children, badly wounded, on the following day, but they were still alive Elizabeth Johanna Rossouw had sixteen wounds, and died next day Adriaan Johannes Rossouw, son of Adriaan, had thirty-two assegai wounds, and escaped with life. He lived on my farm till his eighteenth year (he was my sister's child), and then died of one of the wounds, which had never been completely healed. It was a wound which

he had received under the breast, and it had penetrated
through the shoulder-blade The film of the stomach
remained always exposed, and when he breathed one
could see the film open The third attack was on my
father's bivouac, consisting of five waggons and three
skin tents, and there were three men with it, namely, my
father, Roelof Botha (my brother-in-law), and myself."

An even more piteous narrative is that given by
Mrs Steenekamp—Retief's niece—from whom I have
already quoted· "On the 17th February the Kafirs
attacked us also. Oh dreadful, dreadful night ! wherein
so much martyred blood was shed, and two hundred
innocent children, ninety-five women, and thirty-three
men were slain, and hurled into an awful eternity by
the assegais of those bloodthirsty heathens Exclud-
ing the servants, the number was over four hundred
souls. Oh ! it was unbearable for flesh and blood to
behold the frightful spectacle the following morning
In one waggon were found fifty dead, and blood flowed
from the seam of the tent sail down to the lowest.
Ah ! how awful it was to look upon all those dead and
wounded ! I must also tell you, my dear children, how
it was that the Kafirs could so easily perpetrate the
massacre that night. It was on account of disobedience
and imprudence the greater portion of the people were
on the mission, and others engaged in buffalo-hunting;
others, moreover, were on the road to the Drakensberg,
to assist their families in coming down, so that the
Kafirs found the women and children quite alone

and sleeping peacefully. . . . The Commandant had the
dead buried and the wounded attended to.   On all
sides one saw tears flowing and heard people weeping
by the plundered waggons, painted with blood; tents
and beds torn to shreds; pregnant women and little
children had to walk for hours together bearing the
signs of their heavy flight.   Oh, how weary and fatigued
were those women and children! . . . When the women
came up to us they fell upon their knees and thanked
God for their deliverance from the hands of the cruel
tyrant.   In our encampment there was nothing but
lamentation and weeping."   The district in which these
scenes were enacted was called and still bears the name
of " Weenen," or weeping, and it is therein that yet
heavier carnage—though, thank God, not amongst the
weak and helpless—has been witnessed during the last
twelve months.

The butchery so vividly depicted by Mrs. Steenekamp
by no means closed the tale of Zulu ferocity.   Further
on she says· "On the 10th August we were again
attacked by the Kafirs at Bushman's River.   Their
bands were stretched out by thousands as far as the
eye could see.   It was a terrible sight to witness.   I
cannot describe their number, for one would have
thought that entire heathendom had gathered together
to destroy us.   But thanks and praise are due to the
Lord who so wonderfully has rescued us out of the
hands of our numberless and bloodthirsty foes, and
granted us the victory.   Their foremost band wore the

clothes and had the guns of the killed, and swarmed
down whilst the others surrounded us.   Our number
of fighting men was considerably diminished, for
a portion was with Maritz at Tugela, and another
portion had gone ahead to Port Natal, so that our
strength consisted of only two field commandants and
two field cornets with their men" They, nevertheless,
succeeded in routing the savage hordes, who retired
discomfited beyond the Tugela.

It was of these tragical incidents that I first heard
from the lips of John Tosen, as we travelled in his
waggon to Maritzburg thirteen years after their occurrence He had witnessed them while still a lad in his
teens.   He told us of the morning's shock when the
unsuspecting denizens of the camp were startled out of
their sleep by the fierce Zulu war-cry.   He described
the vain and pitiful attempts of women and children
to shelter themselves in and under waggons from the
spears of the furious savages He gave us thrilling
instances of marvellous escapes. one Boer girl of thirteen, though stabbed in twenty places, lived to a green
old age, the head of three generations   Even more
stirring was his story of the later engagement when,
with a small carronade loaded with nails and bullets,
the farmers kept thousands of Zulus at bay, as they
strove with linked hands to cross the Bushman's River
That was probably the Boer's first essay in the art of
field gunnery, in which, with ordnance from Creusot
they are now so proficient.

The natural instinct of the Cape Dutchman for
border warfare—and all the emigrant farmers came
within that category—was more signally demonstrated
later in the year. Rightly convinced that there could
be no assured peace or security as long as Dingaan
held power over the Zulus, the farmers decided to try
conclusions with him by an expedition the avowed
object of which was revenge and reparation. Mr.
Andries Pretorius, who became afterwards the first
President of the Transvaal Republic, was unanimously
elected Commandant, and well did he justify the confidence reposed in him. The force which thus proceeded
to chastise and vanquish the terror-striking Zulu king,
with his thousands of seasoned warriors all thirsting
for bloodshed, consisted of 460 men and fifty-seven
waggons. Among the former were several "persons of
colour," in whose behalf and for whose protection a
special "ordinance" was issued at the outset. This
small but compact and united force marched in five
divisions, each under its own officers and sub-officers,
but all subject to the leadership of the chief Commandant. A full and elaborate record of the march
was kept by the clerk of the Volksraad, acting as
secretary, and this document, together with the official
report of Pretorius himself, supplies as luminous an
account of the expedition as any student can desire.
Then, as ever since, the Boers entered upon war in a
spirit of exalted religious enthusiasm. Neither Israelite
nor Crusader, Covenanter nor Roundhead was more

constant in the invocation of God's help and in
dependence upon God's favour, than have at all times
been the Boers when engaged in battle. Wrote
Pretorius after his victory: "We had full confidence
in the justice of our cause. Our only hope was in God,
and the issue has proved that 'He who trusteth in the
great God, has certainly not built on sand'"

The narrative of the commando reads more like the
report of a camp meeting in the backwoods than the
story of a critical campaign. Pretorius appears to have
been not less effective as a pulpit orator than his
famous successor. He was ever exhorting and ad-
monishing his men. Calling around him his officers
of all ranks "down to the corporals," he bade them
"behave with courage and prudence when necessary,
reminded them that any design undertaken without
God is frustrated; how every one was to act when
engaged with the enemy; that we as reasonable crea-
tures, born under the light of the gospel, should not be
equal to them in destroying innocent women and children, and that we may pray of God everything which
is not contrary to His great righteousness. He admonished them further to press on the minds of the
men under them to submit every morning and evening
their duties and their doings to the Lord in prayers, and
to spend the holy Sabbath to the honour of God, and
not to use that great name in vain, nor to calumniate
the Most High. . . . Finally he repeatedly reminded us
that 'unity createth power' Amongst other things he

strictly prohibited any one to interfere with Kafir children or women during the conflict or to take them
prisoners "

Whatever views may be held as to the methods thus
pursued by the Boers—and they are as much in vogue
to-day as then—it cannot be denied that they were
amply vindicated by results. In less than three weeks
the expedition accomplished its purpose. In those days
there was not the vestige of a waggon track, but the
route followed was very much the same as that taken
by Lord Chelmsford in 1879 in his advance to Ulundi.
Every possible precaution was taken against surprise.
The Boers were never caught napping. Patrols were
sent out in all directions. Several Zulus who were
taken prisoners were sent to the king with white flags
"to inform him that if he would return to us the horses
and guns which he had taken from our people we
should be willing to enter into negotiations for peace."
No answer was received, and the march proceeded.

At length, on Saturday, December 15, 1838, the
Zulu army was discovered posted on a very difficult
mountain. The rest of the story cannot be told better
than in the pithy words of the Commandant himself.
" On receiving this information I immediately proceeded
there with two hundred men, but finding it unadvis-
able to attempt anything with so small a force, and in
such a place, I returned to camp. The next day, being
Sunday, we intended to remain quiet, but as soon as
day broke upon us we discovered that our camp was

surrounded by, as we thought, the whole of the Zulu forces. The engagement instantly commenced on both sides. The Zulus *fired* upon us, and made several attempts to storm our encampments, and on being repulsed they only retreated for short distances. They stood their ground firmly for two hours, and then were reinforced by five more divisions. At this juncture you will scarcely be able to form an idea of the sight presented to us. It was such as to require some nerve not to betray uneasiness in the countenance. Seeing that it was necessary to display the most desperate determination, I caused the gates of our enclosed camp (formed of the laagered waggons) to be simultaneously thrown open, from which some mounted men were to charge the enemy, at the same time keeping up a heavy fire upon them. The Zulus stood our assault firmly for some time, but at last finding their number rapidly decreasing they fled, scattering themselves in all directions. They were pursued on horseback by as many of our men as could be spared from the camp."

The Commandant started off himself, and shortly overtook a Zulu warrior, with whom, after a brief and bootless parley, he found himself engaged in a fierce hand-to-hand tussle. "At last he closed with me and attempted to stab me through the breast; I averted this by grasping at the weapon with my left hand, but in doing so received it through the hand. Before he could extricate it I seized him and threw him to the ground, but as the assegai remained pierced through my hand,

which was under me as I lay upon him, I had but one
hand to hold him and use my dagger whilst he
attempted to strangle me. At this crisis one of my
men came to my assistance, pulled the assegai out of
my hand and stabbed the Zulu on the spot My hand
bleeding very much I was obliged to return to the
camp, and it was apprehended some of our men had
fallen. However, it pleased the Almighty to give us
this victory without the loss of a single life, only three
of us being wounded. The following day we resumed
our march." On December 22, the commando reached
Dingaan's great kraal, which was set on fire as the Boers
approached, and destroyed There, however, were found
the bones of Retief and his men, and the papers, among
which was found the celebrated "treaty," of which a
certified copy was piously taken and kept.

Though the victory thus achieved did not actually
end the reign of Dingaan it destroyed his power.
During the ensuing year the Boers entered into alliance
with the despot's younger and more placable brother,
M'Pande, and recognised him as the future sovereign of
Zululand. Early in 1840 another commando, also led
by Pretorius, advanced against the fugitive king, who
had established himself amongst the northern mountains. M'Pande, with an army of 10,000 men, co-operated, and by that force another signal defeat was inflicted
upon Dingaan, who disappeared into the forests and was
finally assassinated by some of his own people Meanwhile his brother was formally installed as head of the

Zulus, and the boundary of the new "Republic" was extended northward of the line assigned by Retief's treaty from the Tugela River to the Black Umvolosi, where it enters St. Lucia Bay. These incidents were attended by the seizure of large herds of cattle, and the capture of large numbers of "apprentices," whose services helped to supply the lack of labour which made life in the depopulated territory of Natal so difficult. In spite of the pious professions of the Boer leaders and the artless repudiations of the Boer annalists, Boer methods in dealing with subjugated native races then, as since, practically demonstrated the white man's claim to be his black brother's keeper.

Such were the incidents which made "Dingaan's Day" so memorable an anniversary to the Boer. By him it is kept not only as a day of victory, but as the Day of Independence It is associated not only with the deliverance of his people from the power of a cruel tyrant, but with the deeds and the events by which they purchased their claim to be a free nation In later years it was again identified with the Boer struggle for freedom. On December 13, 1880, the malcontent farmers of the Transvaal anticipated the date by three days, when at Paardekraal, near Pretoria, they proclaimed their independence. More recently, and especially since 1895, the yearly celebration round the National Monument on that spot has been a great popular function. Let me now proceed to describe another even more interesting occasion identified with the fateful day. The immediate succession of more startling events diverted attention from an incident whose pathetic and romantic significance deserved far more notice than it received.

For many months, if not for years, prior to December 16, 1895, endeavours had been made to collect on the site of the Weenen massacres such vestiges as might remain of the victims. From the river-beds, the dongas, and the veld around, as time went on, bleached bones had been carefully gathered and reverently preserved by the neighbouring farmers, together with rusty bullets, implements, knives, and other relics or fragments, from the devastated camps. A movement, carefully fostered and directed by the Dutch ministers of the districts—those Predikants whose influence over the minds and hearts of their flocks has contributed so greatly to present events—was set afoot for the solemn burial of these remains and for the erection over them of a suitable commemorative monument. In both the republics, as well as in the two colonies, subscriptions were collected, and on the date named the solemn ceremony of interment took place. It lasted three days. Families and visitors from far and near responded to the call. They came in waggons, in carriages, on horses; a few by rail. As in ordinary times the Boers troop to their quarterly *Nachtmaal,* or Communion Service, so, though with more pious fervour, they gathered to this patriotic festival. Amongst them were members of the families whose relations had been slain on the spot fifty-seven years before. To them it was not only a celebration; it was literally a funeral. After all these years of exposure and decay, the bones of their kindred were at last to have Christian burial. Summer after summer the scorching sun of South Africa had blazed pitilessly down upon the remains of the pioneers; storms had raged furiously over them; floods had whirled them about; and now, amidst peace and contentment, they were to be laid reverently to rest. There were some—a few—amongst the throng, white-haired and aged, yet hale and keen-minded, who had escaped from the massacre. One old lady bore in her body the scars of the wounds she had suffered from as a child. Among other bearers of names familiar in the annals of the Trek, was Mr. Pretorius, son of the redoubtable Commandant, and at that time a loyal member of the Natal Parliament. Piet Retief had his descendants there. A grandchild of Maritz, the other namesake of Natal's capital, was to have reinterment. General Joubert was present to represent the Government of the Transvaal. The Government of Natal was represented by the Prime Minister and two of his colleagues.

The spot chosen for the monument was about a mile from the railway station at Chieveley, from whence, on the 15th of last December, the forces of General Buller vainly, though valiantly, strove to force the passage of the Tugela, in the face of impregnable

Boer entrenchments. Little recked we then of what history had in store. The weather was bright but sultry. The two previous days had been passed in religious exercises, participated in almost exclusively by the Dutch themselves. About 1200 visitors—mostly family parties—had encamped close to the Blaauwkrantz River Their waggons and tents gleamed cosily amongst the spreading and fragrant mimosa trees All had brought their own supplies, any place of entertainment being miles distant. The public services took place in a huge tent, and there, about ten in the morning, the official visitors from Maritzburg were received by General Joubert and others, and escorted to their places on a rough platform in front of which stood the great square "casket" or box, draped in black, in which had been deposited all that could be found of the murdered Voertrekkers. The rest of the tent was filled with the Dutch visitors, a large proportion of whom were women and children.

Of the service itself little need be said. The Dutch Reformed Church follows very closely the Presbyterian order of worship; simplicity and severity are its prevailing notes, combined, let me add, with the devout earnestness of a religious-minded people. If the hymns sung and the prayers offered were devoid of liturgical embroidery, there could not be a doubt as to their sincerity and fervour. The slow sad cadences of the ancient psalmody were joined in by old and young, and the words of the ancient Book seemed racy of the

E

soil and reminiscent of the past. There were depths of suppressed passion in the extemporised prayers uttered over those crumbling bones, and the written sermon was listened to with profound and unbroken attention. It was a powerful appeal for the unity and brotherhood of the Africander race, and there was, no doubt, in its glowing words a deeper significance than was suspected then.

The service over and the benediction given, all trooped out of the stifling enclosure into the hot midsummer air. Preceded and flanked by representatives of the foremost Voertrekkers, the humble ox-cart which acted as hearse was followed by a cortège nearly a mile long, headed by the Commandant of the Transvaal and the Prime Minister of Natal as chief mourners. Two abreast the procession wound its way over the sun-baked veld, past mimosa, and by donga, the prospect bounded by hills that have lately belched forth shells on beleaguered garrisons and khaki-clad battalions, to where the foundations of the monument awaited the relics that were to rest below. There, the sombre casket was lowered into the pit prepared for it, amidst further hymns and prayers, while reports were read of the steps that had been taken to secure the commemoration. Then came the laying of the corner-stone by General Joubert, followed by speeches from himself and others, all breathing unity and goodwill. One—delivered by the British spokesman—expressed a hope that in the grave below would he buried not only the sacred relics that had been deposited there, but the seeds of all the animosities and discords of the past, and that thenceforward peace, and concord, and common interests would bind together the two peoples and fuse them into one race

Speeches over and function ended, the visitors returned to the encampment. There, in one of the marquees supplied by Government for the occasion, the veteran Pretorius, with his friendly household, entertained the chief guests of the day to a bountiful repast of roast - beef and plum - pudding, and much kindly talk ensued about things past, present, and to come in Johannesburg and elsewhere. Of what passed then this only may be said now, that there was not in General Joubert's mind the smallest apparent apprehension of any imminent explosion, but there was on his part a very strong persuasion that a policy of reasonable compliance with the demands of the Uitlanders would be the best means of meeting the difficulties of the situation. " What is the use," he said to me, " trying to dam up the flowing stream ? It will be all the worse when it bursts through in the end." Wise words and prophetic !

Before luncheon was over the gathering clouds burst in a tempest over the camp. Wind raged, rain fell in sheets, lightning flashed and deafening thunder pealed. The river rose to flood level and trickling streams became almost impassable torrents. It was in such weather that we bade our hosts a hearty farewell, and that the latest celebration of Dingaan's Day came to an end.

Just a fortnight afterwards Dr. Jameson, with his band of troopers, crossed the frontier of the Transvaal and marched on Johannesburg! Four years later the Bishop of Natal buried the dead on the battlefield of Chieveley, slain by Boer shells and bullets on the day preceding.

CHAPTER IV

THE SETTLERS AS PIONEERS

If the old Dutch Voertrekkers won the grateful recognition of posterity for their bravery and heroism in facing the perils of the wilderness, and in doing battle with the pitiless forces of barbarism, the first English settlers of Natal deserved, I think, hardly less credit for the pluck and endurance with which they bore the many trials and disappointments of their new life in a new land. Though they did not come into collision with any of the savage tribes around them, nor win their title to the soil occupied by any blood-bought deed of cession, they nevertheless purchased their right to its possession by the sweat of their brows and the strength of their arms—by patient though often baffled industry, by unflinching struggles against hardship, failure, and adversity, and by the gradual reclamation and development of a desert land. The Boers of to-day, sixty years later, loudly boast that Natal is theirs, by virtue of the bit of paper to which Dingaan set his mark—meaning to falsify it, as he did on the morrow, and of the subsequent victory obtained by Pretorius over the tyrant when the same primitive document was recovered   The British Government and settlers base

their claim to possession upon the prior occupancy of
the seaport by Englishmen, upon the final reconquest
of the Colony by British arms and Boer surrender,
but yet more effectively by unbroken and unchallenged
occupancy of the soil for fifty years. In the making of
Natal, as it exists to-day, a place of enterprise, industry,
and energy, the Boer settler has had but small share.
His flocks and his herds have multiplied by natural
increase, under the peaceful rule of Great Britain, and
with the price of their produce he has been able to add
to his acres and enlarge his untenanted domains. His
homestead and its surroundings have improved somewhat on the primitive type, though not always. In
some instances the force of example has led him to
erect fences and plant trees. His ox-waggons, in charge
of native drivers, have added materially to his income
as carriers of merchandise. But in all that concerns
real progress and development, he has taken little, if
any, part. His race is scarcely represented in the larger
towns. Had he been left alone in possession of the
land, it would have shown few, if any, of those evidences of activity and advancement which now place
it in line with the rest of the civilised world. The
" Republic of Natalia " might have been a Paradise—
of sluggishness and stagnation—according to Boer ideas
and aspirations. It would certainly not be the busy,
prosperous, progressive colony of Natal, the defence and
retention of which have been deemed worth the most
strenuous efforts of a vast empire.

When the British Government formally took possession of Natal, and when British immigrants began in 1849 to arrive in the country, the desire of the Dutch Voertrekkers was to get as far as possible from the reach of the one and the sight of the other. They were glad to dispose of their "farms," or land-grants on almost any terms. The result was that the newcomers were able to acquire holdings of much larger area than those they had expected to occupy. I know cases in which tracts of 6000 acres were sold for a waggon and "span" of twelve or fourteen oxen, wherewith the owner enabled himself to "trek," with his family, into the far interior. A further result was less conducive to the public weal Speculators in many cases purchased these Boer farms at an almost nominal cost, and kept them locked up until such time as they might succeed in obtaining relatively extravagant prices for them. In some cases they were later on thrown into the hands of a great land company, which, in its turn, relet them to native tenants, thus consigning them anew to the occupancy of barbarism A large portion of the best lands in Natal has thus been deprived of the civilising influences of European settlement.

But it is not of absentee proprietorships or Boer drones that I now write. It is of the men, not many thousands in number, who have made Natal what it is My readers know what a motley throng they were, and how devoid of capital or local knowledge Yet they

spread themselves over the country and occupied it.
It by no means followed that the most ignorant—of
farming or commercial conditions—were the least successful. Townsmen sometimes made the best agriculturists. Men who had never stood behind a counter in
the old country occasionally throve as storekeepers or
tradesmen in the new. The first greengrocer in Durban
was a tinsmith; one of the earliest market-gardeners
had been an auctioneer; a leading lawyer in later years
began his colonial life by carrying a hod. Most of our
sugar-planters had been men in business. Schools
were established by persons who "at home" had never
taught a lesson. The category of topsy-turvydom
might be continued indefinitely. The point of interest
is that in a new country the true qualification of success is the stout heart nerving the ready hand. Experience is undoubtedly a good thing, but under changed
conditions and the stress of necessity, it may be re-
learnt without waste of effort or failure of effect.

The purpose which possessed the minds of most of
the early immigrants, was to plant cotton. There were
doubts as to the sufficiency of the American supply of
that staple, and there was a desire that it should be
grown by free Africans instead of by slave labour. Yet
cotton-planting has never prospered in Natal. Some
forty bales were grown by German settlers in 1848, and
some years later several hundreds of acres were planted
by a company, to say nothing of smaller ventures by
private individuals. A small fly, however, and other

pests attacked the crops ; prices fell, and the industry
made no headway. Other pursuits proved more attractive. Of these sugar-planting is the one that has held
its own most continuously. I well remember the sensation that was caused by the first production of sugar
in 1852. The canes, after nearly two years in growth,
had been crushed by most primitive appliances, the
juice being boiled in large three-legged pots. It was
drained and dried in the same crude way, but the
result was unquestionably—sugar—though sugar in its
stickiest and most treacly form. Those specimens were
hailed by the whole community with pride and delight
as being—what they indeed proved to be—the heralds
of a new "industry," to a people ever in those days
on the watch for new products and openings. The
experiment was followed by more ambitious ventures.
Money was scraped together for the importation of
improved plant. A company largely supported by
Cape merchants was established, and if it did little
else, it availed to encourage confidence in the enterprise, and to lead others to engage in it. Though
after the lapse of forty years the industry has not developed the anticipated proportions, it still holds its
own as a mainstay of colonial prosperity, and central
mills, representing a vast outlay of capital, and equipped
with every modern appliance of manufacture, are fed
by ever-growing areas of plantation. The wild and
tangled bush growth of the past has been replaced by
monotonous breadths of rustling cane-field. The Pic-

turesque has made way for the Profitable, and the beautiful coastlands, shorn and trim, have ceased to be natural and romantic.

Civilisation is no doubt a good thing—is any one bold enough to dispute it ?—but it has its drawbacks. If it adds to the fulness and utility of life, it takes from it much of pristine charm. Possibly it was youth—the zest of spring-time—that lent a glamour to the experiences of those days, but one thinks of them now with regret. Earth in her virgin freshness, before axe had stript or man had clothed her, had a grace which one fails to find in spreading field, in measured orchard, in metalled road, or rushing railway car. The free unordered outlines of wild bush and jungle, the winding, scarcely traceable track over hill and down valley, the sudden glimpse of stump-strewn clearance and rude shanty, or of native mealie garden and hive-like huts, the absence of all sounds save the voices of the forest or the veld, the closeness of nature everywhere unconstrained and "unadorned," the strange commingling sense of age and of newness, of immemorial antiquity in the past and of incalculable possibilities in the future —all, even though unconsciously and indefinably, tended to make country rides in the earlier years a joy which is but a memory nowadays. One scrupled not then, after a long amble, to claim the hospitality of any neighbouring homestead, knowing that however bare the larder might be—and bare it usually was—it would be freely at the welcome traveller's service. Where

little was looked for, little was abundance. The
simplest fare sufficeth when hunger sharpens appetite,
and a blanket on the floor, if nothing better were forthcoming, would give a night's sound rest to a tired man.
I never slept better than I did many years ago in a
deserted outhouse, far from the road, to which I had
groped my way in the dark and the rain. My pony
found stable-room in one corner, and I found a bed on
a heap of straw in another corner, in company with a
dog and her progeny already in prior occupation. It is
a fact that, of the hosts of soldiers who have lately been
in the field, those have fared the best who have slept
most continuously in the open, on the bare ground with
only their rugs under and over them.

The spread of sugar-planting led to a social change
of far greater import than was at first realised. Cane
is a product of slow growth and costly preparation.
The industry requires both large capital and a permanent labour supply for its successful prosecution.
The African native, good worker in the field though
he be, after a few months' toil tires of the daily round,
and insists upon returning to the free and idle life of
his kraal. To meet this difficulty steps were taken,
after much negotiation, to import from India indentured
labourers, bound to serve a five years' term with an
employer and to live at least ten years within the
Colony. I well remember one evening late in 1860
watching, from a height overlooking the sea, the ship
Truro sail up to the anchorage. Her white canvas

towered over the blue sea-line, and we all regarded
her as the harbinger of a new dispensation. And so
she proved to be, though in a sense far wider than
we expected. For the system has continued, despite
difficulties and steadily growing opposition on the part
of the European working-classes. At that time all
the trade of the Colony, and especially that of the
smaller storekeepers and "Kafir dealers," was in the
hands of white men, and there were none but English
mechanics and operatives. Now, the "Asiatic" population equals in number the European. Country and
Kafir stores are almost wholly run by Indian traders.
The vending of fruit and vegetables, and to a considerable extent their growth, are the business of the
frugal and irrepressible "coolie," who, after his term
of service is over, settles on the soil, squats in a small,
kennel-like shanty, and lives at a cost which to an
Englishman would spell starvation. Thus it has come
to pass that the poorer classes of settlers have been
elbowed out of the minor walks of trade and agriculture — shopkeeping, market - gardening, hawking,
rough labour of all kinds—and the prospects of Natal
as a home for white men are being gradually narrowed
and restricted. Fortunately, the skilled artisan, the
cultivator and stock-breeder on a larger scale, the clerk
and the shopman, with other superior classes of em-
ployee, still occupy the field, and seem likely to do so, and
it is by them that the steadfast opposition to an indiscriminate "Asiatic invasion" is likely to be sustained.

As the Indian can now acquire the franchise only
under very restricted conditions, the fetters imposed
by law upon Indian immigration are not likely to be
lightly or suddenly relaxed Experience shows, however, that in a subtropical climate indentured Indian
labour is indispensable to successful enterprise in the
field. Whether the colonist likes it or not, the free
and voluntary Indian immigrant or trader finds his
way into the country and silently works on there. As
a purveyor of household supplies, as a domestic servant,
or as a farm hand, he has made himself a necessity
of life, and, as far as one can see, the Asiatic has come
to stay in South-east Africa—at any rate under such
conditions as restrictive legislation may impose

Sugar was the contemporary of other and smaller
industries, which at one time engrossed more attention
than they have done since. Arrowroot-growing for
some years in the later fifties was a favourite pursuit
The tuber with its upgrowth of broad rustling leaves
was scraped or grated to powder, which, having been
cleaned from the fibrous pulp, was exposed in granu-
lated particles, on calico trays, to the sun. Absolute
whiteness and purity from speck or impurity of any
kind are essentials of quality. The process of production is very simple and inexpensive. Women and
children can easily assist in it " Natal arrowroot " soon
acquired an honourable position in the market, and
the industry grew more and more in favour, but its
success and popularity brought about its collapse.

The market was ultimately overstocked, prices fell below a paying limit, and arrowroot was abandoned. The same fate befell the production of cayenne pepper. This condiment is the product of a small, shrublike plant, of which there are many varieties, yielding glistening sac-like pods ranging in size from the tiny yellow or scarlet chilli, of fiery pungency, to the bulkier and fleshier green or crimson capsicum, which in its raw and unripe state is a wholesome and appetising adjunct to the table   These pods, crushed and ground, yield the familiar "cayenne" of commerce.   It is still produced in Natal, but the prices obtainable are hardly remunerative.

Tillers of the soil in old countries, where the capabilities of the earth have been tested and proved by centuries of experiment and industry, know little of the interest which attaches to the agriculturist's work in virgin fields, whose resources are unknown and undeveloped.   Tilth in these regions has the zest of novelty and surprise.   All is uncertainty and speculation.   The seed sown is the matrix of indefinite possibilities.   The sprouting plant is the subject of almost parental hopes and fears.   Promise is often belied by fulfilment.   The unexpected continually happens.   Plants do not always fructify.   Trees sometimes fail to bear.   Sub-tropical countries like Natal, which belong not wholly to either the temperate or the torrid zone, and possess different grades of climate within a relatively narrow area, are natural hotbeds

of experiment. The expectations of their pioneers are
apt to be strangely falsified. Cotton failed, but sugar
succeeded. Coffee, after a prosperous start, fell back
and tea took its place. Wheat, from which two crops
yearly were predicated, has never made headway.
For many years peaches were the staple fruit crop of
the uplands. Summer after summer waggons loaded
loosely with them would arrive in Durban and be cleared
of their contents by eager purchasers at 2s. or 2s. 6d. a
hundred. Now they are less abundant, but the more
wholesome and familiar apple abounds. It was thought
in the early days that hardy English fruits would never
succeed, but now strawberries, pears, and plums are common, though cherries, gooseberries, and currants are
seldom seen. On the coast most tropical fruits have
at all times flourished. Pine-apples, oranges, naartjes,
bananas, mangoes, papaws, guavas, loquats, granadillas,
and avocado pears (daintiest of Pomona's gifts), in their
season, are often drugs, and for miles the hillsides near
the railway are covered with fruit plantations. The
spread of railways and the outgrowth of steamship
lines, with their "cold" chambers, have opened out
markets where none existed in the old days. The first
settlers had to reckon with the absence of markets as
one of the chief hindrances to industry. They could
grow, but they could not sell. The wants of the few
householders in the two towns were soon supplied by
producers in the immediate vicinity. There were no
means of export, and growers at a distance, after

bringing their produce to the port along wretched, unmade roads, would more often than not find no purchasers

In addition to the want of labour and the want of markets, there were, and are still, other besetting drawbacks in the paths of the South African farmer and planter. For many years the sugar-planter's triad of afflictions was known as the three F's—frost, fire, and flood. Strange as it may seem, the first was for a long time a real and recurrent source of dread. Until experience taught otherwise it was assumed that sugar-cane could only be successfully grown in the valleys, along the river-banks. It often happened in those days, before the lowlands had been drained and cultivated, that once or twice during the months of winter hard frosts would visit vegetation in those localities and cruelly nip the leaves of the cane-plants, strong and stalwart though they seemed to be. Many a time has the planter risen at dawn to see his rustling fields blighted by the gelid touch of the crisp, sharp air. In such cases nothing else could be done than at once to cut down the frosted cane and crush it with the least possible delay. In course of time it was found that cane flourished just as well on the slopes and hill crests as on the lower levels, and frost has ceased to be a terror.

Fire continues to be one of winter's perils. After months of drought, plantations became so much tinder, and should by chance any field take fire, and a "hot wind" be blowing, the devastation wrought was widespread if not ruinous. One "Black Monday" nearly thirty years ago will long be memorable for the destruction wreaked through two counties by the ruthless fire-fiend "Fire-breaks" of trees or bare spaces, combined with vigilance in suppression, have greatly lessened the risks of conflagration, but the dangers of grass fires will long be a menace to the tree-planter and pastoralist in the upper districts. Natal has been described as a "vast meadow" Its hills are clothed from foot to brow with crisp and waving grass. The latter often overtops a man's head. From the earliest recorded times it has been the fashion, and a wasteful, barbarous fashion it seems, to burn these luxuriant pastures Old navigators, passing along the sea-coast during the winter months, wrote of Natal as a "land of smoke" To-day the exquisite atmosphere of that season is blurred by the smoke that hangs or broods, like a brown veil, over the prospect. Efforts are made by the farmers, and encouraged by special laws, to regulate the practice, by confining it to certain seasons, and heavy penalties are imposed upon the wilful firing of grass. But it is difficult to prevent either accidental or wanton transgression. Should a fire break out when a high wind is blowing, it is vain to try to stem its progress. On it sweeps over hill and dale, licking up any inflammable thing that may be within its track, leaping over roads, attacking tree plantations, destroying buildings, should they interpose: after dark lighting up the heavens with the lurid glow of its

F

encircling flames, and girdling the mountain sides with
the contortions of its blazing outlines. It is the aim of
most good farmers in these days not to burn their grass
until the spring rains have fallen, and a new growth is
assured : and thus it came to pass the other day that
General Joubert's column of raiders, by firing the grass
between themselves and our own forces, was able to
advance behind the smoke unseen and unmolested, into
the heart of our ravaged uplands. By the same expedient did the retreating Boer forces shelter their
retirement from the Biggarsberg.

Perils by flood are by no means peculiar to Natal,
and they are less formidable than they were in days
when cultivation was confined to the river-sides, and
when bridges and railways and hard roads were
not. Then it was not a rare experience for country
residents to be cut off from communication with
their neighbours for days or weeks. If rains
continued, streams remained impassable, and many a
hair-breadth escape was recorded in attempts made
to ford them. Flood rains in South Africa are
torrents that appear only anxious to make up by their
violence for past times of drought. I remember one
which began at six in the morning and stopped
at nine, when the sun shone forth and a lovely day
of peace and brightness ensued. Yet during those
three hours more than six inches fell, and when
an hour later I rode into town, thirteen miles distant,
the whole country seemed flood-swept. The road

was seamed by gullies, culverts were torn up, and progress even on horseback was only possible over the grass, across country, and along dodging by-ways. On another occasion in 1868, having finished the week's parliamentary duties at the capital, I started as usual for my home at the seaport. There was but one means of conveyance, a so-called "bus," or covered wagonette, which happened that day to be driven by a local magnate who was fond at times of thus displaying his powers as a whip. It rained smartly when we set forth, and it rained more and more heavily as we advanced, until it seemed as if no headway were possible against the driving elements. On we went, however, floundering, jolting, swerving, pitching, abandoning the road for the veld whenever it were possible to do so, sticking fast constantly, breaking harness, lifting wheels out of mud-holes, and appealing to the horses with every epithet of malediction and persuasion. As we changed horses every twelve miles there were alternate spells of activity and depression, but through it all our amateur driver kept cheerful and imperturbable, his spirits rising indeed as the difficulties of the journey multiplied. At the Half-way House the womenfolk inside were asked whether they would stay or proceed, but they all preferred to go on, though evening was advancing and the rain grew heavier as we neared the coast. So on we went, plunging and lurching amidst blinding rain, and evading the shattered roads wherever we could, until darkness fell and progress became merely a

meek trust in Providence. In some places sheets of
water covered the roads on both sides, and nothing but
an unerring instinct enabled our friend on the box to
keep clear of the hidden banks and ditches on either
side. It was a bold and splendid feat of coachmanship,
and the obvious satisfaction with which his performance
was regarded by Mr. C. himself, when towards midnight he drew up at the coach-office, was doubtless his
best reward. A day later it would have been impossible,
as when morning dawned nearly every bridge in the
Colony had been swept away, and the main roads were
impassable by wheeled traffic for weeks.

In 1856 we had had even a worse flood, but as
there were no bridges to be washed away and scarcely
a road worth the name, its effects were not so manifest. Durban, however, was isolated by two raging
streams, and districts that are now thickly built
over and populated were under water. Flood effects
were not then, as they are now, minimised by drainage,
and destruction of property had to be borne with grim
fortitude as part of the unavoidable experiences of life.
With another form of natural visitation civilisation cannot cope. It is still the haunting dread of the fruit-
grower. Thunder-storms can hardly be anywhere more
frequent or violent than they are during our summer
months. In the upper districts they are often accompanied by falls of hail such as Europe rarely, if ever,
witnesses. After a day or days of exceptional heat,
a huge blank blue-black cloud, like a giant wing,

springs up from the west and spreads over the sky.
Deathlike stillness falls. The hot air stifles. A long
band of greyer or coppery cloud sweeps up from the
horizon. Birds dart about and twitter. All nature
seems breathless and apprehensive. Mutterings of
thunder are heard. Then a muffled distant roar seems
to rush onward, and all at once a tornado bursts overhead, wind, rain, and then monstrous hail, all contending together in deafening uproar and stunning confusion Though lightning blazes, the fury of the storm
seems for a few minutes, while at its worst, to arrest
the flash and to stifle the peal, until in a few minutes
the tempest is overpast, and the storm assumes its
normal character. It often, perhaps mostly, happens
that in half-an-hour the sky clears and the sun shines
with surpassing brilliancy, but the jagged fragments
of ice have stript the fruit-trees, and battered down the
crops, if they have not wrought destruction to small
live-stock and outbuildings. These hail-storms, as a
rule, sweep along the heights. Their tracks are comparatively narrow, and sharply defined, being seldom
more than half a mile in breadth. Nothing can stand
against their wild buffetings If the traveller be caught
by one, as I have been, on some exposed stretch of
mountain road, the best thing to be done is to crouch
under the shelter of the vehicle, if it be an open one,
or to get under the lee of any bank or barrier that may
be within reach.

Insect pests are a constant harassment to the Natal

farmer. Cotton suffered from a tiny green aphis.
Coffee was attacked by a grub, or "borer," which
sapped the shrub's vitality and brought about its decay.
Beetles of all sizes often prove destructive in both field
and garden. A beautiful blue moth pierces and blights
peaches White ants attack the roots of many plants,
especially roses, and caterpillars are apt to destroy
bloom and foliage. But the plague of plagues, so far
as insect life is concerned, is the locust. In the very
early fifties the pioneer immigrants were startled by
occasional flights of this deadly visitant. At first a
few odd outfliers—like the Uhlans of the German army
—would flutter about inquiringly, as though spying
out the vegetation, but ere long their numbers would
multiply until the sky would seem alive with the
rustling multitudes, and at last be darkened by the
winged hordes On the flight passed, thickening and
hovering until the whole settled on every green
thing below, covering the earth with a brown and
quivering mantle, drawing slowly onward and leaving
in its wake a stript and leafless desert. In those days
there was little cultivated ground to be thus ravaged,
and, strangely enough, after 1852 the locusts disappeared. Constantly heard of in the interior, they
ceased to trouble Natal, until in 1894 they travelled
downward from the north, in such monstrous swarms
that the Colony was panic-stricken. Crops of all kinds
were devoured In vain did the sufferers strive to
drive off the invaders by the din of clamorous sound.

In vain were tins beaten, sheets of iron banged, and
other noise-creating expedients resorted to. Whenever
the locusts chose to come they came to stay—until
their ruthless task was completed, and the young
crops were devoured. As ruin seemed to threaten the
community, Government was appealed to for succour.
Special plenary powers of action were granted by the
Legislature, and a costly organisation was set on foot.
"Locust officers" were appointed for the several districts; barriers of wire netting were erected; trenches
were dug; rewards were offered, per sack, for dead
locusts The services of the natives were enlisted
and heartily rendered in the common cause. Human
ingenuity was strained by efforts to devise remedial
measures. One inventive-minded colonist appealed to
the war authorities in England for assistance in a
campaign he proposed to prosecute in Natal against
the tenacious foe, by means of mortars and projectiles
which were to scatter destruction amongst the flying
hosts. Unfortunately for his scheme, the local government declined to spend money on the experiment, and
the project fell through. Other plans were tried, however, with varying measures of success. Microscopic
investigation discovered a fungoid germ with which
living locusts were infected, and, dying, spread disease
amongst their tribes. More efficacious, however, has
been the use of poison (a preparation of arsenic), a
process which some planters have found to be quite
effective in ridding their crops of the pest. Partly

because the evil has thus been coped with and partly, perhaps, because familiarity has diminished its terrors, little is now heard of the plague, and though locusts still hover about, they no longer cause a scare.

Insect pests are not noxious to the vegetable world alone. Animal life knows them to its cost. I say nothing about the tsetse-fly, as it has never been known in Natal, though it is rife enough in Zululand, where scientific research is locating its area and securing immunity from its effects. The cattle tick may be less deadly, but it is far more diffusive. Ticks range in size from the pin-point-sized speck, which is so troublesome to mankind, to the large, gross, and distended parasite, as big as a bean, which preys upon the helpless quadruped, and more especially upon the horse, the ox, and the cow. Gathering in the tenderest parts of the body, these greedy bloodsuckers penetrate and hang on to the tormented skin until they drop off in bloated repletion. They are worse in some seasons than in others, but they sap the vitality of their victims, and even horses have been known in bad years to die from their effects. Nothing short of care in picking them off, of vigilant attention, and proper treatment, will avail to counteract the activities of South-east African ticks.

Of the maladies that afflict live - stock generally chapters might be written, as indeed volumes have been published. The first visitors to Natal, long before Chaka had swept off its native population, speak of it

as a land rich in cattle and in goats. Horses and
sheep were unknown before the white man brought
them, but it has always been a land of pastoral abundance. When I first knew the country cattle plagues
were relatively few. Sleek and fat, such herds as there
were did full credit to their pasture lands. About 1855,
however, lung-sickness crept into the country and
ravaged it from end to end. Farmers and carriers
alike were smitten, and stock-raising ceased to be
remunerative. It was not long, however, before inoculation was found to be a safeguard and palliative, if not
a preventive. The virus was applied to the tail, which
dropped off, and for years the comic spectacle of tailless
cattle was witnessed on the roads and in the fields. An
ingenious colonist—he was a cook—proposed to fix
artificial wisps to the stumps that remained, in order
to drive the flies away! Lung-sickness has remained
in the country ever since, but laws have been passed
to restrain its spread, and inoculation and isolation help
to keep it in check, so that cattle thrive and multiply
in spite of it. Twenty years later another epidemic—
red-water—broke out and proved almost, if not quite,
as fatal as lung-sickness had been. But its devasta-
tions were survived. One immediate and compensating
result of these outbreaks was to bring sheep-farming
into vogue. Sheep at any rate were not liable to these
plagues, and farmers turned their attention to the new
pursuit with the eager energy that has ever nerved
them under successive rebuffs and losses. Sheep in

their turn developed diseases which had to be combated with not less patience and vigour. Scab has for nearly thirty years tried the resources of both farmers and legislators. Remedial laws have been passed, and a costly veterinary department created, but the steadfast opposition of the Dutch population has seriously interfered with its utility. Perhaps the only perceptible grievance which the Boer can advance against British rule is the readiness of the Colonial Legislature to pass measures which impose restrictions upon his personal freedom of action, albeit absolutely for his own protection and benefit.

All previous forms of murrain, severe though they may have been, were in 1897 eclipsed by that most terrible type of cattle plague—rinderpest. For years it had been slowly but surely marching southward. Stories of a frightfully destructive malady sweeping off all horned animals in vast districts had come down from the far interior, but so long as the visitation was confined to the distant regions north of the Zambesi it excited only an academic interest. Gradually, however, the plague crept nearer. It entered Rhodesia and played havoc with cattle and game there. It threatened and at last invaded the Transvaal. Then the European communities of South Africa awoke to a sense of impending calamity. The Republican Government took alarm and joined in action. It may easily be imagined how difficult it was to establish cordons and enforce restrictions in the case of a Boer population, but the Dutch farmer's love of cattle overbore even his repugnance to regulation, and the rules laid down were more or less complied with. Traffic was arrested and the circulation of stock interdicted. In Zululand the natives submitted loyally and effectively to all the rules laid down. All the governments actively co-operated in efforts to keep back the common foe. Thousands of suspected cattle were killed, and the most stringent measures were taken to prevent the passage of infected stock. In Natal, wire fences were erected along the western frontier, and all ingress of sheep and cattle forbidden, to the great disgust of farmers who owned land on both sides of the frontier. These measures entailed upon the Colony heavy outlay and individual sacrifice, but the magnitude of the danger silenced all murmuring. But every effort was in vain. With cruel steadfastness the plague advanced. Though the introduction of every conceivable medium of infection was rigorously prevented the pest evaded all barriers. The fowls of the air and the creeping things of the field, possibly the germ-laden wings of the wind, carried it past zones and fences and spread it everywhere. Within a few months the country was swept from end to end. The prize pedigree stock of the European breeder, the dairy stock of the farmer, the "trek" oxen of the carrier, equally with the cherished herds of the natives—to whom cattle mean wives, property, wealth—were all mown down by the destroyer, and for a time the whole

land was corrupted with the reek of rotting carcasses
The patience with which the natives, both in Natal
and Zululand, bore their losses was the marvel of all.
They had been told by their magistrates what to
expect, they knew that their Government had made
stupendous efforts to drive off the plague, they saw
that their white neighbours suffered equally with themselves, and they submitted to calamity when it came
in a spirit of patient fortitude, which was creditable
alike to their loyalty and self-restraint. Then came
the struggle for prevention as well as cure. Joint
commissions were appointed by the several Governments. Bacteriologists were consulted. Experts were
employed. Professor Koch himself came from Berlin
to investigate the conditions of disease upon the spot.
Laboratories for the production of protective lymph
were established, with the result that rinderpest is no
longer regarded with horror and dismay. It has taken
its place along with lung-sickness and red-water and
other controllable ailments to which stock is liable.
The fair hillsides of Natal once more are dotted over
with cattle, and both farmers and natives watch with
complacency the increase of their herds.

Plagues, locusts, drought, fire, storms, failing markets,
and a capricious labour supply—such are or have been
some of the difficulties and drawbacks against which
the settlers of Natal have had to contend. They are
not peculiar to South Africa. They, or their equivalents, fall to the lot of British colonists in other parts

of the world. My only purpose in naming them is to illustrate the circumstances under which a British Colony is built up; to indicate the process by which the British Empire has become so powerful a factor in the world's destiny. Severe though these trials have been, harassing though these troubles have been, they have not in any degree availed to daunt the efforts of the settlers, or to abate their confidence in the prospects of the new land. Despite these experiences life in South Africa has its compensations, and men suffering them are still content to bear the risks of them, while men knowing of them are not afraid to share the lot of their predecessors.

And now another item has to be added to the category of misfortune. The hand of war has had the country in its grip, and not for the first time. In that dark year, 1879, Natal passed through all the rigours of a campaign, but except for one incident— the ever-memorable episode of Rorke's Drift—it was spared the horrors of invasion. Though for three months it was more or less in a state of panic, and for six months was beset by uncertainty and alarm, its soil remained inviolate and its homesteads were un- threatened and unharmed. A savage and ruthless foe menaced the border throughout that period of suspense and peril, but—save for the few brief hours beyond the Buffalo—the Colony was not invaded. Of the thrilling experiences of those days I may speak here- after, as well as of other occasions when the Colony was scared by war's alarms, or threatened disturbances, but not actually chastised by war's fiery scourge Very different is the case now. When I write the country has for seven long months been desecrated by the presence of a foe. After nearly sixty years of peace, the quiet uplands of Natal, where the memories of past massacres had been buried with the bones of the old Voertrekkers, have echoed with the ceaseless thunder of Boer cannonading, and the frequent rattle of Boer rifles, directed against the habitations of British settlers, and the sheltering forces of the Government under whose just and tolerant rule that peace has prevailed. All the many evidences of toil and enter- prise that mark that region are the product of this period. The wire fences that enclose the farms—sure sign of order and progress—the clustering tree planta- tions diversifying and humanising the prospect—the comfortable homesteads and embowering orchards— the herds and flocks and spreading fields—are the tokens and fruits of British rule, and mainly of British industry. So, too, are the thriving townships, Estcourt, Ladismith, Dundee, and Newcastle—all centres of trade, municipal activity, and social progress. So, too, are the coal mines, whose existence and development are so invaluable a resource to a great naval power and maritime empire. So, too, is the line of well-made, stable railway that has helped so materially in the expansion of gold-mining at Johannesburg. Yet all these signs and trophies of Anglo-Saxon colonisation

were for nearly nine months in the hands, or commanded
by the guns, of Boer invaders from the Republics

The graphic pens of home correspondents have told
the story of the war itself—as far as the censor's pencil
would allow—with a fulness and power that are all-
sufficing. The actual daily experiences of the settlers,
however, fell less fully within their province. It is still
too early to attempt any historical narration of them.
Though the tyranny of invasion is overpast, the tale of
loss and suffering is not yet closed. I refer to them here
only to indicate what the feelings may be of the people
who have thus been called upon to witness the sudden
wreck of their lifework. In their case the happening
was altogether unexpected. They had failed to realise
that war was inevitable. They never deemed it possible that the Colony itself would be invaded. The
idea of Boer commandoes swarming over the Drakenberg, and taking possession of the country, never
seriously entered their minds. Though they knew
that their Dutch neighbours and fellow-colonists sym-
pathised more or less with their friends and kinsmen
in the Republics, active and general sedition on the
part of men so void of provocation was scarcely contemplated. In the upland towns residents were so
confident in their sense of security that they never
thought of moving until officially warned or directed
to do so, and this was in spite of the spectacle of
trains crammed with wretched and helpless refugees
passing daily and almost hourly from Johannesburg

In the country farmers were still less inclined to fly. They fancied that the Boer forces would remain near the border, and not until Newcastle and Dundee had been evacuated and Ladismith, after successive battles, been invested and cut off, did the real peril of the situation force itself on the minds of the settlers south of the Tugela. Then, most of them—the British-born, I mean—hastily took flight. First went the women-folk and the children, carrying with them such port-ables as they could dispose of, and then followed the men, who held on to their homesteads until the Boers were actually in sight. Loath, indeed, were the house-wives to leave their domestic treasures to the mercy of Boer raiders. In some cases things were buried, or hidden in roofs, in cornpits, or plantations. In others they were left just as they were, trusting that apparent confidence would prevent spoliation. Cattle, horses, and sheep were in many cases driven off to the deep valleys under the distant mountains, whither the raiders were afraid to follow them. In other instances the owners escaped out of one door as the invaders appeared at another. Six well-dressed and well-mannered Boers rode up one morning to a country store, where some of the refugee farmers were awaiting events, and asked for " drinks," which they paid for. Mistrusting such civility, the British visitors quietly went to the back, mounted their horses, and rode away. Looking round from the hill behind they saw the slopes in front swarming with Boers, and the homestead in the hands of a looting

horde—the vanguard of Joubert's great commando—
which had marched round from Ladismith, unseen
and unsuspected, as I have said, its route concealed
by the smoke from grass-fires purposely lighted, although thousands of British troops were encamped a
score of miles away. On a small scale this daring
inroad resembled Sherman's great march through the
Southern States. It was successful and unchecked as
long as its advance was mainly through country occupied
by Boer sympathisers. Then, when near Fort Notting-
ham, Boer farms were left behind and only British settlers
met with, the hearts of the raiders failed them. Colonial
scouts were encountered, and reports of reinforcements
were received. So the commando turned eastward,
possibly with the view of interrupting communication
with Maritzburg. The country traversed offered goodly
prey. Some of the finest stock-farms in South Africa
are—or were—to be found there. One, belonging to
the Natal Stud Company, has for years carried off the
best prizes at the Agricultural Shows of the Colony
for its exhibits of pedigree animals. All were swept
away. Wire fences were cut or trampled down. The
enterprise and toil of long years were wiped out, and
the homeless sufferers—forced to find shelter where
they might—were left to reflect once again upon the
chances and changes that beset the Anglo-African
pioneer. It is true that in some cases orders were
given upon the Transvaal treasury for the value of
stock or supplies thus seized, and that in certain in-

G

stances there was a marked abstention from undue interference with property, more especially as regards farmers who had chosen to sit still in their homes, but the general experience was one of loss, humiliation, and indignity. Fortunately for the Colony the garrisons of Mooi River and Estcourt were able to arrest and divert the march of the Boer commandoes, though not to cut them off in their retreat, but the injury they succeeded in inflicting upon the loyal colonists can never be adequately repaired. Nor will it ever be forgotten by this generation in Natal that the most reckless and wanton of the looters were the rebellious Dutch neighbours with whom for so many years the despoiled settlers had been living in amity and peace.

Crushing though these latest experiences of trouble and disaster have been, it must not be supposed that the British colonists of Natal will faint or falter in the continuance of their mission as pioneers. The spirit that has enabled them to contend with and to overcome the antagonisms of nature will sustain them in their endurance of the blows and shocks of war. They have won, as we have seen, for the Empire and for themselves the country they inhabit, they have won it from barbarism, and have bequeathed it to civilisation; they have dowered it, through the grace of a wise Imperial policy, with free institutions; they have fought, and many of them have died, in its defence. It is a goodly heritage, and they mean to pass it on as a homeland to their children and their children's children, let us hope, for many generations.

CHAPTER V

THE SETTLERS AS SOLDIERS

LIKE Canada and the West Indies, South Africa has in the past been the scene of much active service on the part of British troops   Purchased in the first instance by armed conquest, British supremacy has been maintained there throughout the nineteenth century at a cost of treasure and of life which in itself may be held to constitute an effective title to dominion.   Were the lives lost and the money spent in upholding British authority there during the last hundred years reckoned up, the sum-total would surprise mankind.   These reminiscences, however, are personal rather than historical, and I only propose to recall incidents that have come within my own experience.

In view of the enormous demonstration of military strength by means of which the Empire is now maintaining and establishing its authority in South Africa, the provision made by Sir George Napier in 1838 for the occupation of Natal seems absurdly insignificant. That able Governor described it as consisting of " 1 captain, 2 subalterns, 80 men of the 72nd Highlanders, 1 subaltern, 1 sergeant, 10 men Royal Artillery, 3 guns; 1 sergeant, Sappers and Miners; 1 assistant

surgeon; 1 commissariat clerk 1 Kafir interpreter."
This little force was placed in charge of his Excellency's
own Secretary, Major Charters, and its object was to
erect a fort at Durban, "to prevent all supplies and
warlike stores from entering that port, by which means
alone," wrote the Governor, " I can prevent aggressions
against the native tribes by these emigrant farmers, and
thus put a stop to further bloodshed and, secondly,
to prevent the emigrants establishing an independent
government, by being in possession of the only seaport
through which gunpowder and other necessary supplies
can be ensured to them." Considering that the emigrants numbered thousands, and had already vanquished, as my readers have seen, the trained warriors
of the Zulu despot, the strength of this little expedition
was modest enough. Yet so powerful were the non-
colonising influences of that time in Imperial councils
that Sir George felt constrained to apologise for the
magnitude of his preparations "Your Lordship may
possibly be surprised," surely this was sarcasm, "at the
amount of force; but in consequence of the information
I have received that there is now a large body of the
emigrant farmers under one Landman, in possession of
that port, and commencing building, &c., I deemed it
necessary to put all idea of resistance, should there be
such, out of the question; and I can at any time reduce
the force, if expedient."

Small as this handful of troops might be, it availed
for the time being to achieve the object in view. The

blockhouse erected by it, and the guns named, were still
standing at the harbour entrance when I first saw it,
eleven years later. And after the Queen's sovereignty
had been fully and firmly extended over the whole
Colony, a garrison not exceeding 450 in all, of regular
troops (apart from the volunteers) sufficed to keep
peace in the Colony for twenty years. During that
period the 45th was the only regiment stationed in
Natal, and some of the best colonists came from its
ranks. Though the rest of South Africa was often in
tumult, the little northern colony enjoyed almost unbroken repose. Two tedious and bloody " Kafir wars "
on the Cape frontier, a campaign in Basutoland, a
struggle with the Boers north of the Orange River,
terrible fratricidal massacres in Zululand, on our immediate border, Boer expeditions against the natives in
the Transvaal, all disturbed or desolated the adjacent
territories, but Natal remained an oasis of peace. Not
an additional soldier was added to or needed by the
garrison. The moral influence of a just and tactful
Government availed, with the aid of local forces, to avert
bloodshed and disorder.

It was at this time, however, that the volunteer movement—destined in later years to bear such memorable
fruit—had its birth in Natal. I believe that to that
Colony belongs the distinction of having been one of
the first communities to lead the way in the modern
outgrowth of citizen soldiership. If not its actual
originator, Governor Pine was the foster-parent of the

organisation, as he was of so many other wise and far-sighted projects. The Crimean War had just begun. The possibility of a call from a Russian privateer was suggested. Then, as now, martial enthusiasm on behalf of the Empire spread from the mother country to its offspring. The Governor found it an easy matter to induce the small nominated and purely official legislature to pass an "Ordinance" providing for the organisation of volunteer bodies. In 1854 the principal residents of Durban, taking advantage of this measure, met and formed themselves into a corps happily designated the "Royal Durban Rangers." I believe that was the first legally constituted mounted volunteer force established in the Empire, since the close of the Great War; at any rate, it was very nearly so. It had but a strength of some fifty or sixty men, but was officered by a captain, two lieutenants, and a cornet. Amongst its members were men who then, and for many years afterwards, held leading positions in the community. These wore a dark blue uniform, with black facings, which were very shortly replaced by yellow facings, when by special permission the corps was allowed to dub itself "Royal." Governor Pine, as Honorary Colonel and Queen's representative, as soon as the Rangers were fully accoutred and equipped, reviewed and addressed them He laid great stress on the fact that theirs was a corps of "gentlemen," and admonished them to act as such on the drill ground and in the field. Races and a ball closed the proceedings of that memorable day.

Despite the encouragement of the local Government, and the personal good comradeship of the regular troops in the Colony, the military authorities did little to help the movement. They looked coldly on it Members had to use their own saddles, and the only equipments forthcoming from the Imperial armoury were some surplus stores in the shape of obsolete swords and carbines The latter were loaded with difficulty, while the blunt and cumbrous sabres were only useful as tests of the endurance and patience of the men using them. Despite military indifference, the Rangers grew in efficiency and popularity. Four years later a handsome little banner, embroidered in scarlet and gold, was contributed by a member of the corps, and, after being consecrated by the Bishop of the Colony, was presented by the Governor's wife amidst much ceremony. This flag was proudly displayed on parade days, and was borne in front of the corps when it escorted Prince Alfred into Durban in 1860 It now hangs in St. Paul's Church.

Fired by so notable an example, other townsmen of Durban almost immediately determined to establish a foot corps for the enrolment of such citizens as might not be possessed of horses. It was as a member of this body—the Durban Volunteer Guard—that my public service, when a lad of fifteen, may be said to have begun. Her Majesty certainly had no prouder subject than I felt myself to be when my name was called out at the first muster of the corps We were a very motley crew, of all ages, sorts, and sizes, but our enthusiasm was unbounded. For a week or two we drilled in the garb of common life, but little time was lost in providing the simplest type of uniform in the shape of a plain blue serge tunic, a home-made peaked képi, emblazoned with the letters "D.V.G.," cast in pewter by a local craftsman. Trousers were supposed to be grey for preference, but it did not matter. Our arms were of the crudest order. As a matter of fact—strange as it may seem—very few of us had guns of our own, and they were mostly fowling-pieces, or other homely weapons. When it was impossible to raise a firearm of any sort, a roughly carved bit of plank was made to serve as substitute; and on one occasion a humorous recruit, of Scottish origin, paraded with a broomstick! Ammunition for some time was provided out of powder-flasks, but the explosion of one in the hands of a careless member led to an appeal for military assistance. The Imperial authorities found that they had stowed away in store a quantity of venerable disused Tower muskets, that had belonged to a disbanded corps of native police. These ponderous pieces, belonging to the "Brown Bess" species, had seen service in the first years of the century. They were enormously heavy, and reached up to one's shoulder. Caps, like small Quaker hats, were served with them. Almost as big as some modern field-pieces, it required the strength—shall I say of ten?—to pull the trigger, while the recoil was such as almost to throw one down. Aiming was a mere matter of chance, and how the gallant soldiers who fought with them managed to hit anybody is a problem yet unsolved. A huge triangular bayonet, heavy pipe-clayed cross-belts, and a capacious cartridge-box, with pouch, completed the equipment. Yet nobody repined under its burden, nor marvelled when five shots out of six failed to hit the target The bullets, by the way, were cast by ourselves, and the cartridges were made up in scraps of paper for each occasion.

Such was volunteering in Natal in the early fifties. We were but a handful of whites amongst thousands of spear-armed and warlike savages, but we slept soundly at nights, and did not regard the future with any perceptible dismay. These preparations for self-defence, primitive though they might be, undoubtedly infused a sense of confidence and security throughout the community, and accustomed a large section of the people to the use of arms. The capital of the Colony soon followed in the wake of the seaport and established the Natal Carbineers, a corps which on many a foughten field has won renown, as shall be shown hereafter It has outlived all its contemporaries, and its name is invested with such a halo of bright tradition that it will not be lightly suffered to pass away The Rangers continued in existence for many years and took part in one or two minor expeditions; but finally merged into the Natal Mounted Rifles, a corps which did good service in the Zulu War, and is still engaged in the present struggle. My own old foot corps struggled

on for about two years, but, without proper arms or
Government encouragement, it gradually languished.
The regulars declined to parade with us on Her
Majesty's birthday 1855, when, nevertheless, we had a
muster of our own, in pipe-clayed belts, and fired a
salute from our ancient blunderbusses, with loyal hearts
and a most loyal cheer. Both officers and men, however, became disheartened by neglect and deprivation,
and the corps may be said to have perished slowly
by inanition. In future years it was succeeded by
other infantry forces, one of which took a prominent
part in the armoured train incident of November last.

Until 1861 the only military episodes that ruffled
the serenity of Natal were the expeditions against the
recalcitrant chiefs Dushani and Isidoi. In both cases
small bodies of regulars, volunteers, and native levies
succeeded in bringing the refractory tribes to their
knees without much bloodshed, and in enforcing the
authority of Government. Both chiefs occupied difficult
positions in broken, hilly country, but the resistance
they offered was brief and weak-hearted. Deposed and
outlawed, they ceased to work mischief, while the
breaking up of their tribes and the seizure of their
cattle had a salutary influence upon the rest of the
native population. Firmness and justice have ever
been the corner-stones of British rule over subject
savage races. In 1861 a more serious menace appeared to the northward. It was then that the little
raw-cloud, which eighteen years later burst in storm

and tumult, began to show itself in Zululand. King
Panda (or M'Pande), first installed in sovereignty as
Dingaan's successor by the Boers, and subsequently
recognised by the Colonial Government, after twenty
years of comparatively peaceful rule, had waxed fat and
slothful.   In 1856 his two elder sons, Umbulazi and
Cetywayo, had waged a bloody struggle for the succession, on the northern banks of the Lower Tugela near
the sea   Both the rival factions met in deadly combat
there, and the younger, a mere youth, got the mastery
His success was partly due to the help of a young
Englishman, John Dunn, destined to play a prominent
part in Zulu history a quarter of a century later.   The
defeated party was driven into the Tugela with tremendous slaughter.   Umbulazi himself and thousands
of his people were slain, and the country reeked for
weeks with the stench of the massacre   Two years
later I visited the spot.   All was then still and peaceful.
Not a hut was visible on the north bank, and, lounging
on the crisp, flowery sward in the soft spring air, it was
difficult to realise that so short a time before such
a scene of butchery had been enacted there   But,
scattered about, bleaching skulls and bones bore ghastly
witness to the fray, and the alligators basking on the
sandbanks of the river had possibly been participants
in its horrors.

Having in such ruthless fashion cleared his brother,
the favourite heir, out of the way, Cetywayo proceeded
to establish his pretensions by orthodox Zulu methods.

He dominated his father and he overawed the people. He let it be known that those who were not for him would be dealt with as being against him. He restored and expanded the regimental organisation that made his uncle Chaka a tyrant and a terror. He enlisted on his side the younger men of the nation, and the older ones he either cowed into submission or drove across the frontier into British territory. During these years many thousands of Zulu refugees found an asylum in Natal. Among them was a young son of the king, a boy called M'Kungu, of whose possible rivalry Cetywayo was suspicious. The lad fled with a brother, and found a home at Bishopstowe, near Maritzburg. Another fugitive, of relatively low estate, called Ngoza, became a henchman of Mr. Shepstone, the Natal Secretary for Native Affairs, had a location assigned him near the Bishop's, and rapidly grew into a personage of importance.

Aware of both circumstances, Cetywayo's distrust was aroused. He dreaded a hostile combination between the English and his boy-brother, and he yearned for some formal recognition of his heirship by the white man's Government beyond the Tugela. The Government decided to gratify him, partly to disarm his fears, and partly to conciliate his goodwill. Mr. Shepstone's rule of policy was to keep peace by staving off evil, and, though the step was criticised at the time, it succeeded in its primary object. As the representative of the Queen he went to Zulu-

land, accompanied only by a few white attendants and
a larger native escort, led by the despised Ngoza. It
was a risky expedition, as Cetywayo and his young
warriors were inflamed with many butcheries and ready
for any devilry Though the British envoy literally
took his life in his hands, he went through his mission
with consummate coolness and intrepidity Surrounded
by thousands of armed and bloodthirsty savages, he
explained to the king and his son the reasons that
had led the Government to recognise the latter as
the lawful heir to the sovereignty. It was desired to
establish settled authority and to prevent the recurrence
of strife and bloodshed. With the dignity that was
natural to him, Mr. Shepstone sought to impress upon
Cetywayo the obligations which this act of recognition
imposed upon him. All went fairly well until the sight
of Ngoza revived the suspicions and provoked the fury
of the young chief, who demanded the surrender of
the renegade, as he deemed him to be. As a matter of
fact, his resentment was aroused by some ill-timed
assumption of authority on the part of one who was
regarded as a "dog." The regiments caught the infection of Cetywayo's rage, and a scene of uproar ensued,
throughout which Mr. Shepstone bore himself unmoved.
At one time, when actually threatened with destruction,
he said : "You may kill me—we are but one or two in
the face of a multitude, but, from the country which
I represent, unnumbered hosts will come to avenge my
death" The unruffled self-possession of the resolute

Englishman overawed and subdued the passionate Zulu.
"Somtseu's" command of temper saved the situation;
the ceremony of recognition proceeded without interruption, and the party returned to Natal free from
molestation.

Cetywayo's suspicions, however, were only lulled—
they were not extinguished.   In a few weeks they
flared up again, and his impis were reported to be
moving about menacingly near the Natal border.
Wild rumours of a possible invasion began to circulate.   Alarm spread.   People grew nervous.   On one
side of the Tugela was an army of 15,000 savage
spearmen.   On the other was a community of three
or four thousand peaceful settlers thinly sprinkled
over the land, with a garrison of about 400 British
soldiers quartered in Maritzburg.   Such a condition
of things was manifestly conducive to panic.   The
Legislative Council was in session.   Its sixteen members were gravely discussing one night the yearly
estimates when a tremendous booming smote the
still air.   It was repeated and repeated.   Discussion
stopped.   Members stared blankly at each other.
Surely those sounds were from the guns at the fort,
and what could they portend but the close approach
of an enemy?   Though the Speaker did not leave
his chair, business was all but suspended, and messengers were sent out to ascertain the facts.   The long,
unlit streets were unwontedly enlivened by groups of
householders, eager, if not tremulous, vainly asking

each other what the disturbance might mean. Time, on such occasions, seems long, but many minutes did not elapse before it became known that the fancied roar of cannon was nothing more than the noise caused by the mischievous turning over of an iron tank on the part of two or three practical jokers!

Though that was a false alarm, it preceded a genuine scare, which for some weeks agitated the Colony. Stories reached town that the Zulus were across the border and marching on Maritzburg, with the express object of seizing the king's son M'Kungu, who had been placed in Bishop Colenso's charge at his mission station near the little city. The bishop and his household with the young "prince" made a hurried flight into town overnight, and many of the farmers forsook their homesteads and sought refuge as they might. The Governor mustered as many of the volunteers as could be got together, and, with a few mounted regulars, proceeded towards the northern border. At Greytown he was reinforced by some of the local farmers or burghers, who were quite ready to take the field against their traditional foe. Though not belonging at that time to an enrolled force, I arranged with a friend to go on our own account to the border in quest of such adventures as might await us there. My companion had the good fortune to possess a Westley-Richards breechloader—at that time a novelty—but I had to be content with a short, muzzle-loading Enfield carbine, the cartridges for which

I spent the greater part of the preceding night in preparing. Thus armed and fairly well mounted, we went
forth merrily in the delicious air of a Natal winter morning, ready for any experience that might be in store.

The road to Greytown, then as now, traversed a
hilly and picturesque country — with bush - crested
bluffs skirting the horizon, rivers and brooks running
through grassy valleys, and boulder-strewn ridges or
kopjes breaking up the landscape. But at that time
homesteads were very few and far between, and the
wire fences which now stretch everywhere were wholly
unknown. It was a free, almost trackless country,
with many bucks and game birds picking or pecking
on the burnt veld. At the start, however, bullets had
to be husbanded for possible sport of a graver kind.
Though some of the farms were deserted, some were
still occupied, especially those belonging to certain
Yorkshire settlers, who were only too glad to regale
us with cheesecakes and custards while we told them
the latest news. Of what was happening on the border
they knew nought, and the only way to find out was
to ride on and discover the facts for ourselves. At
that season, however, and in that buoyant atmosphere,
journeying on horseback is little short of an intoxication
to the young and ardent, so on we rode over hill and
through dale, wondering whether the enemy was over
the next rise, or—where? At last, as the shadows
were lengthening, we saw suddenly rising over the
sharp line of the ridge in front—drawn out in single

file—a native impi! With shields in hand and feather tufts, there was no mistaking the identity of the warriors, while the soft evening wind soon bore to us the long croon of their war-song. As they were but a mile off, or less, the thought of a retreat did not occur to us, nor were we by any means certain that they were Zulus, so we rode forward, somewhat apprehensively it must be confessed; but there seemed no help for it. Anxiety soon subsided as the placable demeanour of the impi suggested no hostile intent, and we were soon assured that it was nothing more than a contingent of our own natives marching to the Governor's camp

The sun was setting when we rode up to the Hanoverian mission station, Hermansburg, where we sought and were gladly given shelter for the night. This is a self-supporting institution carried out on practical lines, combining industry with teaching, in a fashion not wholly unlike the methods of the Trappists. An excellent boarding-school for European boys helps to swell the income of the institution, and craftsmen of all kinds ply their callings. At a patriarchal table we supped, as honoured guests, on porridge, milk, and brown bread, while the pastor eagerly questioned us about the events of which they knew so little, though they were right in the forefront of any possible invasion. Sound was the sleep we soon won on the hard matted floor, with our saddle-rugs to warm us, but rude was the awakening. Sometime far in the

H

night a sudden uproar startled us out of our dreamless slumbers. Stampings and clatterings thundered round the building. Surely that must be an impi outside! We jumped up and looked through the blindless window into the white radiance of the moonlit night, but saw nothing. Groping our way along the passage, we found our way to the door and passed without. Not a moving figure was visible, but the noises continued, though more remotely. We went to where our horses had been tethered and found them gone. Something had frightened them and they had broken loose and stampeded round the house. A weary hour we spent in recovering them, but they were caught at last, and fastened up again, and we slept on till dawn.

Our early ride next morning took us on to the brow of Krantz Kop, a craggy mountain overlooking the great valley of the Tugela. From its summit, only approachable on the southern side, the eye ranges over a superb prospect of hill and gorse—of rock and forests —far into Zululand, which stretches beyond the gleaming river as it winds deviously to the sea. The crest of the hill had been stockaded and roughly fortified. There the Governor and his escort had passed the night. At a humble but deserted farmhouse just below we found fastened to the door a bit of paper notifying that the inmates had heard that the Zulus were "crossing," so had taken flight. The camp itself was also tenantless, and we were considering what to do next, when a mounted body showed itself at no great distance, and

thither we went. It was the Governor with his small
band of volunteers and burghers. From them we learnt
that the reported "invasion" was all a scare—that no
Zulus in force were anywhere visible near the border—
and that messages had been received from Cetywayo,
expressing surprise at the alarm that had arisen.
Whether or not there had been ground for the panic
was never known. Possibly the prompt appearance
of an armed force on the border—though so small a
body — had discouraged any hostile movement: the
Zulus had not forgotten Dingaan's experiences. In any
case there was not then, and never has been—with the
one exception of the attack on Rorke's farmhouse—a
Zulu invasion of Natal under British rule.

In 1865 a somewhat similar incident occurred on the
Western border. The Basutos were at war with the
Free State, and a considerable body of them followed
up some Boers into Natal and looted stock. The
neighbouring farms were panic-stricken. The volunteers were called out and sent to the border and other
preparations were made. The Basutos, however, did not
repeat their venture, and alarm soon subsided. Desultory strife continued between them and the Boers for
several years, until in 1869 Sir Philip Wodehouse was
authorised to extend a protectorate over Basutoland
and terminate a struggle which was demoralising South
Africa. At that time a strong desire prevailed to bring
back the Free State within the pale of the Empire as
the only means of restoring peace, order, and security.

I was one of a large deputation of Cape merchants and others who, in November 1868, waited upon the Duke of Buckingham for the purpose of urging the necessity of that step. Not long before I had proposed and carried in the Natal Legislative Council a series of resolutions to that effect. Strange as it may seem—but illustrative undoubtedly of the methods and temper of the time—the Secretary of State had never seen these resolutions until, on the occasion in question, I handed him a copy of them. No doubt they had been pigeon-holed somewhere in the recesses of the dingy old building which then sufficed to represent the Colonial Empire of Great Britain in Downing Street. The policy indicated was far too comprehensive for adoption in the then existing state of public feeling, and the recognition of Basutoland as a "protected" territory was all that Imperial statesmanship dared venture upon as a remedial measure.

The year 1873, as I have pointed out already, will long be memorable as marking the turning-point of Imperial policy in South Africa. It was then that Mr Shepstone followed up his recognition of Cetywayo in 1861 by his formal coronation of that chief as his late father's successor in the sovereignty of Zululand. For some time past Langalibalele, a chief in North-western Natal, had showed signs of insubordination. Men of his tribe had brought back with them from the diamond fields firearms purchased there, and he refused to have them registered in conformity with law. He had

in other ways evaded the mandates of the Government
and given evidences of recalcitrancy. Unless such mani-
festations on the part of a native chief are promptly
checked they are certain to develop and strengthen;
but it was not deemed prudent to bring Langalibalele
to his bearings until Cetywayo's clamant demand for
installation had been complied with. He wished to be
formally established as king of Zululand by the great
Power that had recognised his heirship. Governor
Pine's first act after returning to Natal in June 1873
was to authorise the Secretary of Native Affairs to pro-
claim Cetywayo. The story of that expedition as told
by Mr. Shepstone himself is intensely interesting, full
of picturesque situations and adventurous incidents,
but it cannot be summarised here. It must suffice to
say that our envoy was escorted by a force of about
three hundred men, including the Durban Volunteer
Artillery Corps, commanded by the late Mr. Escombe,
and two field-pieces. They crossed the Tugela and
advanced to the king's place, where, after many diplomatic delays and much amusing observance of savage
etiquette, "Somtseu" at last, in the presence of the
Zulu regiments, placed on Cetywayo's head a tailor-
made "crown" amidst the salute of artillery and the
shouts of his people. Mr. Shepstone also took occasion
to admonish the king on the duties of his position, and
to obtain from him a promise not to signalise his accession in the cruel fashion of his race, by the spilling of
innocent blood. Other "laws" of humane tendency

were also agreed upon and promulgated, and the king's violation of them formed counts in the indictment against him six years later.

Having pleased and pacified Cetywayo and for the time being dispelled any menace in that quarter, the Natal Government proceeded, after Mr Shepstone's return, to deal with Langalibalele. He had failed to comply with repeated summonses to appear before the magistrate, whose messengers he suffered to be stripped and jeered at. His champions later on declared that he was afraid of treachery. Steps were taken to enforce his submission. A mixed force of regulars and volunteers was sent towards his location. There being reason to believe, and rightly so, that the chief contemplated retirement into Basutoland, a small party of mounted volunteers belonging to the Natal Carbineers was despatched to intercept him at the top of the Drakenberg. It was commanded by Major Durnford, who afterwards fell at Isandhlwana. Two days and nights' forced march took this little band up the trackless heights of the beetling mountain range whose vertical crags wall in the western frontier of Natal. They ascended by the sources of the Umkomas, whose birth-streams tumble down the precipices they spring from in exquisite cascades. The horses had to be led or dragged up the mountain flanks, which never before had been trodden by civilised man. It was a tremendous clamber, up and along almost perpendicular cliffs, one ridge being surmounted only to find yet steeper and

higher ridges beyond. In that clear air distances are
lessened and surfaces flattened, and estimates of ground
to be traversed are altogether misleading. Light food
for little more than a day had been taken, and three
days were spent in the expedition. At one point Major
Durnford fell and rolled fifty yards over stones. Though
bruised and dislocated he refused to be left behind, and
after being tenderly cared for he continued his march
with the rest.

The force started on Sunday evening fully expect-
ing to be at its goal on Monday morning; but all that
day it was scrambling and toiling on, amidst those
verdureless and awful solitudes, where, at an altitude of
over 9000 feet, only nature in her sternest forms was
manifest. At last when day broke on Tuesday morning
the eastern edge of the crest was gained. Fatigued and
famished as they were in the keen frosty air, the spirits
of the thirty-three stalwart troopers rose. They were
near the accomplishment of their mission. Daylight
had not long made visible the curling mists below, the
sun had only just lit up the ruddy peak of Giant's
Castle towering over them on the right, when word
came that the rebels were close at hand. As it happened, the chief, with some of his head-men, followers,
and cattle, had four days earlier fled over the mountains
by the path that had now been reached. Climbing up
Bushman's Pass—a mere groove in the face of the vast
mountain cliff—they had escaped out of the Colony,
and were now being followed by another large body of
the tribe, armed and hostile.

Many accounts have been given of what then occurred, but the actual facts seem obvious and simple.
It was the desire of the Colonial Government to
secure, if possible, the bloodless submission of the
tribe, and with that end in view the order had
been given not to fire unless first fired upon. Major
Durnford, despite his hurts and exhaustion, adhered
inflexibly to his instructions. His little force was
halted in fours while he advanced to parley with the
natives who streamed up from below. The position
could have been easily held by our men, far outnumbered as they were, had they been free to act and to
treat the rebels as a foe, but they had to obey orders.
The kopjes on either hand were, however, occupied
by the natives, who, more and more menacing, closed
round them. The colonists, who knew native methods
better than did their dauntless leader, urged that they
be allowed to fire, but the Major did not flinch in
the implicit execution of his orders. Attended by
three young volunteers and his faithful Kafir interpreter, a Christian native named Elijah Kambula, he
rode towards the foremost rebels and told them they
must all return with him to the Colony and submit.
The only answer was jeer and mockery. The volunteers behind meanwhile grew more and more restless,
and demanded either to fight or retire. Again the
Major warned the natives to lay down their arms, only
to see them press on and round with brandished spear
and furious shout. Fain would he even then have

striven to hold the pass, but his men, recognising the hopelessness of the undertaking, insisted on retiring

In the end the rebels closed in upon Durnford and his immediate companions, three of whom were shot, while the third, being unhorsed, was slain. The Major only saved his life by shooting with his revolver two natives at his horse's head, and then with his men he moved off Falling back at a trot, an attempt was made to rally, but a deadly volley was poured into them at a distance of from ten to fifty yards. Some one called out that they were all being murdered, and the pace quickened. Several instances of individual gallantry were recorded and handsomely recognised by Major Durnford, who wrote subsequently of the solicitude for his safety shown by many of the force during the retreat, adding that, suffering as he was from a slight wound and a bad fall, he would never have returned had it not been for their assistance. They in their turn bore testimony to the soldierlike fearlessness and unselfish demeanour of their leader Of the Carbineers slain, one was a son of the Colonial Secretary. A monument was afterwards erected to the memory of the four brave men who thus perished in the defence of British authority on the bleak crest of the Drakenberg, and not the least honoured of the names inscribed thereon is that of the faithful and dauntless Kambula. After a terrible journey down the mountain the rest of the party arrived nearly a day later, utterly spent and exhausted, at the main camp

The news of this disaster reached Maritzburg all too
quickly, and spread consternation through the little
city. A brooding leaden sky with a still, stifling atmosphere, intensified the gloom. Only a few days before
the young slain volunteers had started on their errand
full of eagerness and gallantry. Fears of a wide-spread
native rising were freely expressed, and instant action
was urged upon the Government. Promptitude in
movement at such a time is ever held to be imperative,
and no time was lost in preparation. Governor Pine
was already in the field with a force that had been
despatched to the neighbourhood of the disaffected
location, and operations on a larger scale were planned.
It is a wild, rugged country. Had the rebels chosen to
make a stand there it would have been no easy matter
to subdue them, especially as the people of another and
adjoining tribe, Putili's, made common cause with them,
or were understood to do so. The fighting men of
both tribes, however, with the bulk of their cattle, vanished over and into the mountains, and the occupation
of their locations was effected after some bloodshed.
They had, however, to be pursued and punished. Had
they been allowed to find an unmolested refuge in
Basutoland there would have been an end to British
prestige in South Africa Two pursuing columns were
at once organised, each being under the leadership of
an experienced Natal magistrate. These little forces
were entirely colonial, either enrolled volunteers or
colonists who enlisted for the occasion. They num-

bered seventy volunteers and 1600 natives. Captain
Allison and Captain Hawkins had no easy task before
them. They had to take their men up the almost
inaccessible mountain sides into a region of rugged and
trackless desolation that had never before been penetrated by white men—a region whose only known
inhabitants in the past had been the tiny untameable
Bushman, the ravening hyena, or the fabled unicorn.
for there tradition had located the one-horned antelope.
Somewhere in front of them, probably lying in wait
amidst Nature's fastnesses, for a sudden spring, was the
fugitive tribe. It was, moreover, the season of storms,
raging up there with indescribable fury, without a scrap
of shelter available. Whatever the difficulties and
dangers might be they were gladly faced, especially by
the men who smarted under the aspersions cast upon
them from certain quarters as a consequence of their
late reverse. The two columns carried their provisions
with them packed in raw hides, on the backs of oxen
which were killed and eaten as the march proceeded,
and as their burdens were consumed.

The story of this expedition was never properly told
either in official despatches or private letters. No
"special" correspondents accompanied it, no postmen
or runners bore back news of it The largest of the
parties ascended the Drakenberg by the more western
passes, the other advanced by the more southerly
route at the sources of the Umzimkulu. Both had a
merry meeting in the clouds, and then disappeared

from sight and hearing, after sending to Maritzburg an
assurance that the objects of the mission should be
accomplished "handsomely and well"—a promise that
was fulfilled to the letter.   And practically nothing
more was heard of the expedition until it had done its
work.   It groped its way amongst the precipices and
defiles, skirting the edges of brawling torrents, camping
at times under the caves of overhanging crags, scaling
nameless mountain heights or scrambling into the
depths of rock-strewn valleys—all void, silent, and life-
less—ever on the alert for a hidden foe, and never beset
by any dread or doubt   The marvellously buoyant
though often icily cold air of South African mountain-
land uplifted and stimulated them   After each day's
hard march they slept the sleep that follows as of right
dutiful fatigue, and they rose at dawn, refreshed and
confident, to resume the chase.   They were not long in
finding traces of the fugitives, and thus guided they
passed farther and farther into the depths of the
mystical "Double Mountains," the twofold mountain
range that divides Natal from Basutoland

And at last their weary quest was rewarded.   One
morning a native visitor apprised them that the rebels
were not far ahead.   They had made for Northern
Basutoland, where a friendly refuge might most confidently be anticipated.   With cheerful hearts therefore
the pursuers pressed on in that direction, until they
reached once again the abodes of men—even though
uncivilised men   The Basutos were astounded at the

apparition of an armed force of white men from a
quarter where Nature's barriers had hitherto been
deemed impassable. The effect produced by such an
exploit was in itself enough to secure a respectful
reception for the heroes of it. The Cape Government,
moreover, with a sympathetic alacrity which Natal
still remembers with gratitude, had sent a body of 120
Mounted Police to the southern flank of Basutoland to
prevent any retreat of the rebels in that direction Any
hope that Langalibalele may have cherished of succour
from the Basutos was soon dissipated. They also loyally
co-operated, and after a brief encounter the fugitives
were surrounded and disarmed Though the rebels had
eluded their pursuers it was only to be captured in the
end. At the first Basuto village reached by the Natal
expedition a hearty welcome awaited them, and huts
were set apart for their accommodation Happier hours
have seldom been passed than were those spent that
night under the thatched roofs of the native loyalists
One of the leaders had carried with him in his saddle-
bag, for use in case of emergency, a bottle of Hennessey's
brandy. It had not been wanted either as a restorative
or a stimulant. His health and the health of all under
him had been perfect. So, pretending to discover the
flask amidst the straw of the hut, he brought it forth
and shared it with his comrades, in grateful commemoration of their safety and success

For, to end the story, the rebels, after some discussion
as to booty, were all handed over with most of their

cattle and belongings to the Natal representatives, who
thus achieved their purpose without firing a shot, and
returned to Natal, with prisoners and stock, a proud
and elated band. The tribe was broken up, its lands
confiscated, and its leaders, tried before a special
tribunal, were sentenced to banishment or imprison-
ment. Langalibalele himself was removed to the
neighbourhood of Capetown, where a farm was set apart
for him, and where he had wives, tobacco, and other
comforts, to lighten his lot in exile. Some years later
he was allowed to return to Natal, and he ended his
days in peace, near Maritzburg.

It fell to my lot, as a member of the Legislature, to
move a vote of thanks to all concerned in the repression
of the rebellion—to Governor, officials, troops, Cape
allies, and loyal natives—and never was parliamentary
duty discharged with truer zest or pleasure. It was
felt by the colonists that the prestige of the Government
had been vindicated, that its authority had been secured
for years to come. And these ends had been established
and that peace had been accomplished, let me add,
without a farthing's cost to the Imperial treasury, under
colonial auspices and by colonial resources only. It is
true that the cost to the Colony was not by any means
confined to the lives lost or the money spent. Both the
Governor and the colonists earned obloquy and discredit.
Sixteen months later the former was recalled under
circumstances I have already described, while the latter
continued for many a day to be vilified as monsters of

cruelty and wrongdoing.   Time, however, the great
rectifier, has silenced these calumnies, and though Sir
Benjamin Pine has passed beyond the reach of misrepresentation, his aims and his policy have been
recognised as those of a far-seeing and high-minded
statesman.   It was largely due to the steps he
sanctioned in connection with these events that the
native population of Natal remained, as they did,
absolutely loyal to the Government during the Zulu
war.   Had Langalibalele been left, comparatively un-
punished, in possession of his chieftainship and location,
there cannot be a doubt that he would have continued
to be a fermenting centre of disaffection and unrest—a
connecting link in Natal between the hostile Zulus on
one side and the nervous Basutos and Pondos on the
other.   The task which the Imperial Government had
to carry out would have been enormously weighted,
and the perils of the colonists terribly enhanced,
during the struggle which six years later ensued.

A volume might easily be filled with recollections
and anecdotes of the Zulu war.   It was Natal's first
experience of war on a large scale.   Although the
colonists had for years been apprehensive concerning
the significance of Cetywayo's preparations and pretensions, they were absolutely without any means of re-
sisting or meeting invasion.   During the three days
spent by Sir Bartle Frere in Durban after his arrival in
1877, he was beset from every quarter by representations
of the urgent necessity for protective and precautionary

measures. Missionaries, laymen, merchants, farmers—all met him with the same story and the same appeal. The world knows what steps he took to face the crisis, but only residents can understand how dire were the effects of that crisis when it actually came. Though the possibility of a Zulu invasion had been perceived and pointed out for years, though Sir Garnet Wolseley four years before had dilated on the blackness of the war-cloud in the north, though Sir Bartle himself most keenly realised the imminence of the danger, no adequate provision had been made by the Imperial Government to guard against the impending peril. Both the Empire and the Colony were taken unawares, but bad as our experiences were, they would have been far worse had Sir Bartle Frere not arrived when, and acted as he did.

It is quite true that both the troops and the colonists entered upon the war with a relatively light heart. Though they correctly estimated the numbers and the hostility of the enemy, they overrated their own ability to vanquish him. They believed that the far out-numbering legions of the Zulu king would be no match for the well-served guns and rifles of trained British battalions. I was present at the Lower Tugela on the 12th of January 1879, when the coast column crossed into Zululand. The river was high, and men and horses had to be carried over by punt. It was a busy and inspiriting scene. On the Natal side, amongst the mimosa bushes, tents, waggons, and contingents were all crowded together. The little roadside inn was

thronged by hungry volunteers and visitors, who soon
stripped it bare of both food and drink.   Beyond the
yellow and swift-flowing stream spread the bare slopes
of Zululand, dotted over by the few hundreds of our
forces, preparing for the night's encampment.   Against
the sky-line a squadron of mounted volunteers were
circling and patrolling.

   While watching them from the little sod-built fort
overlooking the river, a messenger rode up and reported to the colonel in command that an impi of
several thousand Zulus could be seen some miles off
behind a distant hill.   The news caused no excitement, and the crossing proceeded.   A body of native
levies marched in, patient, though curious and scared,
bewildered by the incomprehensible orders of the
British officers placed in charge of them, and plain-
tively anxious to be led by men they knew, and who
could talk their language.   Two or three ladies rode up
with their escorts to watch proceedings, and if possible
to get across the river.   That night we all camped out
in the open, and a merry time we had before rolling
ourselves in our blankets, talking, chaffing, singing, and
otherwise beguiling the eve of a totally unanticipated
tragedy.   Those of us whose duties did not take us
over the border returned townward on the morrow,
confident that all would go well with the advancing
column.   And so it did as far as that force was concerned.   Colonel Pearson's progress was practically un-
opposed for the next ten days, until he reached the

I

Inyezane, and was met there by 5000 Zulus, who
gallantly but vainly strove to surround and overcome
him. After a few hours' sharp but resolute fighting the
Zulus were put to flight, and on the same evening the
column marched on victoriously to Eshowe, where for
ten long weeks they were to be cooped up from touch
or intercourse with their compatriots elsewhere. We
in Durban heard, however, of their success, and for a
few hours were confirmed in our conviction that a short
and easy campaign was in store

Then came the thunderclap. No Natalian of these
days will ever forget the shock of that fateful revelation. People generally were free from extreme anxiety
as to the course of operations. Whenever our troops
had engaged the enemy they had been successful.
At Inyezane they had scored a victory. Farther westward, beyond the Buffalo, they had forced back such
bodies of Zulus as had opposed their march To the
north the "flying column," led by Evelyn Wood and
Buller, was not only holding its own, but making headway in the concerted advance upon Cetywayo's headquarters at Ulundi. All seemed going well. No
telegraphs connected the forces in the field with the
centres of the Colony, and days were taken in getting
news down from the front Then on Sunday afternoon came a vague and horrible rumour. There had
been a great disaster. Lord Chelmsford's column had
been overwhelmed The Zulus were invading the
Colony. At first the story was received with incredu-

lity. I heard it from a military doctor in the street, but I refused to credit it. An instinctive aversion to the "babble of the market," combined with a constitutional tendency to look at the brighter side, closed my ears to the terrible and tragical story. A period of intense suspense followed The actual realities of the situation were for the first time estimated. The smallness of the advancing forces; the magnitude of the Zulu impis; their fierceness and lifelong training; the difficulties of the enemy's country, rugged, roadless and bush-encumbered; the immaturity and inexperience of many of our own regular troops—all were vividly revealed by the lightning-flash of panic. For panic speedily set in. The first definite tidings were brought in by two fugitive volunteers who had ridden down, confused and agitated, from the death-strewn field of Isandhlwana. They reported a surprise, an unflinching stand, a ruthless butchery. Conflicting stories of Lord Chelmsford's separation from a portion of his force, of a successful resistance at Rorke's Drift, of a retirement towards Natal, bewildered the public mind and shook confidence in the whole story Days and days passed before the bald facts filtered through, and the ghastly details were realised. But the horror of the tale only deepened with time, and panic, quiet and breathless, but not the less oppressive, seized upon the Colony.

I have no desire to repeat the oft-told story of the Zulu war. Its incidents are on record in many a volume and public document. My present purpose is

to speak only of the effects produced on the community
by a military misadventure (it was nothing more),
which changed the course of history in South Africa.

Deplorable and disastrous though panic ever is, it
had ample excuse and justification in the circumstances of the time. All the available forces in the
Colony were across the border. Both the towns and
all the villages were practically defenceless. Every
farm was at the mercy of any marauding party. Only
a river that rose or fell with the rainfall protected
the Colony from a Zulu inroad. The attitude of our
own natives — mostly of Zulu origin — should the
country be invaded, was open to doubt. Many colonists
were at the front. The local volunteer corps had
suffered lamentably at Isandhlwana. The Natal Carbineers serving there—mostly young Maritzburg men
—had been cut down, "dying where they stood," under
their dauntless leader, Colonel Durnford. There was
no British garrison elsewhere in South Africa to draw
help from. No ocean cable existed to bear the tidings
of a menaced Colony's extremity. No wonder, then,
that men's hearts failed them, and that women, in
dread of unspeakable horrors, grew pale and anxious,
though never abjectly terror-stricken.

When once the main facts of the reverse were placed
beyond the reach of doubt, the leading men of both
towns bestirred themselves to face the situation. In
Durban a meeting was held, and a Defence Committee
appointed. We met daily and discussed the exigencies

of the moment from every point of view   Opinions
greatly differed as to how the town could best be
defended   Some thought that an advanced line of
defence was desirable, and a body of some fifty mounted
men were enrolled—under Mr. Escombe's captainey—
to patrol the Tongaat, a stream which flowed seaward
about thirty miles from Durban.   They were clad in a
costume of dark brown corduroy—the only material
available—of so pungent an odour that it supplied an
expressive if somewhat inelegant name to the little
contingent   The balance of opinion, however, was
strongly in favour of local fortification, and the whole
town was given up to defence works.   At an early stage
of the proceedings the gravity of them was accentuated
by the advent of Lord Chelmsford himself   After with-
drawing all that remained of his force within the borders
of Natal, he hurried down to Maritzburg and Durban,
to make such provision as might be possible for the
defence of both places.   It must be admitted that his
presence did not tend to allay alarm, as both he and
his officers frankly recognised the seriousness of the
situation and the necessity for action.   Said one of the
latter to me at a meeting of the Town Committee, " I
never saw such a foe, I never heard of such a foe; I
don't think you could meet a worse foe "   After it was
over we rode down the streets with his lordship, pointing out such buildings as might be defensible, and
generally, in no smothered tones, discussing the possibilities of resistance.   Women and children, scared and

nervous, gathered by the roadside, wondering what new and alarming danger beset the town. Before nightfall an idea prevailed that the Zulus had crossed the border and were advancing on the town, and hardly any one slept soundly before dawn appeared. What else could the arrival of the Commander of the Forces, and his words of warning while inspecting the town, portend than some sudden and appalling crisis?

Thenceforward and for weeks all was preparation and suspense. Every large building, no matter what its occupancy, was set apart as a place of refuge should the anticipated onslaught be made. They were loopholed for riflemen, and sheltered from musketry fire or rushing spearmen by sand-bags. For once the natural curse of Durban—its sand—was found to be a blessing. Every available sugar-bag and corn-sack was pressed into service. To this day many of these loopholes remain, objects of curiosity to the visitor, and grim reminders of the past to the resident. The tongue of land known as the Point, where the work of the shipping is done, was barricaded by a wall of timber from shore to shore. Here, should the town itself be overwhelmed and the worst come to the worst, people were to find a final refuge, with such shipping as might be in port, to flee to in the last extremity. All the townsfolk were told off to their assigned places of resort on a given signal. Every townsman was enrolled in a Town Guard, and directed to equip himself with a rifle, for which he had to pay, or hold himself responsible for paying, £2, 10s.

Meanwhile many ingenious townsmen devised their own independent measures of defence. One placed an iron tank in a tree near his newly-built house, from which he proposed to fire at any Zulus who might be audacious enough to attack his dwelling. "At any rate," he said, "before seeing my place destroyed, I shall have the satisfaction of shooting a few of the brutes." What might follow was not apparent. The agent of a local shipping company had a small tug in readiness to carry his household out to sea. Subsequent history was anticipated by a proposal to run an armoured train to and fro past the town, and no doubt had the occasion arisen, and the attempt been made, it would have proved an efficacious method of foiling the wily Zulu. In Maritzburg almost exactly the same measures were taken. Some anxiety was caused in both places by the discovery that corrugated iron sheets—the only procurable material for shield purposes—was penetrable by ordinary musket bullets, but timber was fortunately abundant, and a backing of four-inch deals made the barriers practically impregnable. A daily service of runners was provided to the Lower Tugela—only sixty miles distant—in order that regular and early news might be received regarding the movements of the enemy and the depth of the river. As long as "no enemy in sight" was reported, and the river was said to be "rising," comparative comfort prevailed, but sometimes the Tugela was announced to be "very low," and rumours of "Zulus in sight" were transmitted, to the

perturbation of everybody. On such occasions the
nightly watch was specially vigilant. For weeks many
householders went to bed with their portmanteaus or
bags packed in readiness for an instant flight, and any
noise that might disturb the darkness—a Kafir song, a
rifle shot, a distant thunderclap—caused many a beating
heart and wakeful eye. One Saturday morning, when
passing down the street, a high official, with pallid face
and fluttering scrap of pink paper held in shaking hands,
exclaimed to me, "They've crossed! they've crossed!"
I examined the telegram, having already had a later
one of my own of quite a different tenor, and was able
to point out to my friend that the persons "crossing"
were not bloodthirsty Zulus, but peaceful messengers
with cheering news from Eshowe.

This state of tension lasted fully two months. During
that period the Colony was believed to lie at the mercy
of the Zulus, and, as a matter of fact, it might have
been overrun by them had they chosen to face the
hazard. Several factors happily prevailed to restrain
them from the venture. After Isandhlwana they were
gorged with blood, and like vultures, torpid under
repletion. They returned to their kraals with trophies
from the battle-field, to be "doctored," to feast, and to
rest. They would have left behind them in their own
country, had they moved southward, the garrisons of
Evelyn Wood in the north-west, and of Pearson at
Eshowe near the coast. They had had a taste of British
powers of resistance behind walls or barriers at the little

farmhouse near Rorke's Drift. They knew that the Tugela was frequently in flood, and might bar their retirement were they defeated. More than all, they, and especially the older men, were superstitiously nervous regarding the myterious powers and resources of the Great White Queen, whose power they were challenging and whose people they would have to slay. We did not then perceive these deterrent influences as plainly as we do now. The bare fact of exposure to invasion and massacre was the dominating sensation. The enemy at that time consisted of relentless and brutal savages, from whom neither sex nor age might look for mercy or quarter. The sense of isolation and helplessness intensified the depression of the community. From no point could immediate succour be expected. The home-going mail steamer was ordered to make all speed northward, and to call at St. Vincent, the nearest cable station for the transmission of telegrams. A man-of-war was despatched to Mauritius, the least distant garrison. But not till H.M.S. *Shah* arrived unexpectedly at the outer anchorage, and landed a naval detachment of some two hundred blue-jackets, was suspense relieved, or did nervous folks feel quieted. Never were British seamen hailed with truer rejoicing than were those sturdy sailors as they marched with resolute pride up the sandy roadway, gazed at and cheered as tokens of safety and salvation by their anxious and imperilled countrymen.

And through it all the maligned and misjudged High

Commissioner remained quietly in Maritzburg, calm and watchful, and never despairing, until the arrival of reinforcements justified his departure to the Transvaal from the Colony that will never forget how sympathetically he shared its trials and sacrificed his interests in striving for its security and defence.

CHAPTER VI

THE SETTLERS AS LAWMAKERS

If the foundation of the British Empire is to be traced in the character of its people, Self-Rule may be regarded as its corner-stone, Justice and Law, Liberty and Right, being its buttresses. I use the phrase Self-Rule in its largest sense, as implying self-restraint, not less than self-government. If it confers freedom it imposes responsibility. If it secures Power, it also enjoins Duty. The term Responsible Government was a truthful definition of the system that has worked such wonders in the expansion of Greater Britain. It happily indicates the secret of whatever success has attended the working of free institutions throughout British colonies. It is not bare freedom that has made those colonies what they are, but freedom invested with attendant obligations — freedom weighted with the burden of cares, liabilities, and servitudes that have steadied and controlled the colonists in the exercise of power.

Mr. Froude was pleased to say of Natal and its people, after a hurried visit to the Colony in 1874 :—

" The grain of the old oak is in New England. The English in South Africa are pulpy endogens They

may make a nation some day, but they have a long way
to travel first. . .

"The fact remains that a country which seems to
have been made by nature to be covered with thriving
homesteads and a happy and prosperous people is given
over to barrenness and desolation. Before there can
be a change some authority must be introduced there
which will control both blacks and whites, and bring
the relations between them into a more natural
condition. The sole remedy thought of here is more
freedom and what they call a 'sponsible Ministry.
They look to America and they fancy the colonies have
only to be free, to grow as the United States have grown
America was colonised before the aloe had blossomed."

Like so many other of the great historian's deductions, this judgment is alike fallacious and unjust. His
metaphor is misplaced and misleading, because his
postulate is untrue. Self-government *has* been a plant
of slow growth in Natal, as institutions grow in these
days of rapid change and movement. It would be
absurd to compare the constitutional development of
the colonies with that of the mother country. Colonists
when they leave England have already arrived at their
high estate as British citizens. they need no long process of tutelage and preparation to fit them for the
understanding and discharge of civic duty. They begin
life in the new land fully equipped with the knowledge
and experience of political privileges won for them by
their fathers. They carry with them the roots of the

hardy British oak, and plant them in the virgin soil
of these distant lands, with patient confidence in the
sturdy and steadfast upgrowth   As a matter of fact,
political freedom in Natal has been neither a forced
nor rapid offshoot, as I shall now proceed to show

For thirteen years legislation in Natal was practically in the hands of the Governor, and he was solely
responsible to the Crown.   At first Natal was merely
a dependency of the Cape Colony, and its laws were
mostly " Ordinances " taken over bodily from the Cape
Statute-book.   A so-called " Legislative Council " was
in existence, but it consisted only of the Governor himself, assisted by a few of the chief administrative officers,
together with the Commander of the Forces   The proceedings of this body were never reported, but the
dominancy of the Governor was manifest and admitted, though it was well understood that differences
of opinion at times arose, and that occasionally Downing
Street might be appealed to.   Of any popular voice or
influence, however, there was none, apart from that
right of petition (to the Governor) which is inherent in
all Anglo-Saxon communities   For some years this
autocratic system of rule was accepted as inevitable—
as part of the accepted conditions of the immigrant's
lot—and in truth the struggle for bare existence left
them no time for political contemplations.   Governor
Pine, moreover, being an accessible and liberal-minded
man, prone to progressive ideals, and not afraid of
responsibility, did much to appease the instinctive

craving for reform. He made no secret of his own preference for "liberal institutions," and himself proposed that a popularised legislative body should be established. As newspapers multiplied agitation grew, and the demand for a more representative constitution steadily strengthened. In 1855 Sir George Grey, of all Cape Governors the ablest and most far-seeing, visited Natal, and conferred with its leading citizens. In Durban they took advantage of his presence to present a long and able memorial, setting forth in quiet terms the disabilities under which the colonists suffered. Sir George's subsequent reference to his intercourse with the men of Natal is significant both of his estimate of them, and of the methods which won for him in so unexampled a degree the confidence and respect of South African colonists. After a warm recognition of the intelligence and culture they generally displayed, he laid stress upon the marked moderation with which they framed and pressed their proposals, as affording an assurance that they might confidently be entrusted with a reasonable, yet a liberal, measure of control over their own affairs

This handsome recognition of Natal's fitness for a larger share of political power soon bore fruit. When Governor Scott arrived in October 1856, he brought with him a "Royal Charter," under which a representative Legislature was created. This instrument was welcomed by all the colonists with even greater ardour than the common people of England showed after the promulgation of their own Great Charter by King John, and it has ever since been cherished as the basis and the bulwark of all their liberties. It was but a very modest and carefully restricted dispensation of freedom, but it embodied and affirmed the precious principle, which, according to usage and tradition, when once conferred, can never be withdrawn save by the hand that won it. Henceforward the right to make laws and to vote supplies was vested in a Chamber consisting of twelve elected and four nominated members. The former were to be chosen by registered electors, holding either freehold property worth £50, or paying a yearly rental of £10—a qualification sufficiently wide at that time to embrace most trustworthy residents. A reserved civil list provided for the salaries of the Governor and the heads of the Executive, and set apart an annual grant of £5000 for the welfare of the natives.

This last provision was the cause of an immediate conflict between the Governor and the elective members in the Council. They insisted upon the right of that body to control the whole expenditure of the Government. He vigorously resisted this claim, and refused to submit the disbursement of the sum reserved to the supervision or interference of the Council. The colonists strenuously upheld their representatives in their contention, while the Crown supported the Governor in his attitude. The colonists considered that the sacred principle of control over taxation was at stake, while the Governor held that the right of the Crown to safe-

guard the interests of the unrepresented natives was
not to be impugned. The Council was as persistent in
contending for the power of the purse as the Governor
was in maintaining the right of the Crown to co-ordi-
nate control. Underlying the whole dispute, however,
was the native question, the never-ending difficulty of
South African statesmanship. Governor Scott was
specially charged, as his predecessor had been, to look
after the interests of the native population. He appeared to be imbued with the belief that had so long
prevailed in Downing Street, that the settlers were antagonistic to the natives, were disposed to oppress and
despoil them. His official associates rather encouraged
than dispelled that persuasion. It may be that occasional colonial utterances seemed to justify it The
elective representatives in the Council bitterly resented
the imputation, and protested against the establishment
of a dual system of government in the Colony. They
claimed to represent the natives as well as the colonists,
and they refused to leave native administration in the
unfettered hands of a permanent Crown - appointed
Executive. The contest continued for years. Supplies
were withheld, and deadlocks ensued. The Governor
wrote voluminous despatches, and the Council responded with elaborate addresses and minutes. A
dissolution only resulted in the return of a yet more
intractable majority. The reflections cast upon the
colonists grew more and more offensive, and they were
answered with increasing vigour; but in the end the

struggle wore itself out, and a compromise was arrived at. The Governor agreed to submit, year by year, to the Council a schedule of the sum spent out of the reserve, and that body consented to accept the concession as a vindication of the principle it had fought for. Another conflict almost immediately ensued on similar ground. Shortly after the Colony was established, locations in different districts were set apart for the use and occupation of the natives. They were added to from time to time, and in 1860 they represented an area of two million acres. As a guarantee against encroachment or alienation, it was proposed by Governor Scott to issue titles to these lands to the several tribes, in trust, on the scale of twenty-five acres to each hut or family. These lands were to be paid for at the rate of two shillings per acre, payable in instalments extending over six years.

This measure was no sooner announced than it evoked vehement opposition, both in the legislature and the press. The Legislative Council protested against the preparation and submission of such a scheme without any reference whatever to itself. It was regarded as a high-handed attempt to consolidate and perpetuate the existing system of native management, to confirm the native chiefs in their position and their powers, and to retard the spread of civilisation and the unifying of the law. Colonial opinion had long viewed with distrust what was known as the "Shepstonian policy" in the treatment of native affairs—a policy of "drift"

K

and *laissez faire*, avoiding change and shirking responsibility. The new-fledged leaders of legislative activity desired to improve and regenerate the native, and saw no wisdom in a philosophy which would let well alone and leave the future to take care of itself. They were not opposed to the issue of land titles, but they wished it to be to individuals and not to tribes. They especially objected to a policy which would be calculated "to give a control and preponderating political influence to the clergy and missionaries." Again the battle between the Governor and the colonists raged long and loud Again were the resources of agitation brought into play Again did the Legislative Council strain its powers in order to gain its point After an exchange of very able reports and despatches, references to Downing Street, public meetings, appeals to the electors, and threats of deadlock, a compromise was once more agreed upon. A Native Trust, consisting practically of the Executive Council of the Colony, was created and the native location lands were by law vested in its hands, and there they have remained ever since.

I mention these incidents as they serve to show in what spirit the early colonists received the boon of legislative freedom, and with what sturdy disdain of consequences they exercised their much-prized privileges. Although the immediate outcome was a line of social cleavage which was long in disappearing, the general effect was wholesome and bracing The official and non-official castes might look askance at

each other; the services might look down upon the
tradesfolk; Government House might be out of touch
with the common life of the Colony, but a healthy
political interest stirred the community, and a keen,
perhaps too vigilant, criticism curbed any excesses of
authority. From the very start parliamentary institutions were taken up with a pious regard for old-world
traditions. The burden of citizenship was assumed
with a glad, but not gay, heart. Its duties were discharged with as much seriousness as though the affairs
at stake were those of the Empire instead of a little
colony. Though the range of his powers was confined to the enactment of laws, and in no sense affected
their administration (except as regarded the voting of
salaries), the elector felt his responsibility just as keenly
as though his vote might have helped to save or to
destroy a Ministry.

The election of members was conducted with an
almost grotesque adherence to the ancient forms and
customs, as much so, that is, as the terms of the
charter permitted. There are certain differences in
procedure. Then (as now) candidates were not publicly nominated, but first asked, in writing, to stand
for particular constituencies. This requisition, if
signed by a sufficient number of electors, is nomina-
tion enough, but it must be lodged with the local
magistrate fourteen clear days prior to the day of
election. Attempts were sometimes made by opponents
to delay the delivery of a hostile requisition until the

prescribed limit was passed. It was usual for candidates
to make known their political creeds in advertised
addresses, while the chance of being able to heckle
them at public meetings was as keenly valued as in
other countries. Canvassing a constituency, say of a
hundred and fifty voters, scattered over a district as
large as Yorkshire, was no light, though it might be a
simple matter. Many electors lived out of the reach
of inns, and the would-be member had often to claim
the hospitality of those whose votes he was soliciting.
Colonial senators, therefore, were generally known in
person to most of their constituents. This closeness
of acquaintanceship has its drawbacks. Where "everybody knows everybody" private and personal matters
are apt to influence public relations, and the fact
certainly used to embitter election contests.

They were conducted very much on home lines. There
were committees, and colours, and rosettes. In country
places it was customary to provide refreshment—both
solid and liquid—for the tired and hungry voters, many
of whom had ridden hours and hours in order to reach
the polling offices. These hospitalities were dispensed
without regard to sides. There were seldom public
houses of call at hand, and it would have been
deemed a shabby return to voters for their time
and trouble to send them back hungry and thirsty.
This lavish dispensation of "free drinks" distinctly
tended to enliven the proceedings of polling-day,
while the feeling that he was thus freely enter-

taining hostile voters nourished a sense of magnanimity
in the candidate's mind. Now all such kindly interchanges of good-fellowship are done away with. Bribery
and treating in every form are banished. The Ballot
Act has put an end to open voting. In early days the
course of an election was followed vote by vote, and
many a friendly tussle took place over a hapless
waverer. Men of uncertain mind would keep their
preferences dark up to the latest moment, and after
being entertained and petted by one side would sometimes end by voting for the other. When candidates
were well matched the polling often ran very close, and
in small constituencies every vote was of moment. As
the closing hour drew near excitement grew intense
Horses were despatched ten and twenty miles to fetch
laggards. Special messengers came tearing in from
other polling-places, as in country districts men could
vote in their own wards or districts.

I recollect one case in which the numbers remained
evenly balanced during the three days' duration of the
poll. At the close of the contest, one candidate was
left at the central station, after counting up the latest
returns from the other places, in possession of a clear majority. Only one more return was due, and that was not
thought likely to affect the result. Congratulations
were showered upon the successful man; he was cheered
and complimented, speeches were demanded of him;
he glowed with self-complacency. At last, as darkness
was setting in, the clatter of hoofs was heard along the

road All eyes were bent upon the eager messenger. When he rode up, hot and panting, he shouted out the numbers he had to disclose This final return left the expectant victor just one below his rival!

It will thus be seen that there was no indifference to public life or patriotic duty on the part of the early colonists. They not only valued their privileges but they were prepared to make energetic use of them At that time the test of independence was to be "agin' the Government." A candidate known to have leanings towards the powers that were had but a poor chance He was openly stigmatised as a "toady." He was suspected of social snobbery He was considered to have an eye to the loaves and fishes. A stalwart mechanic once demanded of me before he gave his vote, "Will you accept a Government appointment?" The question seemed ludicrously superfluous, but it evoked a negative so strenuous that I have blushed for it ever since.

Did memory avail me better I might recall many amusing incidents of legislative life in early days. One of the first Speakers—a courtly old gentleman famed for urbanity of manner—once lapsed into slumber during a rather dull debate A loquacious official member just below him desired to rouse his attention, and woke him by a resounding thump on the table. "Mr. Speaker, your ruling is requested on the point of order that has just been raised," mischievously inquired the Hibernian orator. "I beg the hon. member's pardon," blandly responded the unperturbed president, "but the question raised did not reach the ear of the Chair." On a later occasion, when another Speaker had to be elected, rival nominees were proposed by the official and the opposition sides respectively. There was a tie, and neither side would give way. A deadlock seemed imminent, as business could not possibly proceed without a chairman. At last some one proposed that the leader of the opposition—the ablest speaker in the House—be appointed, and before members had time to realise the situation the proposal was unanimously carried. The bewildered politician found himself installed in an office which extinguished his active personality, but he held it for nearly twenty years. During the first session of the little Parliament a certain up-country member, who had dined somewhat freely, presented a petition from his constituents with these words: "Mr. Speaker—Mr Speaker—Mr Speaker, I beg—I beg to present a petition from ——, and to say —to say that—they are a set of d—d scoundrels" That was the first and only time when such a slip of the tongue profaned the atmosphere of a remarkably sedate assembly.

A less unparliamentary but even more diverting ebullition was that of a popular member of Irish extraction, who, thirty-three years later, was stung by repeated interruptions into this stirring apostrophe "Be silent, you cantankerous snarling, pugnacious old ram-cat!" Though colonial representatives are not, as

a rule, so mindful of sartorial observance as their European contemporaries, they are always decently, though
often unfashionably clad. During the second session,
however, a Dutch member who suffered from facial
neuralgia used to take his seat with his head swathed
in a thick woollen shawl. A clerical member, of High
Church tendencies, was wont to punctuate the importance of a debate by appearing in his cassock. Another,
and most genial, member was painfully deaf, and came
equipped with a long ear-trumpet, through which alone,
when helped by a neighbour, he could follow the course
of a debate. As I happened to fill that position, its
duties were often embarrassing, and I have known the
course of debate suspended while I strove to perform
them.

These pages are reminiscent,, and I am writing of
experiences nearly forty years ago, when stately halls
and spreading railways were all dreams of the future.
When the time for opening the annual "session"
arrived members left their flocks, their herds, their
stores, their offices, possibly their workshops, and hied
to the little sleepy capital. Some of them travelled
thither on horseback. The season was usually our
mid-year winter, when we have bright skies and cool
breezes day by day. Delightful those rides were,
starting at sunrise in the sparkling frosty morning, with
the brown or grass-burnt hills spreading round, and the
kindling air uplifting you out of cark or care as your
nag cantered or trotted onward How welcome was

the breakfast of eggs and ham at the quiet roadside hostelry, and how pleasant the easier amble under the mid-day sun, with the more solid meal in store! Or possibly, if the moon were full, the ride would be partly made by night, when the distances seem so illusive, and the landscape so unreal. Were the legislator a family man, he would often make the journey by ox-waggon, and a glorious picnic it was, travelling at the rate of fifteen miles a day, reading, shooting, or bota-nising by the way. Then at night would be the busy camp work—the jovial gathering round the blazing fire, the friendly gleam of the stars through the tent-door, or from behind the waggon-flap.

On reaching Maritzburg the actual business of legis-lation soon began. Our local St. Stephen's, whose planks and rafters — the equivalents of pillars and panels — were familiar to me through long years of contemplation, was a square, thatched, whitewashed building of one storey, with three great staring windows on either side of a big double door. Built before British occupation, by a Boer community of Puritan principles, it looked the Roundhead to the life, with its close-cropt roof, devoid of eaves, and innocent of porch or parapet. In front of this uninviting barn—for it was nothing more—one or two companies of her Majesty's troops would be drawn up; their coats and belts as spotless, their weapons as burnished, as though they were under review at Whitehall. A motley crowd surveyed them with mingled feelings: sturdy English colonists from

the country came in to see "the Council opened," and
to note, too, how their new member might comport
himself; big, listless Dutchmen, thinking no doubt of
their own Volksraad in the brief Republican days.
brisk and dapper townsmen to whom the sight was
no novelty; laughing and chattering natives, with a
sprinkling of Hindoos and a swarm of small boys.
Within was a little "lobby," on either side of which
opened a small room, not eighteen feet square, whereof
one was the "clerk's room," while the other was committee-room, library, refreshment-room, and waiting-
room all in one.   The only other apartment in the
building was the Council Chamber, now thronged with
gaily dressed ladies, who filled the benches provided
for the accommodation of the public, and pressed round
the seats of the members themselves.   The room was
long, cool, and bare, with whitewashed walls and no ceil-
ing, the roof being open to the thatch.   Round a horse-
shoe table were ranged fifteen cane chairs, overlooked
at one end by a low platform, occupied by the Speaker's
chair, covered with a kaross for the occasion, and over-
hung by a rude shield emblazoned with the royal arms.

The Governor's approach was preluded by the
salute of cannon, on hearing which the members filed
in and took their places   The Speaker was clad in his
ordinary clothes, as were the clerk and messenger, but
a lawyer's gown and an academic robe were conspicuous amongst the members.   The military band
struck up the National Anthem as his Excellency dis-

mounted, and, followed by a military and official staff all uniformed like himself, entered the Chamber. The whole assembly rose, and stood until bidden to be seated. Having received a ponderous manuscript from his private secretary, the Governor at once read from it his opening speech. By no means brief or flavourless, it resembled more the "Message" of an American President than a royal speech. It usually took at least half-an-hour in delivery, and dealt fully, and often ably, with the state of the country and the questions of the day. Governor Scott was wont to improve the only occasion he ever had for doing so by lecturing members on their shortcomings in policy and action.

Primitive though the surroundings of the infant Parliament were, members never forgot the dignity of their position. They were as tenacious in upholding the rights and privileges of their new-born legislature as though it had had centuries of prescription to sustain them. Their constant effort was to walk in the footsteps of their British forefathers. The House of Commons was literally to them the "Mother of Parliaments," their model and their guide. May's "Parliamentary Practice" was their Bible. Burke's "Precedents" was their catechism. Both books at all times flanked the Speaker. From their joint tribunal there was no appeal. Personal altercations were by no means rare, but the authority of the Chair was always respected and scrupulously upheld. Sometimes difficulties would arise for which the proceedings of the

Home Parliament supplied no remedy. In 1868 the Speaker went on a trading expedition into what was then the far interior—in other words, the western districts of the Transvaal. His travels took him farther than he had contemplated — to a region where, when early winter came, his cattle were left without grass, and it was impossible for him to return, for he had no horses with him. Thus it came to pass that when the session was opened there was no Speaker, and a deputy had to be appointed. The matter was not much considered, however, as the absence of the chairman was expected to be but brief. But weeks passed on, and the missing man came not, nor were any tidings of him received. At last, before the session closed, he suddenly reappeared, having made all speed from the far frontier as soon as horses were obtainable. He resumed his seat, however, and made his explanation; but one or two members, who thought he should have taken more pains to inform the Council of his movements, raised a question as to the legality of their past proceedings. Precedents were sought. "May" was conned, "Hansard" was explored, but the long records of the English Parliament failed to supply an analogous case, or to lay down any rule of action for the particular emergency. Such a contingency as a Speaker being lost in the wilds had never been reckoned with by parliamentary writers, so, to set at rest all doubts, an Act was passed legalising the doings of the Council during the absence of its head.

During thirty-seven years' experience of colonial parliamentary life, I cannot call to mind one occasion
upon which a member deliberately set at defiance the
authority of the Chair or outraged the proprieties of
procedure. Members have ever been on their good
behaviour, and such "scenes" as now and then have
occurred, though they are most infrequent, have been
usually terminated by an adjournment. Once, a peppery
though easily appeased Colonial Secretary was formally
censured for a sarcastic reference to the domestic relations of another member, but on re-entering the Assembly to be admonished, he cheerfully submitted to
the rebuke, and tendered his regrets with a twinkle of
the eye. In those days official members were rather
prone to assume "superior airs," or their elective colleagues fancied that they did, and sparks of temper
sometimes flew about but as time went on the personal relations of the two sides improved, and a more
genial understanding prevailed. Government House
opened its portals more widely, and the permanent
officials took their cue from their chief. In small
communities small motives are apt to operate, and
where the whole outer world was cut off by a gulf
of distance only bridged once a month by a sea-borne
mail, people had time enough and to spare to brood
over and resent social slights and differences. I could
fill pages with amusing incidents illustrative of colonial
life in this regard as it existed thirty and forty years
ago, but they are best forgotten.

Of the composition of the Council in these days something may be said It was, on the whole, fairly representative of the community. Large property-holders as a rule declined to come forward as candidates, and other classes—lawyers, doctors, farmers, merchants, and journalists—were generally selected and chosen. A colonial "farmer," it must be understood, often signifies the owner of many thousand acres, and a person of considerable culture. From the very first there has been at least one Dutch representative amongst the elected members. A curious end befell one of this class. He was killed in bed by lightning, which struck a gun placed near his pillow The names of Landsberg, Scheepers, Boshoff, Pretorius, Nel, Labuschagne, Van Breda, all show that some of the oldest and best-reputed Boer families were ready to take part in the parliamentary privileges secured to them under the British flag.

They were always free to address the House in Dutch, if they liked, and now and then they did so, though very few of their colleagues could follow them ; but as a rule they preferred to use, as best they could, the alien tongue In either case they were always listened to with unvaried attention and respect. Mr. J. N. Boshoff had taken part in the proceedings connected with the transfer of the unfledged republic to Great Britain. His account of the circumstances which led to the Great Trek is a particularly clear and dispassionate document, and he was one of the first

Presidents of the Orange Free State. A calm, fluent, and sarcastic speaker, he had much weight in the deliberations of the House. Essentially cautious and conservative in his ideas, he viewed with sincere distrust every progressive measure or innovation, especially proposals for railway extension, but though we were frequently opposed to each other, I always recognised his ability and patriotism, even though I might be, as often happened, the subject of his trenchant irony. One of his sons has for many years been Treasurer-General of the Transvaal A nephew is now one of the Judges of the Native High Court in Natal.

The last-named was son of the delightful "Oom Stoffel," as he was familiarly and affectionately called—the elect of Umvoti County for many years. In his time this worthy old member was one of the favourite figures in the House. His English was confused and rather difficult to follow, but it flowed freely from his lips, with really dramatic effects of tone and gesture. Though everybody laughed and smiled at his homely and humorous eloquence, we all awaited some thrust or flash that was pretty certain to enlighten as well as to enliven discussion. In odd contrast to his brother, he was a consistent supporter of railways and progress, while his success in winning votes for bridges, roads, or other concessions to the needs of his constituents was proverbial. The copious notes he made during debate were marvels of originality and spelling, but it may truthfully be said that no man ever sat in the

Council who enjoyed more fully than did he the good-will and affection of his colleagues   Mr Martinus Pretorius, who sat in the old Council as an elective member, as well as in the Upper Chamber of the new Parliament as a nominee, is the son of the old Com-mandant-General of the Voertrekkers and first Presi-dent of the Transvaal Though he seldom spoke, being diffident as regards his imperfect command of English, he was always listened to with manifest interest. That he should sympathise with his fellow-countrymen in their present struggle was in a sense inevitable—one could hardly have wished it otherwise—but all the same he strenuously repudiates any disloyalty to the Queen, though he was arrested after Joubert's raid through Natal, and after a short incarceration was sent on parole to Durban, where he lived for some weeks in a cottage by the sea. General Joubert, it is said, spent two days under his roof during his raiding march southward   I am glad to say that official inquiry failed to elicit any condemnatory evidence against this veteran Africander, who is now domiciled again in his farm in Weenen County.

It will thus be seen not only that the Dutch settlers of Natal have at all times enjoyed complete equality of citizenship and political privilege with their fellow-colonists of British birth, but that they have made free and full use of their rights. Through all the successive stages of parliamentary development there has never been a legislative body without a Dutch representative

in it. Those stages have been gradual but numerous.
The tree of freedom has had slow but solid growth. It
has grown from within, not from without. With one or
two incidental and not vital exceptions, changes in its
structure have been made by itself. In 1873 three new
elective seats were created, and balanced by the addition of another official nominee. I have already written
of Sir Garnet Wolseley's memorable mission in 1875,
when he persuaded the Legislative Council to perform
an act of political self-sacrifice by adding eight "independent" nominees to its ranks. This measure, which
was intended to strengthen the power of the Crown in
the legislative assembly, failed in its purpose because
the new members were "independent" in a sense hardly
contemplated by the authors of the proposal. On many
occasions they voted against the Government just as
readily as they voted for it. One of the most conspicuous in this respect was a Dutch colonist who, in
earlier years, had been a leading Voortrekker, and a
proscribed "rebel." He could never, however, have
been a loyalist at heart, as after the retrocession of the
Transvaal he left his beautiful farm near the Illovo
and went with his family to Pretoria, where a year or
two later he died, happy, as he said, in the thought that
he did so under the republican flag.

This octave of nominees was admirably selected by
Sir Henry Bulwer. They were all men of intelligence,
or property, position, and experience. They thoroughly
fulfilled the qualifications expected of them, but they

L.

were in the wrong place They ought to have formed a
Second Chamber As members of a popular assembly
their freedom from party ties or obligations made them
an incalculable quantity in divisions and an obstructive
factor in deliberations. Though a failure in practical
effect, the five years' working of "Sir Garnet's Nominee
Chamber" was an interesting and useful experiment in
constitutional procedure. Our experience of it led some
of us, later on, to insist upon the necessity of a nominated Upper Chamber as an indispensable condition
of responsible government. After exploring the history
of the past, and studying the examples of other colonies,
in our efforts to frame a constitution that should be
alike free and stable, we could find nothing better than
the creation of a nominated Second or Upper Chamber,
with powers analogous to those of the House of Lords,
as a convenient check upon hasty or heedless legislation. That such a check there must be in the case of a
colony, with a vast native population not directly represented in the popular Chamber, is generally admitted.
Indeed apart from that population the existence of some
brake power, to prevent the hurried adoption of vital,
revolutionary, or ill-considered measures, is as necessary
in a colony as in the old country. Whether some less
cumbrous means of securing it may hereafter be found
feasible remains to be seen.

The lapse of the Wolseley Constitution by effluxion of
time left numbers and proportions as they had been
five years earlier, but the reversion to old conditions

was at once attended by a strenuous agitation for responsible government. It is not my desire to follow the devious course of that agitation during the thirteen years which passed before the change was finally effected in 1893. Like most such struggles it was marked by periods of stress and calm. So far back as 1869, a small concession had been made to the principle of popular participation in government by the addition of two of the elected members of the Legislature to the Executive Council. That this small modicum of control did not work injuriously is evidenced by the fact that it continued unchanged up to the establishment of self-government in 1893. It may also be noted that in later years one of the two members so distinguished was a Dutch farmer. It might be supposed that in any colony the desire for full popular control would be universal amongst the white colonists, but in South Africa it has never been so. A Parliament of two Chambers was established in the Cape Colony in 1852, but twenty years elapsed before, after many a battle, responsible government was adopted. For thirty-seven years Natal colonists were content with their stunted, hybrid constitution. Mr. Froude, in 1874, seemed to think that they were eager for full-fledged freedom, but it was only in 1893 that they agreed to accept the boon, and then it was by the votes of a bare majority.

It took years and years of education to prepare the people for emancipation. The opponents of the change dreaded its effects upon the security and the credit of the Colony. They conjured up all manner of evil consequences. Long endurance of political deprivation and tutelage had weakened their fibre, and made them nervous and apprehensive. Though academically admitting the proposition that self-government was a proper aspiration and patriotic goal, they shrunk from its immediate realisation. "Progress with prudence" was their motto, just as "Freedom with Guarantees" was that of the reformers. Even the latter held that there should be some assurance of continued Imperial assistance to "shelter" the Colony, for a time at any rate. In 1882, however, the champions of responsible government were heavily beaten at the polls on an appeal directly made to the electors, under Lord Kimberley's instructions. For a few years a truce was called, and other affairs engaged the attention of colonial politicians. It may be taken for granted that Lord Kimberley's sudden offer of full freedom took the colonists by surprise. They were still smarting from the effects of two Imperial wars, the Zulu war of 1879, and the Boer war of 1881. They were disgusted with the terms on which Zululand had been "settled," and with the attitude assumed by home politicians and home parties towards South African affairs and interests. They shrunk from making themselves responsible for the possible consequences of Imperial blunders and vacillations. Imperial prestige had suffered lamentably in South Africa by the failure of the Empire to follow up its conquest of Zululand and to establish definite

authority there, and by the surrender of the Transvaal
under the indignity of defeat. A strong party at home
clamoured for the restoration of Cetywayo, a step which
would probably have been taken earlier than it actually
was, in 1881, had the Legislative Council of Natal not
protested against it session after session.

It was only when the interests of Natal were being ruth-
lessly sacrificed in 1886 by the cession of a large part
of Northern Zululand to the "New Republic" that the
party of progress, reinforced by some of its most stalwart
opponents, again took heart and courage, and resumed
the campaign in favour of self-government. Sir Henry
Holland, in the letters addressed to myself, while acting
as Colonial Delegate at the first Imperial Conference,
in 1887 practically and effectively reopened the controversy. Natal desired to raise a new loan, for the
prosecution of railways and other public works. The
Secretary of State pointed out that if such borrowing
powers were to be exercised in the future it must be on
the individual responsibility of the Colony as a self-
governing community. Though the Legislative Council
made no immediately effective response to this intimation, the seed was planted and it soon fructified In
1888 a Select Committee was appointed to consider
and report on the question, and the campaign was
resumed Session after session the controversy was continued. The opponents of change were stubborn and
unyielding, and resisted every step, however gradual,
which might seem to lead towards the goal. At first

the object of the progressives was to ascertain from the Home Government whether they would agree to the retention of an Imperial garrison for a certain time after responsible government might be established. Only with the greatest difficulty could the majority be persuaded to submit this question. When the answer came, it was a gentle intimation that the Colony had better make up its mind on the main issue before details were dealt with. The contest then proceeded in earnest on both sides. The "Forwards" and the "Antis" ranged in hostile camps. Evenly divided as the parties were, neither gained much advantage. In the session of 1890, however, there was a general rallying for a decisive effort. The life of the existing Council was about to run out, and it was decided to make the "cause" a battle-cry at the next elections. An academical proposition, therefore, was submitted to this effect. "That while this Council is unable to accept the suggestions offered in Lord Knutsford's despatch for the protection of native interests in the event of a change in the constitution of Natal, it nevertheless claims for the Colony full control of its own affairs and of all sections of the population, in accordance with the constitutional powers exercised in all colonies where responsible government has been established."

May I be pardoned for adding that the occasion was made memorable to myself as being identified with the longest speech it has ever been my misfortune to deliver. It lasted two hours and three-quarters, and was immediately denounced by one of our most bitter and vehement opponents as "one of the finest specimens of flatulent verbosity, misrepresentation, humbug, and high-falutin' that had ever been listened to in this world" I daresay he was right, but for nearly ten years any free discussion of the question in the Council had been barred, and the pent-up torrent could not be stemmed. A long and lively debate lasting many days followed, but it ended in the adoption of my motion by 12 votes to 10

Having thus secured parliamentary recognition of the principle, we went to the country with a definite cause and platform. Henceforward the contest was open and straightforward. All the resources of election energy and strategy were called into play We "stumped" the Colony from end to end, told off candidates for every seat, and flooded the electors with literature. So did our opponents. Such struggles are much the same in their features throughout the Anglo-Saxon world Whether amidst the crowded cities and quiet hamlets of England, or in the void spaces and wild habitudes of Africa, the same methods are employed, the same passions aroused. While it lasts the conflict is keen and all-absorbing; men think and speak of little else But when all is over animosities are forgotten, and social composure is restored We submitted to the electors the simple issue "yea" or "nay," for or against responsible government, and we won fifteen seats against eleven. Though not an over-

whelming it was a solid and impregnable majority,
strong enough to enable us at once to proceed to the
preparation and enactment of a Bill Of the difficulties
that attended that process it is not for me to speak
here. Though we were a united party, as regards
the main issue, we were by no means at one on points
of detail, such as the creation of a Second Chamber,
the distribution of seats, the representation of the
natives, and the reservation of power to the Crown
This last was, indeed, the most contentious difficulty
we had to dispose of. The Home Government insisted
upon the reservation for the royal assent of all bills
dealing with native interests. Our opponents at once
declared that it was intended to withhold from the
proposed administration the control of native affairs.
The objection was somewhat inconsistent with the
position they took up as opponents of self-government,
but it sufficed to perturb the colonists and to foster
distrust in our own party Day after day this and
other debatable questions were discussed and re-
discussed in Committee-Room No VI., where the
fifteen "Forwards" met to hammer out the provisions
of the new Constitution They were all very much
in earnest, and their differences were not easily
arranged. Again and again we seemed in peril of
fatal rupture, but loyalty to the cause in the end
prevailed, and we succeeded in carrying through the
House, inch by inch, such a measure as seemed likely
to satisfy both the Colonial Office and the colonists.

The former very properly insisted upon the adequate recognition of the constitutional prerogatives of the Crown. The latter, not versed in the working of constitutional procedure, with its silences and implications, and dependence for construction upon age-long usage, desired to have in black and white effective safeguards against usurpation and encroachment.

The cable was freely employed as a medium of correspondence and reconciliation, but it was at last decided to send a delegation to Downing Street with a view to the personal discussion of the questions involved. Two of us were deputed to undertake the duty, and in April 1892 I left with my colleague, Mr. Sutton, on a congenial, but by no means easy mission. Fortunately for us and, let me add, for the Colony, the duties of that mission were lightened by the sympathetic reception, open mind, and cordial assistance accorded by Lord Knutsford and his official assistants. They listened with full appreciation to all we had to say concerning feeling in the Colony, and the doubts, anxieties, and apprehensions of people there, and they were not less frank in pointing out the necessary requirements of the Crown, the demands of home parties where native interests are concerned, and the absence of any real ground for the dread of undue Imperial interference in colonial concerns. The result of our negotiations was the final preparation of a revised Bill, which was to be submitted to the electors, after its adoption by the local legislature, as an unalterable

whole This last condition undoubtedly saved the
situation. Had it been open to meddle with the details
of the Bill, it is fairly certain that it would never have
gone through in a form acceptable to the Home
Government. There would have been a change here,
and a change there, and the measure would have been
wrecked piecemeal As it was we were able to carry
" the Bill, the whole Bill, and nothing but the Bill,"
through the House, thanks to our still undivided
majority, and it was then submitted to the country.

Of the electoral contest which followed I could give
many amusing reminiscences, did space permit. It was
the most exciting and exhausting in my experience.
In 1882, when Mr. Escombe opposed me on the same
platform, and accomplished my defeat, the struggle was
in my own case confined to the borough itself, but ten
years later, when we both fought together, we had to
spread our energies over the whole Colony. Durban had
now become the stronghold of the Forward Party, and
could be left to take care of itself, but the outlying constituencies had to be braced up and wooed. Meetings
had to be addressed, one week at Newcastle in the far
north, and the next week at Harding in the far south.
To reach the latter place a post-cart journey of a hundred
miles had to be faced, along roads the perilous nature
of which, in the dark, must be experienced in order to
be understood. A furnace-like hot wind blew during
the first two stages of this journey, and the horses of my
trap knocked up in the depths of the magnificently

precipitous Umkomas Valley, and I had to walk all the
way to Ixopo, twenty miles off, in the face of a fiery
blast Two nights later the open two-wheeled post-cart
started with us hours before dawn, scrambling and
crawling along a misty mountain-track, whose dangers
were mercifully hidden from sight by the darkness and
the sleet At the meeting held the same day, in the
billiard-room of the country hostelry, about twenty
Griqua half-castes formed part of the auditory. Having
votes, they had a right to be present. They listened
quietly enough, and afterwards assured me of their
sympathy and indeed I had specially for their benefit
descanted upon the benefits that would accrue to the
coloured population from being governed by men who
knew and lived amongst them. They were privately
interviewed, however, later on, by an agent of the other
side, and, so I was told, voted to a man against us And
that would be the common experience had natives votes.

An even more interesting meeting, in the light of
recent events, was one held at Springfield, on the Tugela,
where our forces were fighting the other day. I travelled
thither overnight by rail as far as Frere While passing
through Maritzburg I was told that the meeting I was
to attend—it had been called by our party—had attracted the attention of the other side, and that our
opponents would muster there in special strength were
it known that I was to be present I was asked, therefore, to keep unseen in my carriage. The door, though
locked, was often tried during the night, and from time

to time, at stations we passed, I could hear whispered inquiries as to whether I had joined the train or not. The guard professed ignorance. We reached Estcourt after midnight, and there the question of my whereabouts was eagerly discussed just outside my window. On we went to Frere, where, about three in the morning, I emerged in the darkness. There, too, got out the two hostile emissaries. It was some time before they made me out at the other end of the train, which left us helpless in the veld. As it turned out, our opponents were my best friends, as they knew the locality better than I did, and with the personal kindness I at all times experienced at their hands, they took charge of my movements and my bag. The rough shanty which there served as store and inn was some distance from the station, and would certainly never have been reached without this friendly aid. After much knocking we roused the inmates, slumbering heavily after a revel, and were glad to stretch our limbs on the bare floor for the few hours preceding daylight. One of the first sights I witnessed on going out into the crystalline morning air was the figure of one of my fellow-travellers, standing out on the skyline, towards Chieveley, rehearsing the stock speech with which he was a few hours later to pulverise the reckless advocates of self-rule.

A neighbour had arranged to drive me to the place of meeting at Springfield, on the Little Tugela, several miles distant. On our way we called at the farm of Mr. Pretorius, to whom I have already referred. His long, thatched dwelling-house looked homely and comfortable, with its adjacent orchard, its corn-fields, and its large "dam" or pond, lively with wild water-fowl, near at hand. It was a "clearing up" day, and the plain but solid furniture of the sitting-room was being aired in the sun Around the walls of that apartment were framed lithographed portraits of the chief Boer leaders in the war of 1881, some of them kinsmen, all of them compatriots, of our host. They had been printed in Holland, which is the real nursery of Africander ambitions and designs After a substantial breakfast, prepared specially for us, and a little chat with our hostess, we took Mr. Pretorius on with us to Springfield, and I did my best to dispel certain doubts he harboured as to the proposed constitutional change. It may seem strange, but it was the case, that the Dutch colonists of Natal were by no means eager to join the party of progress. They were bewildered by the conflict of opinion amongst the English electors; they were suspicious of the intentions of the Imperial Government. and they were greatly influenced by the story, so sedulously propagated, that all control over the natives was to be retained by Downing Street. I am also inclined to think that they saw no attractions in a measure which might popularise British rule and diminish any cause of discontent therewith.

Springfield at that time consisted of but three or four scattered houses, near a lately erected bridge, on broad open ground, skirted by the towering cliffs and toothed

crests of the Drakenberg The meeting was held in a
building which served as courthouse on the occasion of
magisterial visitations.   Thirty or forty people crowded
it, and others clustered round the doorways and the
windows.   An unusually large attendance of Dutch
farmers lent special interest to the gathering, and the
speakers on both sides were duly mindful of the fact.
Amongst the auditors was the oldest Dutchman in
Natal, one Oosthuysen.   He had been with the Voertrekkers through the massacres of Blaauwkrantz, and
had fought against Dingaan in Zululand—a white-
haired, gentle-mannered octogenarian—fully conscious
of the benefits he enjoyed as a British subject, though
very possibly a republican at heart.   There were no
evidences at that meeting, however, of disaffection or
recalcitrancy.   The one or two Boers who spoke dealt
with local grievances, common to both races ; but, as no
suspicion of coming events was in the air, any sinister
significance in their utterances was unsought and
unsuspected.

And that was our general experience throughout
the campaign.   At Ladismith we had in the chair
a leading Dutchman, recently under arrest as a rebel.
At Newcastle I attended, by request, a meeting of
the local Vereeniging, or Union — a body essentially
Africander or Boer in its composition and aims.   Its
proceedings were all carried on in the Dutch language,
and resembled those of a religious body rather than of
a political association.   Hymns were sung, and prayers

of inordinate length indulged in. Some of the speeches left a ring of hostility in the ears and a flavour of alienship in the mouth, and I left the meeting with a feeling that I had been a foreigner and an interloper Was it fancy or forecast ? Be that as it may, the final issue of the contest was decided by the Dutch vote, though not all at once As far as could be ascertained under the ballot, the Dutch electors voted for the "Forward" candidates, and thus turned the scale. The numbers actually, though in two cases erroneously, returned by the magistrates were fourteen for and ten against self-government.

A special session was immediately summoned to enable the new assembly to record its verdict on the measure I think that, perhaps, the gloomiest moment of my political life was that when, after all our efforts and hopes, we found ourselves confronted by an impregnable majority of four. The tables had been reversed. In the last Council we had been a solid phalanx of fifteen, now we had shrunk to ten Our opponents lost no time in pressing their advantage home. We contended for delay until the disputed election returns should have been disposed of, but in vain. On points of procedure the majority were supported by the Government members, who had, under instructions from Downing Street, abstained from voting on the main question. The "Antis" had the power in their hands, and did not hesitate to use it. They introduced into the reply to the opening speech words which practically extinguished discussion. There was nothing for it but to submit, and await the result of the election trials. So the session ended with apparent failure to our cause. The work of nearly twenty years seemed to have gone for nought. The Forwards by no means lost heart, however They were resolved to wrest success out of temporary defeat. They provided the most strenuous professional advocacy at the election trials, which were held before an able and impartial judge, Sir Walter Wragg. Fortune smiled on them. In both cases the disputed returns were upset. So far as votes were concerned, there had been a substantial majority in each case recorded for the Forwards, but papers had been spoilt or rejected by the polling or returning officers The judge overruled this action, and in the end the defeated candidates were placed in their rightful positions at the head of the poll. Henceforward all was plain sailing Again the Council was called together, and the Bill, which we had brought from Downing Street, was passed in its integrity without amendment Immediate sanction was given to it, and on the 4th of July 1893 Natal took her place as a self-governed colony

This rapid retrospect of parliamentary development in Natal leads up to three conclusions. (1) That self-government has been no mushroom upgrowth, begotten by sudden impulse or popular passion, but the slowly matured result of arduous effort and deep conviction; (2) That the people of the Colony have always tempered

their love of liberty with a prudent regard for wholesome checks and safeguards; and (3) That, as between
English and Dutch, the principle of racial equality and
common citizenship has ever been carefully observed.
Mr. Froude's forebodings have proved as baseless as his
sneers were unjustified.   There is much more of the
oak than the aloe in the constitutional framework of
either the Cape Colony or Natal

Nor will a study of Natal legislation during the last
forty years indicate any failure in these respects.   The
fruit on the whole has been worthy of the plant.   Many
of the laws passed may, in their construction, betray
signs of inexperienced or faulty draughtsmanship.   That
was an inevitable condition of colonial circumstances.
The principles embodied in these local statutes are,
nevertheless, in accordance with modern British juris-
prudence, while the whole superstructure rests upon the
solid, time-tested basis of Roman-Dutch law.   The combination of ancient maxim with British practice and
colonial instance, in so far as it is stable, elastic, and
comprehensive, may confidently challenge criticism.   As
a rule the measures sent home have seldom called for
correction by the law officers of the Crown, and I was
surprised to find how little amendment was required in
the last Constitution Act, notwithstanding the manifest
difficulties attending its preparation.   On one occasion
Natal gave the lead to the Empire on a question of the
utmost delicacy.   The Immigration Act of 1897, which
was designed to deal with the Asiatic invasion from

M

British India, has been accepted as a model throughout the Colonial Empire.

So much has been said about the bribery of legislators in the late South African Republic, that it is pleasant to be able to make a contrary record in the case of a neighbouring British Colony. Looking back for forty years, I can unreservedly say that at no time in the history of parliamentary institutions in Natal can I recall any instance of legislative delinquency in this respect. I am not aware of any attempt having been made to corrupt the virtue of our representatives, nor, indeed, of any lapse of that sort having been suggested. "Concessions" have seldom been favoured in Natal, and when on public grounds they have been agreed to, their acceptance has usually been regretted. If any irregularities of this kind have occurred they have not offended the public eye or ear. The arts of lobbying have been conspicuous by their absence. Venality in public life is, most assuredly, not a colonial characteristic. The offer of a "present," if only as a "souvenir," would be no passport to parliamentary or official favour. Natalians have come to regard purity in politics as a quality to be prized and cherished, and ever may it be so.

It is no easy matter for a legislature to cater for the needs of three alien races living within an area so small as that of Natal. The European, the Asiatic, and the African are all domesticated on the soil of a country not much larger than Scotland. These three great types of the human race all jostle and intermingle with each other Even the European is divided into two classes, the English and the Dutch. Side by side with the statute and the common law of the Colony stands native law, of which I shall say more by and by. It is a codified structure, based upon habits of life and ideas of morality wholly at variance with those of the white man Yet it has to be administered and enforced, and is from time to time modified, to meet changing circumstances or special requirements The task of the Colonial Legislature is therefore far more complex and embarrassing than that which falls to the lot of most Anglo-Saxon lawmakers elsewhere It calls for sympathy and indulgent criticism, and when mistakes are made, as they must be at times, they should be judged with due regard to the conditions under which they were committed

CHAPTER VII

THE SETTLERS AS TRADERS AND CIVILISERS

HALF a century ago, in 1850, when I first knew Natal, the import trade of the Colony was valued at £111,015, the value of goods exported was £17,106. The imports were brought to Durban in small sailing-vessels, most of which came from the United Kingdom, while the rest were coasters. Towards the end of 1850 the first merchant steamship seen in these waters, the *Phœnix*, brought up from Capetown a party of merchants and other visitors from Capetown, anxious to spy out the land, and to assess its capabilities as a seat of trade. Two years later the General Steam Shipping Company placed a small steamer, the *Sir Robert Peel*, on the coasting service. She ran in conjunction with that company's regular monthly service between England and Capetown. Several years after that the decline of trade was so serious that steamers ceased to run regularly on the coast, and we had to depend upon small schooners for the delivery of our mails. Home dwellers can but faintly imagine the interest which attached to the arrival of the mail from home. It was the one event of the month. A flag hoisted on the tall flagstaff of Lloyd's Agent betokened the approach of

the mail, and the people of the town at once rode or
walked to the landing-place, content to wait there for
hours on the chance of being the first to hear the news
Up to 1854 war prevailed intermittently in the Cape
Colony, and then the Crimean War broke out, so that
we had stirring events to anticipate and to read of.
Now the daily paper serves up to us at our breakfast
tables news of the night before from the whole world.

Commerce in those days was conducted on the
simplest and most primitive lines.   Little distinction
existed between the wholesale importer and the retailer.
Most dealers were " storekeepers," a generic title that
covered all classes of commodities and transactions.
Even then, however, that inland trade which has been
the mainstay of progress and prosperity in Natal was
germinating   Its headquarters were in Pietermaritzburg.   Its agents were locally known as "smouses."
A smouse is, or rather was, for he is known no more in
those latitudes, a glorified pedlar.   He was a merchant
on wheels   His warehouse, or pack, was an ordinary ox-
waggon with its team of fourteen oxen.   In this was
stowed away a carefully chosen assortment of such
goods as might catch the fancy or suit the needs of the
Dutch farmers in the interior—coarse brown or black
sugar from Mauritius, bean coffee from Rio, rough salt,
brown bar soap, moleskin for the dopper's garments,
printed calicoes of flaring hues for his womenfolk :
cheap earthenware " cometjes," or little basins — the
equivalent of coffee cups ; baftas and punjums, the

unbleached materials for underclothing, bar lead for bullets, and buckshot in small bags, for the chase—the mere rudiments and raw materials of the crudest civilised requirements. With these would be packed away beads, brass wire, and clasp knives for the artless natives of the wilderness. Thus equipped, the smouse or trader would go forth on his mission of barter. Produce, of sorts, not coin, was the object of his quest. He would disappear for months, wandering about the inland deserts at his own sweet will, trekking, regardless of time, from farm to farm, where he would be the only visitor from the outer world the whole year round. In exchange for the wares he had to dispose of, he would receive the hides of cattle or goats, the skins of antelopes and wild beasts, rough tubs of stale butter, in later years parcels of unwashed sheep's wool, or goat's hair, possibly a little roughly dried and pressed tobacco, all that the Boer settler had to offer as an equivalent for the things he needed.

There was fascination about the life, with its utter freedom from all constraint, its healthy, hardy experiences, its abundant chances of adventure and sport. At that time the vast inland plains were thickly thronged by countless hordes of antelope—eland, hartebeest, wildebeest, quagga, springbuck, rheebuck, and all the rest—bounding joyously from sunrise to sunset across the untenanted and uninvaded veld. Hyenas and jackals prowled around the trader's outspan after nightfall. Lions would often provide a more perilous diversion.

Giraffes and ostriches would invite to the chase, and birds innumerable offered sport for the gun and food for the evening meal. Men of gentle birth and culture were wont to try the life as a relief from the burdens and shackles of civilisation, and sometimes it weaned them altogether from the chafing associations of the past. One who tasted of these delights, celebrated them in spirited verse. For many years an honoured civil servant of the Colony, he still lives an octogenarian in Maritzburg, and often has he in times past enlivened festive gatherings of his fellow-colonists with words which aptly illustrated the care-defying life of the itinerant trading adventurer.

The smouse was the forerunner of the country trader. He was a necessity in years when villages and townships were conspicuous by their absence. Bloemfontein, Smithfield, Winburg, and Potchefstrom were fifty years ago the only centres of population worth considering in the two republics. They were soon supplemented, however, by other places. A trader would sometimes settle down and become a resident "winkelaar" or storekeeper, or merchants in Durban and Maritzburg would establish branch trading-stations in suitable localities, and these in turn would gradually attract other residents and competitors, and blossom into urban settlements. The country store would usually be a place of accommodation for travellers and way-farers, and the popular resort for the neighbouring farmers. Religious services would be occasionally held there by itinerant predikants, a post-office would be opened, and a Government office attached. Then would follow the laying out of a township, the appointment of a landdrost, and the erection of a church. Thus it came to pass that towns which are now historical Harrismith, Bethlehem, Cronstadt, Vrede, Zuringkrantz, Pretoria, Heidelberg, Rustenburg, Lydenburg, Standerton, and other republican centres, came into being and grew into importance, and thus it was "the Natal trader" or storekeeper and merchant planted and nourished the commerce for the retention of but a share of which he has had to fight so strenuously with rival communities in later years. Just as the British settler in Natal strove, as we have seen, with all his might to develop new industries and enrich the soil with new products, so did the British trader act as the pioneer of commercial activity in the states of the interior, and cater for the requirements of consumers there, scanty and simple though at first those needs might be. For many years by far the bulk of the trade done with the northern districts of the Free State, and the whole of the Transvaal, was in the hands of the men who had established it, the importers of Natal.

That trade was often accompanied by contingent risks of heavy loss. Credit was a large factor in operations, and buyers were often unable to pay their debts. Disease or starvation would destroy their cattle, scab would ravage their fleeces, crops would fail, drought and locusts would devastate. Storekeepers had of necessity to provide a margin for the misfortunes of their customers, and those customers would seek to protect themselves by a corresponding increase in prices demanded for their produce. Hence arose the practice of "verneukering"—by which buyer and seller each sought to get the better of the other. The process has given a malodorous notoriety to South African trading customs, but it was mainly a natural product of the time, and is disappearing with the spread of railways and the growth of competition. I fear that it had its root in the congenital depravity of human nature. The Boer was pleased to get a higher price for his produce, even though he might have reason to suspect that the difference would be made up in the accounts. The storekeeper was content to offer a higher price for produce or to accept a lower price for his wares, knowing that he could compensate himself in other ways. That such a method of doing business was improper, and indeed dishonest, need not be argued, but the impulse to overreach in commercial transactions is not, I believe, confined to infant communities, or to semi-civilised conditions.

The itinerant trader's operations were by no means restricted to dealings with Boer settlers. They embraced the whole native population. After the missionary the trader may take rank as civilisation's earliest pioneer. Wherever a native tribe exists he finds his way. To many men the allurements of Kafir trading surpass those of any other calling. Its absolute free-

dom from constraint or convention is seductive and
enthralling. In too many cases it also proves to be
deteriorating, if not debasing. It is impossible to mix
only with savages for weeks and months, and years,
without sinking in the social scale. The natives are
wont to live in broken though beautiful country, where
roads are not, and where wheeled traffic is impossible.
In such regions the trader's stock has to be carried in
bundles on the heads of his bearers. Thus accompanied
the vendor travels on foot from kraal to kraal, by narrow
footpaths that scale the hills or skirt the precipices, or
thread the bush-clad gorges and valleys. At night, if
so disposed, he accepts the friendly shelter of a hut,
and for food he is content with the provender supplied
by his packs or his gun or the kraals he visits. In
many cases he encamps with his waggon or cart at some
convenient spot near a running stream, and sends his
boys out with their packs to do the huckstering. For
weeks or months at a time he may never see a white
man. His companions are natives, and natives only.
Except the dumb dependents around him, the beasts of
the field, and the fowls of the air, or the many voices of
exuberant nature—

> " The sun, the moon and the stars, the seas, the hills, and the
> plains "—

are the only associates of his daily life. Well for him
is it if higher innate influences avail to counteract
the grosser seductions of the savage life around him,

to keep his life clean and his heart sound. If in too
many cases lapse has been the outcome of such an
existence, it has also at times been identified with the
deliberate acceptance of the native code of morality,
with its definite restraints upon indulgence and excess
I speak, of course, of times that are vanishing, and of
experiences that are past.   In most of the native territories—Zululand, Pondoland, Swaziland, and Tongoland
—settled stores will now be found scattered throughout
the country.   They are places where anything can be
bought, from a box of matches to a bottle of gin or a
tin of salmon   They have largely superseded the
travelling trader.   In many instances they are kept by
the ubiquitous Asiatic, who is gradually if stealthily
overrunning South Africa   Perhaps it is as well for the
moral status of the European in a land of black men
that his race is fast ceasing to be represented in the
lower walks of trade, and that responsibility for "ways
that are dark" shall be transferred to the less sensitive
shoulders of yellow competitors.

As years went on the inland trade of Natal developed
a new form of enterprise.   In the early fifties the transport work of the Colony was all done by a few regular
carriers and by casual waggon-owners.   The ordinary
vehicles employed were tented waggons drawn by spans
of twelve or fourteen oxen and holding about two tons.
The common charge was £3 for a load from Durban to
Maritzburg and 30s. for a load back   Rates for other
journeys were a matter of arrangement.   As trade

increased and roads improved, better organised facilities
were provided. Open waggons with projecting "bucks"
or frames were constructed, and the weight of loads increased by degrees to three, four, five, and even six tons.
The production of sheep's wool necessitated more commodious means of conveyance for the bulky but light-
weighted bales of that staple. After lung-sickness had
swept off by thousands the trek oxen of the Colony,
the rates of transport rose to abnormal figures, and as
much as 16s. per cwt. was paid for carriage between the
seaport and the capital, a distance of fifty-four miles.
Then it was that transport-riding became a systematic
pursuit. Only at times were owners seen driving their
own waggons. They mostly employed white and coloured
drivers, and many waxed rich and prosperous. Farmers
found carrying more lucrative than stock-raising or
cultivation, and the agrarian interests of the Colony
suffered by the consequent diversion of energy. In the
winter, however, the business was almost suspended.
Drought, frost, and grass fires destroyed the pasturage,
and it was impossible to work the cattle—starved, flesh-
less, and feeble—along the dusty roads. Such spans or
teams as might now and then be seen straining forward
at that season—otherwise so glorious—were miserable
spectacles. "Cruelty to animals" seemed imprinted on
their bony, lash-scarred, quivering bodies. To see such
a team towards the end of a half-day's trek, writhing
under the detonating whipcracks of a callous driver,
with heaving chests and gasping breath and doubled-up

backs, striving to drag a load up some steep bit of road, was to feel that trade was purchased at too horrible a cost. And thus it was that year after year, prior to the advent of railways, trade with the interior was practically at a standstill   Merchants regulated their indents accordingly, and the middle months of the year, from April to October, were periods of stagnation and depression   Imports and revenue alike fell off   Stocks up-country got depleted, and prices of all edible commodities advanced in proportion as distance from the port increased and as the dry season lengthened. As the demands of consumers in the inland states developed, so did the need of capital to lay in stocks large enough to provide for them grow, and thus it was that the element of credit became a controlling factor in South African commercial enterprise.

Up to the year 1853 all business transactions in Natal were matters of barter or money. Payment was made in kind or in coin. Treasury drafts issued by the Army Commissariat Department upon the military chest were the chief medium of remittance to English creditors. A local Fire Assurance Company at first afforded a little relief in the way of exchange, but the absence of ordinary monetary facilities soon became so serious a drawback that local enterprise rose to the occasion, and two banks were established. One of them, the Natal Bank, still flourishes, having triumphantly survived the many critical experiences of our commercial history. The establishment of banking opera-

tions at once lifted up the conduct of trade to a higher
level. The loose and primitive methods of earlier times
were succeeded by conformity to the principles and
practices of a more advanced life Progress in usage
was also attended by abuse of opportunity. Facilities
of accommodation led to perilous indulgence Promis-
sory notes became popular instruments of purchase.
Though for many years the bank rate of discount was
never less than 12 per cent, it was gladly submitted to
by an impecunious community The renewal of bills
was a common resort, and the endorsement of them
by friendly hands was an act of reciprocal assistance.
Much of the commercial difficulty which at times
beset the Colony was due to the lavish, not to say
indiscriminate, negotiation of " paper " by local institutions. The custom had its effect on social life, and
the earlier debates of the local legislature were often
enlivened by vehement denunciation of " bank parlour
tyranny " as exercised in the interest of a favoured few
to the detriment of the unblest many. As time went
on and banks multiplied, all these processes and effects
gradually disappeared, and to-day are only remembered
as legends of the past. Bank directors are no longer
the powers and personalities of yore. With the advent
of great Imperial institutions business has drifted into
ordinary, legitimate, impersonal channels, and is conducted between the bank manager and the customer
as it is in other large communities. Natal colonists,
nevertheless, feel proud that their one local institution

has been able to hold its own—almost alone amongst other colonial banks—with such tenacity and success in the face of outside rivalry, and at one time in the teeth of a political attack from without which the resolute interposition of the local Government alone availed to frustrate. The survival and prosperity of the Natal Bank afford another example of that patriotic purpose and energy which it is my desire in these pages to commemorate and emphasise.

The railway system of Natal has been developed on lines much more scientific than have been adopted elsewhere in South Africa. The principle of connecting local centres and following established trade routes has not been sacrificed to the fetish of inland trade—important though that is, and advantageous as it has proved. The several lines more or less follow existing traffic routes. The main central line bisects the country from east and west, connects Durban with Maritzburg, Estcourt, Ladismith, the Coal-fields, and Newcastle, and only branches out at Ladismith so as to tap the two republics, each by a direct line. When the first responsible Government took office, the principle so far adopted was amplified and extended. Trade requirements having been provided for as far as the border, the first step taken was to complete the connection to Johannesburg, and thereby to connect the Natal system with that of South Africa at large. This having been accomplished, by steps indicated in my next chapter, the internal

development of the Colony itself was accepted as a rule
of policy. Parliamentary sanction was obtained for the
construction of lines extending coastwise from Durban
to the Tugela and from Durban to the Umzinto, as the
first section of a line to the Lower Umzomkulu, which
is now under construction. The needs of the upper
districts were met by a line from Maritzburg to Greytown northward, and to Richmond southward, while the
Natal section of an extension from Dundee to Vrijheid
in Northern Zululand was also authorised. These proposals were cheerfully assented to, and are all now in
progress, the Coast and the Richmond lines having
been completed and opened for traffic, while the Greytown line has just been completed.

A yet more important project was also initiated by
the same administration, and legislative authority has
subsequently been obtained for its execution, namely, a
line to connect the Natal system with that of the Cape
Colony, advancing through Griqualand East from the
border railway system of that country. The importance
of this undertaking from a political, not less than an
industrial point of view, cannot be overrated. It will
link the two seaboard colonies directly by the most
potent of all unifying agencies, and will give Natal the
shortest and most direct route to the southern seaports
and centres. It will also traverse the fairest and most
attractive region of South Africa, and strike, through
the native territories which now so largely absorb that
region, a civilising and pacifying agency which will soon

revolutionise their conditions At present, if a Natal colonist desires to travel overland by rail to Port Elizabeth or Capetown, he has to pass through both the late republics and to journey round two sides of a triangle. Whatever may be the fate of those inland states, the necessity of a coast line between the two colonies is instantly made apparent by a glance at the map. The precise route to be taken by that line has yet to be determined. It may be connected with the coast line, or it may take an inland direction, but that it will be soon carried out is beyond doubt. Nor is much time likely to elapse before the north-coast route is continued into Zululand, where large coal and mineral deposits await exploitation. A home company has undertaken both these operations.

All these lines are now practically in the hands of the State, and with one exception have been carried out by the Government. Experience in the case of the north-coast line did not encourage any further departure from the rule of State construction and State control. Neither as regards economy nor convenience is private intervention found preferable. Whatever may be the case elsewhere, in Natal the State ownership of railways has been justified by results. It is true that the Colony has been fortunate in having the services of an exceptionally able and energetic manager, but the Cape Colony can also point with satisfaction to corresponding results. I have no desire to burden my readers with figures, but it may suffice to say that at the end of last

N

year (1899) 545 miles of railway had been built at a cost of £7,267,000, and earned, over and above all working charges, a profit representing 4 per cent. interest on capital outlay. And this was in spite of the paralysing effects of three months' actual war, and the seizure of 150 miles of line by the enemy. In 1898, when the Colony was at peace, the profit earned was a little less. Having been a most persistent advocate of railway extension, in season and out of season, from the earliest date of action, I may be excused, perhaps, for some exultation over the remarkable economic effects of the policy that has been pursued. Never are the taxes of a people better laid out in a new country than in the provision of cheap and easy facilities of transport. By no other means is civilisation more effectually advanced. Under no other influence does the wilderness so soon blossom like the rose. By no other policy is the maintenance of law and order more successfully secured and assisted.

Apart from the stimulating effects of railway extension upon trade, revenue, and industry, the influence thereby exercised upon social development is, in a new community, especially remarkable. People living outside the towns are no longer confined, for the greater part of the year, to the seclusion of their more or less remote and isolated farms. They are able to move about and mix amongst their fellow-men. They are able to see a little of the outer world, and to rub off the rust of rusticity. Their outlooks are widened, and their

orbits enlarged. Their political interests are expanded,
and their prejudices abated or corrected. In the case
of the native population, these influences are still more
manifest. The natives of Africa take to railway travelling as readily as do the natives of India. The carriages
provided for their accommodation—covered, airy, and
commodious—are usually crowded with a chattering,
merry, snuff-taking and munching crowd, many of
whom are in the primitive garb of barbarism—a motley
of beads, tatters, and cast-off clothes, while all bear
their bundles, bags, and mats, and sometimes their pots
and pans. Thanks to the railway, they are now able
to travel to Johannesburg in a day, a journey which,
twenty years ago, would have taken two or three weeks,
and to earn there wages so high that they are able, after
a few months' work, to return to their kraals with bags
full of coin to invest in cattle and in wives. But of
that I shall write hereafter.

Railways are of only limited value if they have not
a port to start from. Long before railways were seriously thought of, the necessity of an improved harbour
was recognised in Natal. Less than thirty years ago I
have heard intelligent and influential colonists express
their disbelief that a line of railway would ever be constructed between Durban and Maritzburg. As to an
extension to and over the Drakenberg, such an idea
was scouted as fantastic and chimerical. I never heard
such scepticism expressed concerning the feasibility of
improving the harbour of Durban. The little, almost

land-locked sheet of water, some twelve miles in circumference, bare at low water, but at high tide a
rippling or burnished lake, has been recognised as a
possible haven from the earliest times. Though Vasco
da Gama discovered the coast of Natal on Christmas
Day, in 1497, and named it in honour of the Nativity,
he does not appear to have landed or entered the inner
bay; but succeeding navigators referred to it as the
"River of Natal," with " a mouth wide and deep enough
for small craft, but at which is a sandbank, with at
highest flood not more than ten or twelve feet of water
This river is the principal one on the coast of Natal, and
has been frequently visited by merchant vessels. The
East India Company would have taken possession years
past but for seeing at the mouth of the port a reef or a
sandbank that no galliot without touching could get
over without danger, so that a small vessel could not
safely go in there."

This was in 1687, and what Batavian enterprise
shrunk from attempting then, British push and
energy have triumphantly accomplished since. As
a matter of fact there is no river worth the name
running into the bay, though two small streams,
having their rise in the adjacent hills, enter it at
the upper end. There can be little doubt that at
one time the sea flowed between the Bluff promon-
tory and the Berea, and that the southern end of
the channel, which separated these islands from the
mainland, gradually silted up, leaving at the northern

and more exposed front a slake into which the tide ebbed and flowed with a current strong enough to keep the entrance more or less clear, though not to sweep away, unaided, the sand deposited there. Nature had thus provided the "makings" of a harbour, if not a harbour in the proper sense itself. Fortune willed that in 1850 a shrewd Scottish engineer who had served under Rennie, one John Milne, should arrive in the Colony concurrently with another shrewd Scotchman, Governor Pine. The keen eye of the one detected the possibilities of the place, and the large mind of the other grasped them. Small though the revenue of Natal was at that time (£29,338), Mr. Pine did not hesitate to authorise a small appropriation for the commencement of re-medial operations. They were urgently called for. The "bar" was on its worst behaviour, and even small coasting schooners could only, with much difficulty and after long delays, cross that barrier and get inside. Mr. Milne's plan was simple enough. He sought to strengthen and regulate the tidal current by construct-ing a little breakwater on the north side of the entrance running parallel to the rock-tipt Bluff, and to prevent the drift of sand into the inner channels by running out little groins of wattlework and broken stone into the bay.

With the few pounds at his disposal, the resolute old engineer succeeded in attaining results which were full of promise; but worse times came. The local exchequer emptied as the demands upon it multiplied.

Another Governor came who was less favourable than
his predecessor to Milne's plans, and they were practically suspended, while controversy raged over the
respective merits or demerits of different proposals.
I have no intention of reviewing these interminable
discussions even in outline. It is enough to know that
the primary principles laid down by John Milne in 1850
have been more or less adhered to. They have assuredly been vindicated by results. For though the effects
of tidal scour have been immensely aided by the employment of modern dredging appliances, it cannot be denied
that the extension of two parallel piers has been attended by results such as the most sanguine advocate of
harbour improvement never dared to contemplate. In
1896 Sir Charles Hartley, as the highest authority on
such questions, visited Natal, and subsequently, in conjunction with Sir Wolfe Barry, a not less commanding
authority on dredging operations, submitted a report
which generally approved of the principles that had
been followed, though certain modifications in detail
were recommended. For some years past opinion in
the Colony has been divided between those who depend
on tidal scour and those who depend on dredging, for
the extermination of the " bar." As a matter of fact,
both processes have been concurrently pursued, and
both were approved by the eminent experts I have
named, and it is by continual reliance upon both that
the harbour of Durban will be made hereafter accessible
to vessels of the largest tonnage.

From 1880 to 1893 the presiding genius of the
harbour was the late **Mr.** Escombe, whose sudden
removal on the 27th of last December was justly
mourned as a public calamity and a grievous personal
loss. Throughout that period he gave up his time and
his energy to what became the dream of his life, the
creation of a first-class harbour As chairman of a
reconstituted Harbour Board, through all these years
he contended against opposition and discouragement,
and when on the establishment of responsible government that board, with other boards, was swept away,
he had the satisfaction of knowing that his unselfish
and disinterested labours had borne imperishable fruit.
Since then the course of improvement has proceeded
without interruption.   The gain of depth has been
continuous, 27 feet at high tide is a common record.
Within the bay channels have been deepened, wharves
built, steam cranes, shears, sheds, and all other
appliances and facilities provided A flotilla of steam
dredgers and tugs is kept constantly at work During
this war, transports of the largest tonnage have been
brought inside without delay or difficulty, and have
discharged their freights, whether of troops, ammunition,
or stores, from the water-side into railway trucks that
have carried them straight to the front, so that men
landed at Durban one morning have sometimes been
fighting the next day near Ladismith.   During the
Zulu war all the transports had to be discharged into
lighters at the outer anchorage and travel over a

turbulent bar at much cost of time. money, and difficulty. There seems no reason to doubt that, by patient persistence in the present policy, the harbour entrance will ere long be so deepened that vessels of the largest tonnage will be able at all times to steam over the bar and be berthed at the wharves. Unfortunately for the Empire, not less than for the Colony, the seizure of our coal-mines by the Boers at the outset of the war, nullified the enormous advantage which their possession would otherwise have conferred on both.

The coal-mines of Natal have come to be regarded as the natural complement of the seaport in any estimate of the future which awaits the latter. They have been a product of slow and difficult development. For many years local geologists declared that coal of commercial value would never be found in South Africa. Stratigraphic evidence was all against it. They said just the same about diamonds. Scientific authority was not wanting for other deductions. In 1867 Sir Roderick Murchison wrote me a note in which he referred confidently to the probable existence of large coal deposits in the country. For more than half a century an outcrop of anthracitic coal has been known to exist on the sea-coast, forty miles from Durban. Much money has been spent in exploration at this point and elsewhere near the shore, but without satisfactory results. The other carboniferous indications occurred 200 miles inland, the intervening country having been

denuded by glacial and fluvial action. In their case
the cost of transport presented insuperable obstacles to
development, and until railway communication was established all mining enterprise was futile. Since the line
was completed to Newcastle, both capital and energy
have been freely expended in the opening up of coal-
mines, and the supply now equals the actual demand
Coal is delivered into the ship's bunkers at Durban
at an average cost of 20s. to 25s. per ton. It is good
steam coal, and all the regular liners use it constantly.
Durban is thus a coaling base for the commerce of the
world, and for the navy of the Empire. One of the
first results of the war was to destroy this advantage and paralyse this industry. and the fact that it
was possible for two hostile republics in the rear
thus to cripple the resources of the Colony and the
Empire, is in itself a sufficient reason why such a possibility should be prevented in the future. England
cannot afford any more than can South Africa to hold
an endowment of such priceless value at the mercy
of a reckless and antagonistic power There is every
reason to hope that coal will do for South Africa what
it has done for every country where it has been mined
in adequate quantity. At Johannesburg it has been
found and worked within arm's length of the gold mines,
to whose economical development it has enormously
contributed Its existence has been proved at many
other points. Found as it is in conjunction with or
proximity to both precious and baser metals, it cannot

fail in the near future to make the southern continent an area of manufacturing activity, which will supply its agriculturists and pastoralists with the markets they need. But it is especially as a means of fuel supply for the sustenance of sea-borne trade and of naval power that the coal-fields of Natal are of Imperial interest and value. Associated with a fine harbour and a wide-spreading railway system, they form a possession which the world may envy, and a heritage which the Empire may well guard and cherish.

Trade, banks, railways, harbour, and mines, these are the solid and appraisable tokens and elements of national prosperity. They represent the labours, energies, and struggles of the British settlers of Natal during half a century. They may not be the things which the old Boer Voertrekkers had in view when they vainly strove to set up a bucolic republic in a region so richly endowed by nature with the resources of a busy and progressive civilisation, but they are the fruits of Anglo-Saxon activity in a virgin field, and they represent the claim which the Empire and its children have to the possession and control of the soil. They are not all, however. The settlers have established other claims to the ownership of the land they live in. The evidences of civilisation are not confined only to the constituents of material wealth and advancement. There are higher gains than commercial progress and industrial expansion. Some of them have, I hope, been already indicated in these pages. Others I can

but glance at.   Education has not been neglected.
Schools have multiplied. Government from the very
first has done something for the mental culture of the
colonists, though it has never made school attendance
compulsory.

In 1850 a free school was established in Maritzburg
and in Durban, so that no one in those centres could
even then plead inability to get a child taught the
rudiments of knowledge.   Little by little these primitive institutions have expanded and out-stretched,
until for many years past a public school fabric has
embraced the whole Colony.   Dr. Mann was the first
to give form and scope and character to the system
An enthusiast and a student, he left his mark in
the sixties upon the colonial mind   I accompanied
him once or twice, as a young but admiring friend,
upon his tours of inspection, and very interesting
expeditions they were.   Ambling along the bridle-paths
that connected outlying centres in secluded districts,
the good doctor's companionship was not less enter-
taining than profitable, for to him nature was an open
book, and his work a delight   Like all true colonists,
he lived in the future not less than in the present.
"All the wonder that should be" was ever present to
his mind.   The tiny barnlike structure, in which the
few humbly clad children gathered under their homely
teacher to learn such rudiments of knowledge as he
or she could teach them, became in the doctor's
presence the birthplace of a future seminary, and the

wondering but eager-faced little pupils, struggling with their alphabets and primers, their slates and copy-books, amidst the sylvan surroundings of a South African wilderness, were the coming citizens of a new state, the heralds of a new order. Sometimes arrangements would be made for the instruction of the elder folk in the form of a popular lecture on some scientific or literary subject, which would be handled by the doctor with wonderful ease and graphic charm. After his departure a lull took place in educational activity, but it fell to Sir Henry Bulwer's lot to lay the foundations of the system which still prevails in the Colony with ever-increasing acceptance and success. The High Schools, the Model Schools, the Primary Schools, the farm schools, and the assisted schools of the Colony, bring within reach of nearly every child teaching of varying degrees of fulness and excellence, at a cost that shuts out no one. And that instruction is open to all, irrespective of nationality or creed. Dutch is taught wherever it is wanted, though English is, and ever has been, the language of the Colony; but though the Dutch residents often clamour for the use of their own tongue, when instruction is provided in it the advantage taken of the facilities afforded is miserably small. Natal is also the scene of many private schools, chiefly of a higher class, which are carried on with much success, and of these the Huguenot seminary at Greytown, an establishment of Dutch parentage, affords evidence of a growing desire on the part of the Dutch population to secure educational advantages for their daughters on a more distinctively national and religious basis than is possible under the strictly unsectarian public schools.

Though there are public libraries and museums in Durban and Maritzburg, it cannot be said that in either respect public activity in Natal has been quite up to the level of some other colonial communities. Perhaps with the growth of wealth the example set by private munificence elsewhere may bear fruit in edifices and collections of monumental magnitude. Agricultural associations, on the other hand, are amongst the earliest offshoots of co-operative activity. For long years past every district has had its agricultural society or planters' association. Their annual shows, dinners, and balls form the chief events of the social year, and the management of them by committees gives scope for participation in public life. Race meetings are not less universal and popular. Rifle associations and shooting-matches are means of bringing together the scattered residents of country districts in friendly rivalry. All these gatherings are made occasions for picnic excursions, the jollity and pleasantness of which must be experienced to be appreciated. They promote amenity of social intercourse, and in their primitive freedom and gladness of life recall the days when " Merrie England " was something more than a memory. That the Dutch settlers of Natal may more and more take part in these meetings, forgetting in them the rancour of past events, must be the hope of all who desire that race hatred shall pass away.

Much might be written about the outgrowth of municipal institutions in Natal and South Africa Their germs were developed at a very early date both in Durban and Maritzburg, where English and Dutch pioneers lost little time in associating themselves for purposes of common action. The old Town Committee and Heemraden were the precursors of the full-blown incorporations of municipal boroughs, under the responsible control of Mayors and Town Councils, which have done so much to extend the visible traces of civilised life in South Africa. The history of these bodies is indeed the history of the Colony. They have been a most excellent training-school for public life and representative energy, and have relieved the central government from burdens and duties which would have greatly enhanced the cares of administration. They have given to the country well-ordered, well-controlled, healthy, attractive, and beautified centres of population, where all classes, from the half-naked native to the gaily clad dame of fashion, commingle without discord in the relationship of daily life.

It would be possible to fill many pages with stories connected with the public festivities, or rather, let me say, the public "feeds," of the Colony in its earlier years. In nothing is the Englishman more loyal to his traditions than in his observance of gastronomic ordinances. No matter where he may have been transplanted—in southern continents just as ardently as in northern islands—he "celebrates the occasion," whatever it may be, by the consumption of food and drink. In sober and religious circles the function takes, or took, the form of a "tea-meeting," where good folks of all ages disposed of vast quantities of tea and cake as a preliminary to graver exercises in the shape of speech, hymn, or prayer. More secular celebrations, and especially those of political significance, were represented by "luncheon" or "dinner." The former was often dignified by the name of "collation" or "dejeuner," just as the vaguer but more grandiose term "banquet" came into vogue as civilisation advanced. "Public dinners," however, grew for some years into disfavour on account of the rowdyism that sometimes marked them. One or two of those gatherings degenerated into noisy orgies, thanks to the presence at them of a few roysterers who made uproar of the proceedings, and for some time they were abandoned. When Governor Musgrave arrived a strenuous effort was made in Durban to give him a seemly welcome, and a civic banquet was organised, though with fear and trembling.

Respectable citizens, anxious to impress her Majesty's new representative with a sense of their intelligence and self-control, were nervously anxious to guard against any excess of festal hilarity. Tables and tickets were all planned and numbered with careful regard to the maintenance of order and the restraint of revellers. The event fully vindicated the preparations. Though

the toast list was of portentous length, it was gone
through without a hitch or a halt. Order was supreme.
The illustrious visitor admitted himself to be most
agreeably affected by the admirable behaviour of his
entertainers, while they were so delighted by the success
of their endeavours that after the guest of the evening
had taken his departure they signalised their satisfaction by a march round the room singing the popular
chorus of the moment. So keen was the enthusiasm
that one of the sedatest of the townsmen found himself
at the end minus the coat tails that had yielded to the
ardour of his neighbour in the procession! Having
thus re-established the reign of order, colonists again
resumed the practice of banqueting, and never again
lapsed into impropriety. The tendency, indeed, has
been rather the other way. A very able and popular
governor complained to me on one occasion of the lack
of warmth and enthusiasm. It is not easy on these
occasions to reconcile local or sectional differences.
When the first bridge over the Umgeni River, which
divides the counties of Durban and Victoria, was opened,
the people of the town and the people of the country
both wanted to celebrate the occasion in their own
fashion. Neither would give way, and as the bridge
itself was not available as a neutral banqueting ground,
two luncheons were held, one on either side of the river.
The dual function entailed obvious strain upon the
principal actors—and speakers—on the occasion, but it
averted a deadlock.

Perhaps the most imposing banquet ever held in the Durban Town Hall was that given to President Kruger, when he visited the seaport in connection with the opening of the Natal Railway as far as Charlestown on the Transvaal border. We were all eager to obtain or to receive from the sphinx-like potentate some assurance or indication of his readiness or intention to extend the line as far as Johannesburg. When he rose to speak every ear was bent amidst breathless expectancy for the hoped-for word. The reporters gathered near the great man so as not to lose or misinterpret the fateful utterance. The oracle spoke, through his interpreter, and spoke at some length, but he said nothing that left us a bit wiser as to his wishes, purposes, or thoughts. Unfortunately for us, perhaps, Oom Paul drinks milk only on such occasions, and he was not betrayed into any verbal indiscretion. Only three days before I had seen him at a ball at Newcastle, where the Governor undertook to chaperon him round the room. The ladies present—most of them—were clad in the, perhaps, not too redundant garb of modern fashion. Certainly not exceptionally so, but the vision of those undraped shoulders was a palpable shock to presidential innocence. Before he was half round the room he developed acute indisposition, and hurriedly retired from a scene that outraged his primitive sensibilities. His pregnant comment on the spectacle I prefer not to repeat.

CHAPTER VIII

THE SETTLERS AS NEIGHBOURS

NATAL is but a small red patch on the map of the South-east African seaboard. It is so small as to seem almost lost amidst the vast parti-coloured spaces of the great continent. Any one ignorant of its whereabouts would have difficulty in locating the garden colony. Elbowed in between the mountains and the shore, it has a breadth ranging from one hundred to one hundred and fifty miles, and for fifty-four years its coast-line stretched for the same length, bisected by the 30th parallel of south latitude. In 1897 the province of Zululand was incorporated with the little colony, and its sea frontage was thereby doubled. Its northern frontier now abuts directly upon the southernmost boundary of Portuguese possessions. Arrangements for this acquisition of territory were amongst the last official duties I had to discharge before relinquishing office in 1897. I recall this fact with satisfaction, inasmuch as it helped to rectify that inadequacy of area which has always irritated the Natalian mind. Lord Rosmead once said that Natal had a heart too large for its body. The remark was not unkindly meant, but it rankled, and, for reasons which will be shortly specified, it bore a somewhat sinister significance.

Though Natal may be diminutive in size, it will, I think, be admitted by my readers that it is not lacking in productive energy or political activity. In its case nature has compressed within a narrow compass the physical conditions and capabilities of many lands. Mere breadths of the earth's surface do not in themselves constitute greatness. Small countries are often the most wealthy and influential. Great Britain by the side of Russia is a pigmy, but as a power and a producer she is coequal. Victoria represents but a little slice of the Australian continent, but she contends with New South Wales for primacy. Acre for acre, Natal could sustain a population many times larger than that of the Cape Colony. Though her area does not much exceed that of one or two of the Cape magisterial divisions, her trade bears a proportion of one-third of that done by the whole sister and senior colony.

But it is in respect of interterritorial position and relations that Natal's strength as a factor in South African politics has to be recognised. Contracted though her borders may be, they touch those of every other South African State save one. On the south lies the Cape Colony, as represented by Pondoland and Griqualand East. Then comes Basutoland, behind its barrier of well-nigh impassable mountains. The Free State follows, where the mighty Drakenberg subsides into a more broken and less forbidding range. Then

advances the Transvaal, starting where Majuba sentinels
the junction of the two republics, and doubling round
to the south and the east, along a frontier so angular
and disjointed that the one aim of its delineators seems
to have been to take everything from Natal, and give
all to the Republic. That section of the border-line
affords melancholy evidence of the recklessness with
which British and colonial interests have been sacrificed to expediency, timidity, and nescience by Imperial
representatives in the past. Then, when this zigzag
frontier—so typical of zigzagging policy and purpose—
terminates in North-west Zululand, the boundary of
Portuguese dominion is reached, and followed until it
ceases with the sea. It will thus be seen that Natal
comes into direct contact with the greater and older
sister colony, with the independent British territory
of Basutoland, with the two late republics, and with
the Portuguese possessions. With Rhodesia there is
no propinquity, while Germany's new colony in South-
west Africa is separated by half the continent from the
eastern seaboard.

To Natal, therefore, a policy of isolation has never
been possible. She has always had her neighbours to
consider and reckon with. The earliest British settlers
at the seaport, adventurous as they were, entered into
compacts and treaties with their Zulu neighbours. In
1828 King Chaka appended his mark to a document
whereby he charged an Englishman named King and a
chief, Sotobi, to proceed to " King George's dominions "

on a friendly mission, and after offering his Majesty
"assurances of friendship and esteem," to negotiate
with him "a treaty of friendly alliance between the two
nations." The same document granted to King, in
return for services rendered, "the free and full possession" of the country at and near the sea-coast and port
of Natal, "together with the free and exclusive trade"
of all his (Chaka's) dominions. A like grant was made
subsequently to Lieutenant King's successors at Port
Natal, both by Chaka and by Dingaan. We know of
the later treaties entered into between Dingaan and
M'Pande, successively, to the emigrant Boers, and also of
the later engagements entered into between M'Pande and
the Government of Natal. All these documents serve to
show the solidarity of interests that has always existed
between Natal and her savage neighbours to the north
in Zululand. They were gradual precursors of the
final covenants entered into after the country had been
conquered by Sir Garnet Wolseley, and of the ultimate
act of consummation, embodied and ratified in the law,
by which Zululand became part of Natal.

Already the countries known as Amatongoland and
Zambaansland had been annexed to Zululand, much to
the chagrin of President Kruger and his colleagues. For
years they had coveted those territories, not so much
on account of any particular endowments of soil or
resource, but because their acquirement would give the
Republic a foothold on the seaboard. Access to the sea
has ever been the cherished desire and purpose of Mr

Kruger. It was as a means to that end—as a long step towards the ocean—that he so persistently and strenuously strove for the absorption of Swaziland. An independent harbour—"my own port"—has been the dream of the old President's life. To gain that he planned, intrigued, and temporised, alternately yielded and insisted, covertly operated and openly contended. That he was wise and shrewd in doing so no one can deny. With a port of his own he would have been master of the situation. He could have snapt his fingers at all proposals of customs union, and pursued without a halt his policy of republican absorption and aggrandisement. As a maritime state he could have claimed an international status which it would have been difficult to dispute, and might, by enlisting naval co-operation on the sea, have changed the fortunes of the war.

Fortunately for South Africa and the Empire, Imperial vigilance has succeeded in thwarting this ambition and in blocking the republican march to the sea. I say "fortunately," not because of any ungenerous desire to crib and cabin the development of an inland state, or to blast the success of a just and laudable aspiration, but because events have shown in what a spirit of exclusive and hostile dominancy the craved advantage would have been employed. Had Tongoland fallen into the hands of the Transvaal, or any point along the coast-line been acquired without attendant checks or conditions, the Republic with its vast command of money—wrung out of the gold industry—would have been able, by constructing a port, to set South Africa at defiance. Though the sea-coast between Durban and Delagoa Bay at present offers neither open harbour nor safe anchorage, there are certain points where skill and money would avail to create the one or to secure the other. Protruding capes or reefs, resembling on a smaller scale the Bluff at Durban, offer shelter from southern seas and gales, and are flanked by lagoons or river-mouths which are capable of being dredged and deepened. Only in its hold upon the south-eastern seaboard has the Government of the Empire shown true foresight in its treatment of territorial questions, and in that respect it has to thank the vigilance of local representatives rather than the observance of any settled policy for the salvation of its interests.

In 1884 Sir Henry Bulwer, Governor of Natal, autho- rised the planting of the flag at St. Lucia Bay at a moment when another power seemed on the point of get- ting a foothold there. On the 7th of May in the follow- ing year Count Munster, German Minister at St. James's, formally notified to Lord Granville, who was then Colonial Secretary, the readiness of Germany "to with- draw her protest against the hoisting of the flag at Santa Lucia Bay, and to refrain from making acquisi- tions of territory or establishing Protectorates on the coast between the Colony of Natal and Delagoa Bay." Though this understanding safeguarded British interests on the eastern shore, it was attended by a definite sacri- fice of British claims on the western side of the conti-

nent, where Germany was granted an enormous sphere
of influence, extending from the south Portuguese
frontier to the northern frontier of the Cape Colony
on the Orange River. The complaisance with which
the Colonial Government of that time acquiesced in so
vast a circumscription of its territorial limits has yet
to be satisfactorily explained. Had Natal possessed
the control of its own affairs at an earlier period, it
may be confidently assumed that the northern frontier-
line of that Colony would have been defined on intelli-
gible and patriotic, if not exactly "scientific" principles.
Its interests, and those of the Empire, were simply
given away by those who were responsible for the work
of delimitation.

Though the line of the Tugela and its affluent, the
Buffalo, has at all times been scrupulously recognised as
the boundary between Natal and Zululand, no care has
at any time been taken to prevent the gradual curtail-
ment westward of the latter territory. Little by little
the Boers of the Transvaal were suffered to creep eastward. The districts of Wakkerstroom, Utrecht, and Piet
Retief were absorbed by the Transvaal. Had the natural
line of the Drakenberg been accepted from the first as
the western limit of British dominions as far as the
frontier of the Portuguese possessions, these encroach-
ments would never have occurred; but Imperial aspirations stopped short at the Buffalo, and the Republic was
allowed to wander eastward at its own sweet will. Years
before the Zulu war, Cetywayo repeatedly urged the Colo-

nial Government to take possession of the disputed territory intervening between Zululand and the Republic,
but the Imperial Government persistently declined to
sanction any such measure After the Zulu war, any
frontier whatever might have been insisted upon, but
under the Wolseley settlement the only aim of British
statesmanship seemed to be the reduction of Imperial
responsibilities and possession to the narrowest limits

That this policy was viewed with great disfavour by
the colonists need not be said The local legislature
again and again lifted its voice in protest against
arrangements in regard to which it had neither part
nor lot, nor vote. It was asked for a contribution
towards the cost of administering the country, but it
declined to commit itself in any way which might be
held to imply approval of measures which it deemed
inimical to the future peace and order of South-east
Africa Meanwhile the Boers, presuming on British
apathy, found their way into the fine pasture-lands of
Upper Zululand, and remained there. They are as apt
in stealing a march diplomatically as they are in doing
so in the field. It would be too long a story to tell
here of the events which led to the establishment of
the "New Republic" and the recognition of that ridiculously contorted frontier-line which now disfigures the
map. The Boer piously acts upon the principle that
possession is nine points of the law—where he sets his
foot, there he means to remain He has scored many
diplomatic successes in South Africa, but none has

been more disastrous to British interests than was the
cession of the New Republic in the teeth of strenuous
opposition on the part of the Natal Legislative Council.
How completely that surrender was disapproved by the
colonists and their representatives—impotent though
they were—will best be indicated by the resolutions
adopted by the Legislative Council in 1886. Early in
the session members were made aware, by the presence
of three leading representatives of the "New Republic"
in Maritzburg, that important negotiations, about which
they were being kept in the dark, were afoot, and they
thus expressed themselves —

"1. That this Council, as representing the Colony of Natal,
claims a voice in any settlement of a question so vital to its
interests as is the future disposal of Zululand, including the
reserve and the control of the trade route to Swaziland and
the north.

"2. That this Council protests against its persistent exclusion from any definite information concerning the negotiations that are going on between the Special Commissioner,
the Boer settlers, and the Zulu chief.

"3. That while this Council does not ignore such just
claims as the Boer settlers may have to land in Zululand, it
respectfully asks that the provisions of the arrangement
that has been submitted to the consideration of her Majesty's
Government be communicated to the House prior to any
decision being come to thereon."

Later on, when it became known that negotiations
had actually been concluded, a yet more emphatic
protest was recorded :—

"1. That this Council is of opinion that the interests of Natal have not been duly considered and conserved by his Excellency the Governor, as Special Commissioner for Zululand, in the negotiations which preceded the Agreement entered into on the 22nd of October, in disregard of the resolution passed by the House on the previous day; and this Council feels keenly that it was not frankly treated by the Government in regard to this question during the early part of this session.

"2 That this Council reiterates the readiness of this Colony to undertake the government of the Reserve and Eastern Zululand, as the only means whereby stable peace and order can be established in those territories; it is convinced that the strong desire of the Zulu people is to come under the government of this Colony, and it asks his Excellency, should he have any doubt on that point, to take such steps as may satisfy him as to the temper of the Zulu people in regard to their union with this Colony.

"3. That this Council accepts the offer of her Majesty's Government to act in concert with it so far as regards the future of Eastern Zululand and the Zulu Reserve.

"4. That this Council is of opinion that the terms accorded by her Majesty's Governments to the Dutch settlers in Zululand make it doubly necessary—not only in the interest of the Zulus on either side of the Tugela, but in the interests of the Colonists of Natal, and of British influence in South Africa—that her Majesty's rule should be immediately extended over the remaining portions of Zululand, including the Reserve.

"5. That this Council is prepared to pass a Bill for the extension to Eastern Zululand and the Reserve of the Laws in force in Natal, such Bill to have effect whenever her Majesty's Proclamation may incorporate Eastern Zululand and the Reserve with Natal.

"6. That this Council strongly urges the extreme importance of providing, in any convention that may be entered into
between her Majesty's Government and the Dutch settlers
in Zululand, for the unrestricted passage of goods through
their territory, free of duty or transit dues in any form."

Though Lower Zululand was thus saved to the
Empire that had spent so much blood and money in
its conquest, it was only by the skin of its teeth. The
attitude and action adopted by the colonists throughout all these events have been abundantly vindicated
by events. Until Great Britain openly and definitely
annexed such part of the country as remained un-
appropriated there was continuous trouble, disorder,
and insecurity The independent kinglets set up by
Sir Garnet Wolseley were perpetually quarrelling or
fighting with each other So long as Dinizulu's claims
to sovereignty were allowed to operate, intrigue, conflict, and occasional bloodshed prevailed. His trial and
removal to St. Helena were followed by a period of
comparative quietude, but there was no proper or stable
settlement of affairs before annexation was effected.
The history of this period cannot be more clearly or
succinctly summed up than in the words of the "Colonial Red-Book," which bears the hallmark of official
and Imperial authenticity —

"The territory between the Umhlatusi and the Natal
frontier was constituted a native Reserve under the supervision of a British Commissioner, and it was arranged that
locations should be provided in this Reserve for any of the

Zulus who might be unwilling to again submit to the restored King Cetywayo, who had at his own request been allowed to visit England, where the decision of the Government was communicated to him, and by him formally accepted, and who was re-installed by Sir Theophilus Shepstone on the 29th January 1883, in the presence of 5000 Zulus.

"His enemies, headed by Usibepu, proved more formidable than he or others had anticipated, and after a struggle of some months he was overthrown and his kraal destroyed. He took refuge in the Reserve, where he lived practically under the care of the Resident, until the 8th of February 1884, when he died. Soon after his death, his followers, the Usutus, finding themselves no match for Usibepu, called in some Boer adventurers, with whose assistance they inflicted a crushing defeat on Usibepu, who took refuge in the Reserve. As a reward for this service the Boers received a grant of land, in which they established the 'New Republic.'

"Finding that the Zulu people were unable to form any orderly administration of the remaining territory, her Majesty's Government decided, with the general assent of the Zulus, to declare their country to be British territory, which was done in May 1887. Some disturbances occurred soon after in connection with an attempt to set up Dinizulu, a son of Cetywayo, as king; but it was soon checked, and Dinizulu and some of his indinas were removed to St. Helena, while others were imprisoned or fined."

The change which at once ensued in the conditions of Zululand, after annexation was proclaimed, bore splendid testimony to the character of British rule over subject native tribes. Quiet replaced unrest. The chiefs ceased to worry and harry each other. Imperial

sovereignty was implicitly accepted. War's pursuits
were abandoned, and the people betook themselves,
under the sheltering wing of the Great Mother, to the
ways and the works of peace. The Resident Commissioner (Sir Marshall Clarke), with his magistrates,
became the recognised centre and embodiment of
supreme authority. Justice was faithfully administered,
and the land greatly prospered. The efficacy of a firm
and fixed policy was once again demonstrated. When
one thinks how simple and easy a thing it is to carry
out such a policy—when one realises how beneficent
and abounding are its results—the marvel more than
ever strikes one that it should have been left to colonial
representatives to urge its necessity and its wisdom upon
the cultured minds of Imperial statesmen.

Although Natal was originally an offshoot of the Cape
Colony, the relations of the two communities have not
been marked by much filial regard or parental solicitude.
Each has stood upon its own dignity and interest. The
Cape has never forgotten that it was the senior and the
larger colony. Natal has always been ready to resist
and resent interference, encroachment, or assumption,
on the part of the sister state. Natal was annexed to
the Cape Colony in 1844, and declared a separate colony
in 1856, but it was not until 1876 that the boundaries
of the two colonies actually touched each other. Before
that date they were separated by the territories known
collectively as Kafirland, occupied by the Galeka, Fingo,

Tembu, Pondo, and other tribes. This is perhaps the fairest region of South Africa. Generally resembling Natal, its climate is a little less tropical, and its features somewhat more expansive. The broad sweep of its uplands gives place near the coast to broken and bush-clad valleys, through which brooks and rivers rush turbulently to the sea. It is a land of rich pastures, primeval forests, and picturesque aspects full of sylvan charm. Early visitors wrote of its beauties with delight, but, strangely enough, of all parts of South Africa it has been the least invaded or molested by the white man. Thickly occupied by more or less warlike, and often hostile native tribes, it has been left to them as a happy hunting-ground, and only within the last ten years has it all been brought definitely under British rule.

During the last two decades of the first half of the expiring century Great Britain had the good fortune to be represented in South Africa by three Governors of singularly high-minded aim and purpose. Sir Benjamin Durban, Sir George Napier, and Sir Peregrine Maitland, were all inspired by a noble conception of Imperial duty. Of the first two I have spoken elsewhere. The last made his name memorable by a series of treaties with the chiefs of Kafirland—with the heads, that is, of the Galeka, the T'Slambie, and the Gaika tribes, and with Faku, the paramount chief of the Amaponda nation, and throughout his life the faithful and unswerving ally of the British Government. The scope and character of

these historical documents imparted a monumental significance to them, as examples of high-minded, humane,
and generous statesmanship

It is greatly to the honour of Imperial rule that the
undertaking thus solemnly entered into was loyally
observed both in spirit and in letter, as long as faithful
observance on the part of the native signatories rendered
it possible and easy to do so   Only when the chiefs and
their tribes had, by acts of open hostility and aggression,
practically torn the treaties into bits, was it necessary to
depart from the policy that had been laid down, and to
deprive the natives of the independence which, by their
own infatuation and folly, they had sacrificed.   And
even then scrupulous care was at all times taken to leave
the misguided people in the undisturbed occupancy of
tracts of country far more than sufficient for all their
requirements   In its dealings with the native tribes
within and beyond its own frontiers, neither the Imperial
nor the Colonial Government has any cause for self-
reproach on the score of humanity or justice.   So far as
the Pondos are concerned, the policy of indulgence and
non-interference has indeed been carried to the point
of weakness and peril   So long as Faku lived and
ruled, no occasion arose for any change of attitude   He
was always able to control his people, and ready to
comply with reasonable remonstrance or representation.
But his successors, Umqikela and Sigcau, men of inferior character and resolution, needed firmer treatment and a less tolerant hand   Had they been left

less severely alone, much trouble would have been averted.

As in the case of the northern frontier of Natal, so on the southern border, the local government—owing largely no doubt to its lack of genuine responsibility—showed fatal apathy in safeguarding the interests of the Colony. Just beyond that border—the line of the Umzimkulu River—stretched a zone of sparsely occupied and unclaimed territory, known as No Man's Land. Faku would have been glad to have seen it occupied by the British Government, but various reasons—mere political inertia being perhaps the foremost—barred the way. In 1855 Adam Kok, chief of the bastard tribe of Griquas, was invited by Sir George Grey to take up his abode in the western part of this territory. This proposal was intended partly to compensate the Griquas for their loss of territory on the south-western border of the Free State, and partly to stop the incursions of the Bushmen, who made the fastnesses of the Drakenberg in that direction a base for their predatory raids upon the farmers and natives of Natal. The Government of Natal acquiesced in this arrangement, and the country which has ever since been known as Griqualand East passed into other hands. The Griquas settled there, and established the township of Kokstad, named after their founder, and it flourishes to-day as the seat of a chief magistracy.

Like most half-caste races, however, they were difficult to deal with, and after Adam Kok's death in 1875 the

P

territory became a centre of unrest and disaffection. Its people were in direct and frequent communication with Basutoland, by means of the mountain passes which connect the two districts. Faku had passed away, and elements of distrust existed amongst all the surrounding tribes Fear prevailed that as Natal had been deprived of a natural and proper chance of expansion to the westward, she might lose any possibility of a modest extension eastward on the seaboard. The administration of government happened to fall into the hands of a sagacious and active-minded ruler of colonial origin—Colonel Bissett—and he readily operated in the desired direction. In 1865, therefore, with the sanction of the Colonial Office, he travelled down to the district immediately south of the Lower Umzimkulu, accompanied by a field-piece and a small military force, and he there proclaimed the adjacent territory annexed to the Colony of Natal, and named it Alfred County, after the royal prince on whose escort he had ridden to the Colony five years before This act of annexation only added about a million acres to the area of Natal, but it extended the coast-line by about twenty-five miles, and more than that, it shut out any other power from obtruding itself there. To a people thankful for small mercies it was a distinct contribution to their self-importance, and until Zululand was annexed it was the only territorial acquisition which Natal at any time could boast.

Gradually, though, the two colonies were creeping towards each other. Nine more years passed before

they were actually conterminous. In 1876 letters-
patent were issued, annexing "No Man's Land," or
Griqualand East, to the Cape Colony, and henceforward
British rule extended without a break from Table
Mountain to the Tugela River. It would be too long a
story to tell were I to describe the devious steps which
led to the unscientific and unsatisfactory arrangement
of frontier between Natal and its great neighbour. Geographical fitness and political convenience would have
placed that frontier along the line of the Umzimvubu—
or better still of the Umtata. Both rivers run considerably south of the present boundary, and the latter, or
southernmost, would have been preferable, because it
would have embraced the whole of Pondoland and its
people, and being unnavigable, would have been free
from possibilities of friction in connection with fiscal
or harbour regulations No such prescient or statesmanlike considerations governed, however, in these
days the course of events. Natal was the smaller and
weaker colony, her Government had not the strength
or initiative which responsibilty and representative
character imparts. The Cape has at all times pursued
its own interests with relentless inflexibility; at any
rate when the interests of Natal have seemed in conflict
with its own enrichment or aggrandisement, or with its
own lines of settled policy.

This is a grave allegation, but it points to a fact that
has materially influenced South African history during
the last thirty years. The Cape would probably attempt

to rebut it by a reference to its efforts in behalf of
Customs Union. That shall be dealt with shortly.
We are now considering the distribution of territory
and the definition of boundary, and in doing so a
glance at the historical relations of the two colonies
seems desirable.

Natal, as we have seen, was originally an offshoot or
dependency of the Cape Colony. Its very earliest
settlers, whether of British or of Dutch origin, came
from Capetown or Port Elizabeth. Its places of
business were in the first instance established by Cape
merchants. Its first officials were taken from the Cape
service. It was natural, therefore, that Cape colonists
should take a parental, if not a proprietorial, interest in
the infant community, and should, as years went on,
regard with some jealousy or distrust its efforts to
escape from tutelage, and to compete with themselves.
That was but the fulfilment of a law of nature, an
exemplification of the mother instinct which is aroused
when the fledgling takes to flight, or the whelp seeks to
forage for itself. Where our Cape friends have erred
has been in not adequately realising the inexorability
of this law. Like some parents, they were slow to
perceive that the child must grow, and that the mature
offspring would inevitably assert its powers and protect
its interests. The Prime Minister of the Cape Colony
once said to me on a certain occasion, in the presence
of other representatives of South Africa; "Yes, but you
must remember that you are the little Bear, and that

we are the great Bear." My response was: "True, but please also remember that the little Bear will grow, when you have ceased to do so." Whether justly or not, an impression prevails in Natal that the desire of our colonial neighbours has been to prevent the growth of Natal, and thereby to restrict its capacity for effective independent action. They have certainly done their best to prevent our expansion southward, at the cost of grievous hardship and injustice to their people in Griqualand East, and of injury all round. The contour of the frontier between the colonies is nothing less than a scandal. In order to reach Alfred County from Maritzburg the traveller has to pass through twenty miles of Cape territory, a tongue of country having been allowed to cut off one portion of Natal from the rest of the Colony.

But it is in the treatment of Pondoland that the differences between the two colonies have been most acutely accentuated. The natives of that country, without being exactly warlike or courageous, are fond of war in a predatory sense, and ever since the death of Faku have been split up into tribal factions. That old chief was a firm believer in the value of an alliance with his Natal neighbours, of whom he knew much more than he did of the Cape people. While he lived there was little trouble, but after he died difficulties began. The paramountcy of the recognised successor was disputed, and intertribal conflicts became frequent. The moral condition of the tribe—never satisfactory—deteriorated.

Witchcraft, with its attendant abominations, got rife, and vice flourished more flagrantly than ever Stock thefts multiplied, and traders lived in terror of spoliation. Bloodshed was frequent, and a state of chronic internecine warfare developed on our immediate border. From time to time appeals for intervention came from our own settlers The Government of Natal, however, was powerless to act In 1885 Sir Henry Bulwer had brought the whole question before the notice of both the Secretary of State and High Commissioner in a most able and exhaustive despatch, but without avail in so far as any recognition of Natal interests was concerned Whatever action was taken was in behalf of Cape interests and aims. In 1886 an agreement was entered into between the chief Umqikela and the Cape Government, by which the latter acquired practical control over St. John's River and port. This was in 1888 followed up by a secret undertaking which left the Cape Government in full command of the situation, and barred Natal from any power of interference, either in behalf of its own interests or in behalf of peace and order. Yet the former persistently abstained from any exercise of its powers in the prevention of outrage and disorder.

This was the position of affairs when the first Responsible Ministry took office in Natal, in October 1893. Embarrassing though it was to be at once confronted by such a task before it had settled down to its new duties, the administration at once took such steps as were possible in order to protect the Colony. The situation brooked no delay. The combatant forces of the contending tribes were fighting not only on our border, but had actually crossed the small stream which divides Natal from Pondoland. Our settlers and our natives were being panic-stricken, and the most serious results might be expected to follow any further inaction. Colonel Dartnell, the head of the local defence forces, was despatched to the southern border with a small body of the Mounted Police and a Maxim gun, and instructions to use his own discretion in guarding the border. That able officer did his work as capably and well as he has at all times performed duties entrusted to him. His appearance on the frontier, and the display of armed force he at once made, kept the combatants on their own side of the river, though on one or two occasions parties of them crossed under his eyes. A Pondo impi, estimated to number 14,000 men, was over-awed by the handful of police and the solitary Maxim, and confined their operations to Pondo territory. So far as the safety of the Colony was concerned, there was soon an end to apprehension; but public opinion throughout Natal clamoured for more repressive measures, and urged further action upon the Government. The latter was taunted with subserviency to the Cape authorities, and the immediate occupation of Pondoland by an adequate colonial force was, in certain quarters, vehemently demanded. To have complied with that demand would in effect have been to go to war with the Cape Colony and the Imperial Government, but a good many excited people failed to realise this fact as clearly as their Ministers did, and the controversy was continued on paper or on the wires. The Natal Government was determined that the Cape Colony should be compelled to do its duty, by effectively exercising the responsibilities it had voluntarily assumed The following extracts from the Minutes, with which Natal Ministers at the time sought to protect the interests of their colony, serve to illustrate the situation as between the two colonies. It must be remembered that it was only after correspondence had been going on between the two Governments for three months that the Natal Ministers had been informed of the arrangements entered into several years before between the Imperial and the Cape Governments.

"Ministers are glad to learn from these documents that steps are at last to be taken by the High Commissioner and the Cape Government to put a stop to the scandalous condition of things that has for years past prevailed, and that has been repeatedly represented by the Government of Natal as being a disgrace to civilisation and a reproach to British rule in South Africa.

"Ministers observe that the measures which it is proposed to adopt correspond with those that Natal would have been prepared to carry out had effect been given to the policy indicated in Minutes recently addressed by them to his Excellency and the Imperial Government. It will be seen from those Minutes that the original proposal of Ministers was in favour of conjoint action by the two Colonial Governments in the pacification and settlement of Pondoland; failing that, it was proposed that Natal itself should undertake the duty, acting on its own responsibility and at its own cost.

"It was only when the Secretary of State informed his Excellency by telegraph on the 10th February that her Majesty's Government fully recognised the right of the Cape Colony to 'claim to administer the whole of Pondoland, if it should see fit to claim the whole,' that Ministers became formally aware of the true facts of the situation. In then pressing upon the High Commissioner and the Cape Government the necessity of an immediate exercise of these long-dormant responsibilities, they did so without any prejudice to the just claim of Natal for a voice in the final settlement of Pondoland, a country with which this Colony is and has been identified by ties of the closest proximity, interest, and association. They repeat what has been frequently said before by the Government of Natal, that the relative interest of Natal in Pondoland and its affairs is greater than the interest of any other community or Government, and they submit that the Government of this Colony had full right to be consulted before the claim or right of any other Government to exclusive consideration should have been conceded."

"The Imperial Government has informed his Excellency that the claim of the Cape Colony to the whole of Pondoland was admitted years ago. The High Commissioner had informed this Government that he only is responsible for control in Pondoland. Cape Ministers, in their Minute of the 20th February last, have stated that 'in truth, responsibility for the ultimate settlement of Pondoland has been imposed upon successive Cape Governments.' The evils and outrages to which his Excellency the High Commissioner refers in the despatch now under consideration are evils and outrages that have prevailed for years past, that have been repeatedly recognised by the High Commissioner, and that have been again and again advanced by the Government of Natal, as reason for active intervention. Had Natal been free to do so, her Government would have been prepared, some time ago, to take steps to terminate these scandals and to establish order in Pondoland. It is owing to the failure of the Cape Government to undertake the effective exercise of the responsibilities imposed upon it, that Natal has been called upon to bear this extraordinary expenditure and suffer all the other losses and inconveniences that have in consequence arisen.

"In conclusion, Ministers desire to repeat :—

"1. That on grounds of equity, political convenience, past associations, and geographical position, Natal has a right to be consulted and considered in any future partitionment of Pondoland.

"2. That the neglect of the Cape Government to give effect to the claim to Pondoland recognised years ago by her Majesty's Government has entailed upon Natal heavy expenses and losses which might otherwise have been prevented.

"3 That this neglect strengthens Natal's original claim to be considered in the settlement of Pondoland.

"4. That any settlement which may be entered upon without the concurrence and in disregard of Natal must necessarily be unstable in its character, inasmuch as a powerful section of the Pondo nation has expressed a strong desire to be brought under the rule of this Colony; and, further,

"5. That such a settlement could only tend to estrange the two colonies, and to retard the establishment of that concord which is essential to the future welfare of all South Africa."

The end of this correspondence was reached when the Cape Government decided to fulfil its obligations, by restoring order and imposing authority. Under the circumstances it had only one other course before it, namely, to retire from the field and leave Natal to undertake the task—and to hold the country. That Colony was quite prepared for both contingencies, whatever immediate strain might have been imposed upon its resources. Its success in governing the large native tribes within its own borders justified confidence in its capacity to rule the Pondos as well. That people, though numerous and turbulent, are soon cowed by an exhibition of organised force, while their internal dissensions weaken their strength as a fighting unit. Natal, moreover, would have been powerfully assisted in any operations that might have been undertaken by its own native levies and by other tribes. No occasion arose, however, for such a demonstration, as the Cape Government aroused itself to action, and established its authority over the disturbed territories. Its Government was not prepared to let Pondoland go. Mr. Rhodes in the earlier stages of the controversy was Prime Minister, and that territory was too valuable a counter in the game of statecraft to be handed over to the rival Colony. At that time he cared no more for territories in Kafirland than he did for "niggers." His projects of expansion lay in other directions. But Natal was believed to covet Pondoland, and Natal had yet to be brought within the Customs Union. So important a diplomatic factor must not, therefore, be thrown away.

The eager and persistent desire of the Cape Government — through successive administrations — to bring

Natal within the scope of a Customs Union is best
explained by the trend of interior trade. In earlier
years the volume of that trade was relatively insignificant. We have seen how it began, and how it grew,
and how large a share Natal had in its development.
After the opening up of the diamond-fields in the
early seventies, Kimberley suddenly became a centre of
business and activity as well as the fountain of un-
calculated wealth. And so it remained for many years.
But Kimberley was only a little farther from Cape
ports than it was from Durban, and politically it
belonged to the Cape Colony. At first Natal merchants
did their best to compete for the trade of so opulent
a mart, but they soon, except in one or two instances,
retired from the contest. When railway communication
was established between Capetown and Diamondopolis,
any chance of successful competition was at an end.
But in 1887 a far greater mine of wealth was revealed
at Witwatersrand in the Transvaal, only 430 miles from
Durban.

Natal men were largely concerned in the earlier
gold discoveries at that point, as they had been indeed in the first developments of the diamond-fields.
As mining pioneers they have ever been in the van.
They were the most active explorers of the " River
diggings " in the Vaal, long before Colesberg Kopje
disclosed its treasures. They organised and carried out
the gold-hunting expeditions to the Tati and Shashi
gold-fields beyond the Limpopo in 1868. They were

the first to work at the Pilgrim's Rest and Macmac
gold-fields near Lydenburg in the seventies. They toiled
at the still infant gold-fields of Marabastad, near Zout-
pansberg, in the Northern Transvaal They were the
foremost in opening up the gold-fields of Swaziland.
It was from Durban that Carl Mauch and Thomas
Baines set forth, as far back as 1867, to investigate
the gold formations of Matabeleland and Mashonaland,
before Mr. Rhodes, a youth, had left Natal for the Vaal
River; and it was the said Thomas Baines, whose
remains now rest in the cemetery at Durban, who
obtained from Lobengula the cession, under his own
seal, of the gold-fields which now form the centre and
backbone of Rhodesia.

The experiences of these adventurers from Natal,
who during the two decades which ended in 1887
pursued in all these regions the quest of the golden
fleece, would form the subject of an epic quite as
thrilling in its way as any story of classic fame. Like
the gold-seekers of California, twenty years earlier, they
were the modern Argonauts. They went forth from
the Colony to find the wealth they had failed to win
there, lured on by that hunger for swiftly gotten riches
that has been so powerful a factor in the industrial
expansion of mankind. To most of them the goal
proved a mere will-o'-the-wisp. Many lost whatever
they had sunk in the venture. Some returned ruined
but wiser men. Most were disappointed. A few were
lucky; one or two made fortunes, though more by

speculation than actual "finds." Very little alluvial
gold was found anywhere. Quartz reefs too often
"petered out," or proved unpayable. Much money
was wasted in fruitless operations. In 1867 Mauch
returned from Matabeleland and reported that when
he saw there the quartz reefs, known by him to be
gold-bearing, stretching out in all directions and
glittering in the sun, he was dazzled by the vision of
incalculable wealth thus revealed to his eyes. It was a
perfectly truthful description of his own emotions, and
results elsewhere at Johannesburg have vastly tran-
scended his glowing words; but it was not borne out
by immediate developments, and the revulsion which
ensued for a short time paralysed confidence in the
gold resources of the continent, but the quest was soon
resumed and continued. Though the first colonial gold-
seekers gained little themselves by their devious and
dogged explorations, they laid the foundations of the
industry which has latterly reached dimensions so
colossal, and has so enormously influenced the history
of South Africa and the Empire.

What diamonds and Kimberley did for trade in the
seventies, gold and Johannesburg did on a much larger
scale in the later eighties. Witwatersrand became the
commercial centre of South Africa; the chief seat of its
financial and industrial activity. The first pioneers
there, as elsewhere, were mostly Natal men, as the
names of some of the oldest and most lucrative mines
still indicate. Both in trade and in gold development

the little Colony could claim to have been in the van of
enterprise, and it was bound to be so, both by reason of
old associations, and by virtue of close proximity. The
Rand was only 130 miles distant from the Natal border,
but it was separated by the whole area of the Free
State from the Cape Colony. From the very first,
therefore, Natal contended for its proper and legitimate
share of the trade which its people had heretofore
commanded. All the policy and efforts of its Government, its legislature, and its merchants, were devoted
to the retention of that share. To that end the Colony
loaded itself with debt for the extension of its railways
and the improvement of its harbour. As long as the
iron road from the seaports of both colonies kept outside republican borders, Natalians had nothing to fear.
As long as trade to Johannesburg was dependent only
on the ox-waggon for any section of road traffic from the
several ports, Natal could compete confidently with her
neighbours. As long as neither colony enjoyed any
advantage of customs tariff over the other, both were
on equal terms in the race. The Cape Colony, however,
wanted something, and a good deal more than an equal
share. It wanted a lion's share, and some of its leading
politicians did not hesitate to say so. Had their claims
and assumption been more equitable and moderate,
friction between the two colonies would have been
much less severe. It is only fair, and it is right, to
record that Natal never sought or contended for more
than her proper share of the interior trade, a share

which experience, often tested, has computed at a third of the whole. To have been content with less would have been a reckless sacrifice of whatever advantages geographical position and past activity had secured to the Colony.

Although the questions of railway extension and customs charges were closely correlated and inter-dependent, the fiscal condition of the two colonies was by no means identical. The revenual requirements of the Cape Colony and its political exigencies made a much higher tariff necessary in its case than was called for in Natal. The latter colony had always, so far as circumstances permitted, supported a policy of low duties and free trade. Though it did not recognise the claim of the inland states to any definite share of customs revenue, it kept tariff rates as low as revenual necessities would possibly allow. It bore the whole cost of road and railway construction through a very difficult country, and of harbour improvement in the case of a bar-bound port. The disadvantage which this policy entailed upon the Cape was keenly recognised by the senior colony, and after several abortive attempts in the same direction, the Cape Government succeeded in convening a conference of representatives in January 1888, for the purpose of considering the practicability of establishing a South African Customs Union. At this conference, the Cape Colony, Natal, and the Free State were each represented by three delegates. The Transvaal declined the invitation, and thereby frustrated any chance of complete success which might have attended the movement. President Kruger and his associates had another game to play. Their aims took a different direction. The completion of their own line of railway to Delagoa Bay, and the acquisition, were it possible, of controlling or preferential rights there, were the cherished objects of their ambition. They had already secured from Portugal treaty rights which guaranteed to the Republic the entry of all goods through Lourenço Marques on a transit charge of three per cent. That rate had, therefore, become a governing factor in the tariff charges of both the colonies, and the Transvaal had no intention to restrict its advantages, or to fetter its hands, by any new engagements with its Anglo-Colonial neighbours. Yet without its participation any Customs Union claiming to be South African in its scope must surely fail. It was like closing all the front entrances to a house, while the back door, free from barrier, remained open. Cape statesmen did not see this as clearly as their Natal neighbours did, but the knowledge came in time. The Cape Conference met, however, as a tripartite gathering, and for three weeks did its best, under Sir Gordon Sprigg's presidency, to hammer out a tariff that should be acceptable to three parties, each of which had a separate axe to grind.

The Cape Colony, as we have seen, was handicapped by geographical disadvantages and the necessity of a relatively high tariff. Natal was determined not to

Q

forego the advantages it possessed of a shorter trade
route and much lower customs duties. The Free State
was bent upon getting the best terms it could out of
both the maritime colonies, and was especially insistent
on its claim, as a right, to its full share of customs dues
paid upon sea-borne goods passing into its own territory.
These three positions were clearly not easily reconcil-
able, but it was a happy augury for future developments
that the representatives of interests so divergent were
able to enter upon the discussion of them with a
strenuous and honest desire to work out a solution of
the problem on the basis of a common end—that end
being unity

The Conference sat with closed doors, and the public
knew nothing definitely of its proceedings until the
official minutes were published after its termination.
It then appeared that the principle of a uniform tariff
had been agreed upon as essential to the successful
working of any union   Any other system would have
meant the establishment of border custom-houses, which
would have stultified the object of the Conference. The
next point to be decided was the proportion of revenue
to be paid to the inland, consuming state, or to put it
the other way, to be kept by the maritime states, as the
equivalent of the cost of collection and of port charges.
This was finally fixed at three-fourths in the one case
and at one-fourth in the other. It will thus be seen
that the Free State stood to gain enormously under any
circumstances, even although its representatives affected

to exercise a lofty magnanimity in waiving any claim
for the repayment of amounts paid in the past. They
chose to ignore the vast expenditure incurred by both
colonies on account of harbour improvement and railway extension. These two questions having been dealt
with, it only remained to settle the details of the tariff.
This, as may be imagined, was no easy business. It
was, all through, a struggle for high rates on the part
of the Cape and for low rates on the part of Natal.

As the Free State only wanted as much revenue as it
could get, and was not averse to have its consumers
taxed through the custom-house, its influence naturally
went with the older colony. The household needs of
Boer farmers are so small that the incidence of customs
taxation falls as lightly as can be on them. The
interests of South African wheat-growers were to be
protected by a substantial duty upon imported grain
and flour, while a sop was thrown to Natal in the form
of a rebate on imported sugar. Although the principle
of free trade in South African products was established,
the Cape could not bring itself to the sacrifice of revenue which would have been entailed by the complete
inclusion of Natal-grown sugar within that category.
In that case the duty on local produce was only reduced,
not abolished. This incident is worthy of note as show-
ing how carefully the whole scheme had been arranged
and was manipulated for the more particular advantage
of the Cape Colony and the Free State, and to the
consequent detriment of Natal. The delegates of the

latter Colony, however, in their anxiety to promote
the cause of union, after doing their utmost to reduce
the duties, item by item, made a last fight over the *ad
valorem* rate on goods not enumerated, being the bulk
of the whole. This was set down in the draft bill at
sixteen per cent. Successive efforts were made by
Natal to fix it at nine, ten, and eleven per cent, the
existing Natal rate being seven per cent. The Cape
would not recede a fraction below twelve per cent., and
that rate was ultimately adopted. Reluctant as they
were to accede to a tariff so hostile to Natal interests,
and so certain to be opposed in, if not rejected by that
Colony, its representatives up to the last refrained from
accepting the onus of wreckage. They warned their
associates that the proposals were almost certain to be
refused, but, as a demonstration of their anxiety to
bring unity about, they agreed to sign the Convention,
as being the best result that could be obtained, after a
keen and continuous struggle between the advocates of
a low and of a high tariff. They distinctly declined,
however, to pledge themselves to recommend their
adoption or otherwise.

It is only necessary to add that the forebodings of
the delegates were instantly and amply justified by
results. Even before they had time to return to the
Colony the murmur of protest became audible. Though
every effort had been made to keep the work of the
Conference secret, until the time prearranged for its
disclosure, information leaked out, and no sooner were

the proceedings published than an outcry arose from all
quarters—from the press, from the local Chambers of
Commerce, from representative bodies everywhere—in-
dignantly denouncing the Convention as utterly inimical
to Natal interests, as a reversal of its policy in the past,
as destructive of its trade with the interior, and as
fastening upon the consumers of the Colony oppressive
fiscal burdens from which they had hitherto been free.
So unmistakable and overpowering was the outburst of
popular feeling that the Convention dropt, stillborn, so
far as Natal was concerned.   When the local legislature
met, a few weeks later, it was not so much as discussed.
Silent contumely was the only reception it had from
that body.   Public meetings had already, by unanimous votes, pronounced unqualified condemnation of
the measure   In my whole political career I never felt
so completely isolated as I did in Durban when called
upon as a local representative, and one of the Conference
delegates, to address a crowded meeting of the electors
called to discuss the Convention.   Every man in the
hall, whether past ally and supporter or old opponent,
I knew to be vehemently opposed to the obnoxious instrument in whose preparation I had been called upon
to take part.   It was an anxious and difficult, and to
me a critical moment, but the consciousness of having
striven only, with my colleagues, to promote the cause
of South African unity, to uphold Imperial interests,
and at the same time to safeguard colonial interests as
far as circumstances would allow, bore me up on the

occasion. Personally I felt no cause for self-reproach or regret. I had signed the Convention simply as being an embodiment of the best terms that could be obtained under the circumstances. It was for the Colony to accept or to reject it. In view of the state of public opinion, there could be no question as to the result. The Convention was impossible, and I said so; and the electors seemed satisfied. All the same, I thought then, and I still think, that the Colony made a mistake in so summarily turning its back upon the proposals. Had it condemned the tariff as it stood, but expressed a readiness to reconsider the question on a revised basis, it is quite possible that the other two parties would have paused before giving effect to its provisions, and have agreed to another conference, with a fuller understanding of the popular feeling and prevailing policy in Natal.

But it is idle to discount unfulfilled possibilities. Events took their course. The Convention came into operation. The war of tariffs began. Both the Cape and the Free State Governments established custom-houses on the Natal border, to collect the duties on goods sent from, or through, what became practically a foreign country. Natal at once responded by making such rebates of duty on its side as might be necessary in order to retain trade. It could not, however, afford to do this in heroic fashion. It could not dispense with customs duties altogether. A community of 60,000 Europeans was unequal to bear on its own shoulders, in direct imposts, the whole burden of maintaining the local administration and of providing for costly railway extensions and harbour works. It was impracticable, therefore, to make Durban a free port The tariff had to be regulated from time to time so as to tax local consumers and to relieve foreign customers Each Colony watched the fiscal action of the other with feline vigilance, in eager desire to retain and to extend its business with the Republics. So far as the Free State was concerned, however, Natal had to witness the diversion of nearly the whole of its existing trade. Its merchants were unable to compete with their Cape rivals. Some of them sought to meet the situation by establishing branches at Port Elizabeth, but the revenue and carrying trade of the Colony suffered all the same.

Meanwhile the trade of Johannesburg grew in volume and value, and became month by month the aim and centre of all colonial enterprise. As long as there was any zone of intervening country between the Rand and the nearest railway terminus, Natal was able to hold its own in the race for trade with its competitors in the Cape Colony and Delagoa Bay. Even when the Cape and Free State railway system had reached the Vaal River, a distance of thirty-seven miles from Johannesburg, Natal could still operate successfully from its terminus at Charlestown, 130 miles distant. The Cape Government succeeded, however, at last in arranging with the Government at Pretoria for the

completion of its line, though not before President
Kruger's own line from Delagoa Bay had been opened
for traffic.   By what means this stroke of policy on the
part of the sister Colony was effected has never been
quite clearly explained, but that it was accomplished
to Natal's great detriment, and possible ruin, experience
soon demonstrated.   Competition under such circumstances became hopeless.   A ton of goods landed at
Capetown, or Algoa Bay, and conveyed straight by
railway to Johannesburg itself, had an enormous and
obvious advantage over a ton of goods landed at
Durban, carried by rail as far as the Transvaal border,
and then unloaded into an ox-waggon, and carried forward by that slow and costly method of transport
to its final destination.   Still greater was the disparity
of advantage between the short railway route from
Delagoa Bay and the broken route from Durban.   It
thus seemed, in 1893, that at last the sister Colony had
compassed the ruin of Natal trade, and that Natal,
being at the mercy of its neighbours, would be forced,
in sheer desperation, to join in the Customs Union
against which it had fought so hard.   Its import trade
dropped in three years from £4,417,085 to £2,236,738.
In estimating the significance of these figures, it must
be remembered that Natal had spent nearly seven millions on railway extension, and had saddled itself with
a yearly interest charge of more than a quarter of a
million.   This great burden had been incurred solely
in order to retain a share of the Transvaal trade.

Without that trade the railway would not earn enough to cover its working expenses. That outcome would spell ruin to the Colony, and crushing taxation of its people.

Dark though this prospect might seem to be, and dire though the case of the Colony undoubtedly was as regards actual and imminent results, one factor had still to be reckoned with—the spirit and determination of the people. Though baffled for the moment, they were not beaten. They were bent as stubbornly as ever upon getting back their hard-won heritage. The trade which had been decoyed from them by intrigue and stratagem was to be recovered by other methods. The Government of the Transvaal was once and again approached. Twice in 1892 delegates from the Natal Government visited Pretoria for the purpose, if possible, of arranging for the extension of the Natal line. Though Cape diplomacy had succeeded in getting priority of construction for the Cape and Free State line, Natal claims were not regarded with unkindly eyes by Transvaal politicians, and certainly not by commercial classes in Johannesburg. Natal had at all times cultivated friendly relations with its northern neighbours, and shown continuous readiness to co-operate in all matters of mutual concern. The splendid reception accorded to President Kruger in 1890, on the occasion of the opening of the railway to Charlestown, had left a pleasant flavour in the mouth. But there was one stumbling-block—one barrier to united action. Natal

was still under Crown rule. Its emancipation from
Downing Street leading-strings had not been complete
The republican rulers shrank from allying themselves
too closely with a community whose responsible administrators were appointed by England. Though a large
number of Natal electors to the last failed to see it, the
fact that its form of government was the chief bar to
railway extension weighed more and more with the
colonists and their representatives, and contributed
largely to the acceptance of Responsible Government
in 1893.

The champions of that cause had insisted that the
change was necessary to the attainment of the great
and common colonial desire Events soon justified
their contention The first business devolving upon
the new administration was to save the Colony from
the threatened ruin.   Ministers at once sent one of
their number to Pretoria, supported by the official
head of the railway department, and they never rested
until the object was accomplished.   It took five months
of patient negotiation to secure success, but it was
achieved.   A Convention was signed by all parties in
March 1894, and the earliest duty of the new Parliament, when it met in ordinary session in April, was to
ratify the agreements They were no hastily prepared
or unworthily conceived covenants.   They bore on their
face no evidence of selfish purpose or grasping aim.
They were based on the principles of fair play and fair
dealing.   The idea which permeated them was the re-

cognition of what may be called a policy of "thirds"—a just division of traffic between the three great routes. Delagoa Bay, Natal, and the Cape Colony were each to get a third of the traffic, and though it was manifest that Natal's share would be the heavier and least profitable portion of the carrying trade, the Colony was content. So long as its own share of the volume was secured, it had no desire to deprive its rivals of any incidental advantage which might fall to their lot

On October 15, 1895, the line from Charlestown to Johannesburg and the central South African railway system was completed, amidst mutual rejoicing—as I shall describe hereafter—on the part of both Governments and communities. It at once justified its construction by bringing back the diverted trade, by restoring the balance of revenue, and by putting Natal on an equality with its neighbours. Equality of position was all that it had fought for, and equality being won, brought with it revived prosperity and financial relief.

The railway problem being thus solved, it was perhaps natural that the customs question should be taken up again How far the growing prosperity of Natal may have influenced the minds of Cape politicians I do not pretend to say, but it probably availed to inculcate a desire for closer union and friendlier relations with a community so well able to defend and advance its own interests. In October 1897 the first Natal Parliament expired by effluxion of time, and the result of the

elections was to place in power what is known as the
"country party"—the party, that is, which favours
the direct protection of local industry, as distinguished
from a strictly free-trade policy. It followed, perhaps,
as a natural sequence that another Customs Conference
was held in Capetown early in 1898. Again the two
colonies and the Orange Free State were represented,
and again the Transvaal Republic was conspicuous by
its absence. On this occasion the Natal representatives
fell at once into line with their colleagues, and the
result was the accession of Natal to a Customs Union
based upon a revised tariff. The altered circumstances
of the case enabled the Natal delegates—including the
Prime Minister—to exercise much greater influence
than their predecessors had been able to use, ten years
before, upon the modification of rates and details
Substantial reductions were effected in certain items—
the *ad valorem* rate being reduced from 12 to 7½
per cent, but duties were still retained upon flour meat,
and some other food-stuffs, though free trade in South
African produce was made general on all products and
manufactures. Some of the duties on drinkables and
luxuries were increased, and the free list was materially
expanded The whole tariff, however, may be said to
have been framed on protectionist principles, and as
such it has been regarded with great disfavour by all
free traders in Natal, as well as by the consumers of the
towns Their representatives in Parliament numbered
only 12 against 22, when the final vote for ratification

was recorded, and the Convention came into force with little organised opposition How far its existence will be affected by recent events is a matter of speculation, but as confederation in some form is a political necessity of the immediate future, a common customs tariff appears certain to follow But it will embrace the whole of South Africa, and will thus be a union tariff in the proper sense

Rapid though this survey may be, it suffices to show how little real community of action there has been between the two British colonies. Rivalry rather than brotherhood has marked their relations. Children of the same mother, they have not been by any means members of a happy family They have both been suitors for the favours of their republican cousins in the interior. Though each has had the same end in view, it has not been a common interest. The Cape, as the older and larger colony, would fain have made its younger and smaller neighbour subordinate to its policy and subservient to its interests Natal, with its essentially British inspirations and strong individuality of existence, has refused to be coerced or "squared." For a long time many leading Cape politicians saw a cure for existing evils in incorporation. They favoured the idea of complete absorption Natal in their eyes was, as regards size, no larger than one of their great western divisions. The easiest way to overcome its rivalry or opposition would be to take it over. Thus had British Kafraria been disposed of—why not Natal ?

Sir Hercules Robinson in the earlier years of his governorship strongly supported this view. He naturally desired, after the retrocession of the Transvaal, to consolidate British interests in South Africa, and he thought that the accession of Natal would materially strength English influence and voting power in the Cape Parliament. One prominent member of the late Cape Ministry also took that view. Other statesmen—with truer precision—would fain have sought the same results by other methods. Sir George Grey, Sir Bartle Frere, Mr. Paterson, and later on Sir Gordon Sprigg, would have pursued unity by means of confederation. That also was Natal's policy. At no time would her representatives have agreed to incorporation. In their opinion that would mean effacement, if not extinction—submission to hostile tariffs, and subordination to an unsympathetic and jealous majority. Neither English nor Dutch settlers desired that the country should lapse into the position of so many Cape divisions or magistracies. So strong and instinctive was this feeling that no Governor or individual at any time had the temerity to submit the proposition in a concrete form. It would have been hopeless to do so. The outcry which greeted and scouted the Customs Convention of 1888 was an expression of the passionate regard which Natalians cherish for their independence as a colony, and their individuality as a people. That regard has been stigmatised as selfish and narrow. Natal politicians have

been freely denounced by their colonial neighbours as
parochial in their aspirations, as "wayward" in their
demeanour, as wanting in breadth of view and grasp of
duty. They have been taunted with allegiance to the
parish pump instead of to the loftier ideal of a united
South Africa. These aspersions have not troubled them
much, as they have known best what their hopes and
purposes are They can confidently appeal to records
in vindication of their honest and earnest desire for
union More than that, they can show by their dealings
with the Republics how ready they have been to take
the initiative in promoting a large and comprehensive
policy of confederation, and it now becomes necessary
to consider the relations of Natal with its republican
neighbours in the interior.

CHAPTER IX

THE SETTLERS AS NEIGHBOURS (*continued*)

PRECEDING chapters will, I trust, have made it clear how closely the interests of Natal have been intertwined with those of the inland States. From the time of the Great Trek onward the Boers and the British settlers—the Africander burgher and the Anglo-Saxon settler—have been more or less in intercourse. They have from the very first done business together, and up to the day of Majuba they may be said to have shared common political rights in both the Colony and the Republics. In earlier days, however, the British resident in either State cared little for the acquisition of burgher rights, and "the franchise" was a cry seldom, if ever, heard. The political condition of both territories, notwithstanding, became an object of interest to Natal politicians at an early date. In both countries the withdrawal of British sovereignty had been followed by a gradual but steady outgrowth of confusion and disorder. In the Free State the Boers were continually at war with the Basutos. That people possessed the finest wheatlands in South Africa, and a country that has been well described as the South African Switzerland. After more than ten years of desultory, intermittent warfare, the Boers, taught by experience and emboldened by partial successes, stormed some of the mountain strongholds which Sir George Cathcart had failed to capture in 1854, and the Basutos retired into yet remoter fastnesses, leaving the more open arable country in the hands of their enemies.

This "conquered territory" was annexed to the Free State and sold to the farmers, while the French missionaries, who had long laboured amongst the natives, were ejected from their stations and despoiled of their property. This wanton and wholly unjustifiable proceeding was vainly protested against at the time. The peace thus won was only transitory. The Boer forces were withdrawn from the scene of their conquests, and the Basutos again reoccupied their country and recultivated their fields. Then followed more robberies, more reprisals, and war again, with further attacks upon and capturing of mountain strongholds. The Boers seemed not unlikely to extinguish their stubborn foes, when Moshesh—of all South African chieftains the most astute and farsighted — represented his case to the High Commissioner. Negotiations ensued, which finally ended in the cessation of hostilities and the acceptance of Moshesh and his people as British subjects. This proceeding, as might be imagined, was bitterly resented by the ruling party in the Free State. They refused to negotiate with Sir Philip Wodehouse, threatened to seek the interference of the French or the Russian

Emperor, and finally despatched two Commissioners to
England to protest against the action of the British
representative just when they seemed on the point of
reducing the Basutos to absolute and unconditional
submission. The deputation met with no encouragement from Downing Street, but was told that her
Majesty's Government approved of all that Sir Philip
Wodehouse had done, and had empowered him to take
such further steps as he, with his local knowledge,
might deem necessary.

It was at this stage that the Natal Legislature was
moved to intervene in behalf of peace and order.
Although the Home Government had been wise enough
to sustain its representative in his acceptance of Imperial responsibility, no provision was made whereby
that policy might be effectually upheld. I may quote
here the following passage from an article I contributed
at the time to a leading English Review. " It will be
at once apparent that the acceptance of the Basutos as
British subjects entails the likelihood of complications
with the Free State. Unless Moshesh succeeds in
curbing the thieving propensities of his people better
than he has done so far, there will be more robberies
and more reprisals. What will be the position of the
British Government then ? Is it prepared to maintain
in Basutoland a police force large enough to keep the
Basutos in order, or does it intend to see the Boers
again marching into the territory of its new-made
subjects, laying it waste and appropriating it to their

own purposes? Unless some definite and extended policy be adopted, one or other of these alternatives seems inevitable. In the Cape Colony and Natal public opinion is very unanimous regarding the policy to be pursued. Neither of these colonies cares to have Basutoland if one or other of them is to be responsible for the good conduct of the natives."

Natal, as we have seen, had already suffered directly at the hands of these people, when in 1865 a large body of Basuto marauders crossed the border in pursuit of cattle said to have been driven there by citizens of the Free State. Though this raid cost the Colony £9000, no compensation was ever made for that outlay. The colonists, moreover, had suffered in other ways. During the later years of the Basuto war all the courts of the Free State had been closed, and no debts were recoverable. Nearly half a million sterling was thus due by Free State consumers to merchants in the Cape Colony and Natal. To meet this emergency paper "bluebacks" had been indiscriminately issued, and as these notes were made legal tender, a ruinous depreciation had been the result. As in the Transvaal, so in the Free State there was no effective security for social order or legal redress, while the relations of the white and the black races were becoming more and more embittered by the spectacle and the experience of constant strife.

The absence of good and effective government in the two republics, resulting as it did in paralysis, disorder, and warfare, became at last so great a scandal and so

injurious a condition, that the Legislative Council in
1868 was moved to action   A direct proposal in favour
of the annexation of the Free State led to the final
adoption of the following modified resolutions.   They
are worthy of note as embodying the views of all
British colonists, as well as of the more intelligent and
moderate-minded Natal Boers at that time, and as
being the first formal utterance in favour of the policy
of Confederation on the part of any South African
Legislature

"That the interests of the two South African British
colonies, viz. the Cape Colony and Natal, are in many
respects so closely united with the republics situated on their
respective borders, that a union of these under British rule
could scarcely fail to conduce to the material welfare of the
whole, both as a means of promoting an interchange of
friendly relations amongst them, as well as of providing, by
judicious combination, for their adequate security and confidence in time of danger, and establishing and regulating
commercial intercourse on a permanent and satisfactory basis
to all parties

"That the comparative dependence of these republics on
the Cape Colony and Natal, together with the similarity of
the religion, laws, and customs of the white inhabitants to
those of the same classes inhabiting the two latter colonies,
favour the belief that sooner or later they will be desirous of
coming under the dominion of the British Government

"That the Council is therefore of opinion that, with a
view to furthering the objects set forth, it would be highly
desirable for her Majesty's Government favourably to consider any proposal which the authorities of these republics,
being empowered thereto by the inhabitants, may put forward,

affecting their annexation to either the Cape Colony or Natal, or embracing suggestions with respect to any other form of allied or separate administration deemed suitable by the majority of the white inhabitants of such States."

These were amongst the resolutions of whose existence, some months later, her Majesty's Secretary of State expressed to me his entire ignorance, as I have stated elsewhere.[1] No attention appears to have been paid to them, nor did anything come of them, as a few weeks afterwards a general election led to a change of Ministry, and Mr. Gladstone came into power In any case it is doubtful whether they would have availed, at that time, to influence the course of Imperial policy. They were weighted, it is true, with South African knowledge and experience, but they carried with them only the insignificant authority of an obscure colony. I wrote thus of them at the time in the pages of the *Westminster Review*:—

"It must not be supposed that the policy foreshadowed in the foregoing resolutions would entail a fraction of Imperial expenditure upon the mother country. These States would be just as able to pay the cost of their own government as they are now, far better able, in fact. Give peace and security, law and order to them, and they would soon yield a revenue ample for all requirements. With a governor over each of them, specially selected for the post, having under him officers and advisers chosen with equal discrimination, a police system could be organised and maintained at the cost of the inhabitants sufficient for all purposes. The people

[1] Chap. VI.

ask for neither Imperial troops nor Imperial money; they only ask for that 'moral' power in the conduct of affairs which British rule confers.

"Nor must it be supposed that any practical accession of responsibility would be thus assumed by the Home Government. In point of fact, England is already responsible for the disorders of those regions, and directly suffers for them. If no change be made these disorders will get worse and worse, until the time arrives when interference will become not a matter of choice, but of necessity, and cost not the mere exercise of a little statesmanship, but possibly a large Imperial outlay. 'A stitch in time saves nine.' It will assuredly do so in this case. For unless England is prepared to cast off her other colonies at the Cape, as she cast off the Free State, she cannot divest herself of Imperial obligations on their account."

Though a brighter dispensation was at hand, the doctrines of Manchester were still in the air, and South Africa was left to drift on aimlessly towards un-shaped destinies. The little spurt of Imperial activity for which Sir Philip Wodehouse had been responsible in Basutoland, put an end for the time being to the ravages of war there, and enabled that wisest of all the republican rulers, President Brand, to devote his energies to internal administration. That the opinions of Sir Philip as High Commissioner entirely accorded with colonial sentiment, his words when proroguing the Cape Parliament in September 1868 abundantly demonstrate. "Speaking entirely on my own responsibility, giving expression only to my own opinions, I may say that I regard the measures which severed from their

allegiance the European communities in those regions to
have been founded in error, and that it will be a blessing for all if, with their general and hearty concurrence,
they can be restored in a general sense to their former
position." In both cases, it should be remarked, the
suggestion of reannexation is made contingent upon
the assent of the inhabitants themselves No policy of
violence or aggression was indicated. That the attitude
of Natal and its legislators was correctly appreciated in
the Republic was shown a few years later. After his
return to the Colony in 1873, Governor Pine, at the instance of the Legislative Council, addressed to President
Brand a letter in which he gave expression to warm
assurances of amity and goodwill in connection with,
and in acknowledgment of the friendly co-operation of
the Free State authorities in facilitating the capture of
Langalibalele President Brand and his Volksraad responded to this friendly advance in the same spirit.
"Having heard the correspondence referred to, the
Rand rejoices that the relations between the Colony of
Natal and the Orange Free State are on such a satisfactory footing, and hereby gives expression to the hope
that the ties of friendship between the two countries
may be drawn more closely, and that both may continue
to increase in prosperity and happiness."

What might have happened as a consequence of
these cordial interchanges, had history pursued its
normal course, can only now be inferred. How far
the acuter forces of republican feeling would have

succeeded in thwarting the conciliatory influences that were at work amongst moderate men in the direction of closer union under the British flag, had South Africa been left severely alone to work out its own destiny in its own way, must remain a matter of conjecture. A new political cycle was at hand. An era of Imperialism was about to dawn. The events which supervened on the crushing of Langalibalele's rebellion swiftly followed each other. Bishop Colenso's crusade against the colonists and their Government was followed by Mr. Froude's ill-starred visit, and his despairing commentaries on British colonisation and British rule. Then came Governor Pine's recall, Sir Garnet Wolseley's five months' mission, and the great historian's reappearance in South Africa and his triumphal progress through the Boer districts as the apostle of Dutch Africanderism.

This was speedily succeeded by Lord Carnarvon's invitation to a London Conference, at which the Confederation of South Africa was to be discussed. Had that proposal been submitted by more tactful methods it might have borne the desired fruit, but it was foredoomed to failure by the conditions of its birth. The Cape Parliament, following the lead of its first Prime Minister, Mr. Molteno, who was quite content with his sphere of influence in the Cape Colony, refused to entertain any scheme of confederation, and practically declined to take part in the conference. President Brand, less uncompromising, accepted the invitation, but was forbidden by his Volksraad to discuss or to consider the question of confederation The only two really free agents, therefore, would have neither part nor lot in any discussion of the great question of union Natal, on the contrary, was ready unreservedly to take part, and sent its three delegates to London Though Mr Molteno accompanied them in the same ship, he was resolute in his refusal to put in any appearance at the Conference table.

When, therefore, the meeting was held, under Lord Carnarvon's presidency, there were present Sir Garnet Wolseley, Mr. Froude, the three Natal delegates, and President Brand, who, however, invariably retired whenever discussion drifted towards the forbidden topic. I may be allowed to say, however, that nothing in its way could be better than the good temper and dignity which marked the President's demeanour and attitude throughout the proceedings. It was evident that under such circumstances the Conference must prove abortive in so far as the definite adoption of any concrete scheme of union might be concerned, whatever the results might be as regards the interchange of opinions and experience. After a few meetings the Conference lapsed, and left no public or Parliamentary records to tell of its work or existence It was followed, nevertheless, by three notable and pregnant incidents Sir Theophilus Shepstone returned at once to South Africa, bearing the comprehensive Commission under which a few months later

he annexed the Transvaal Republic to the Crown
Six months later Sir Bartle Frere was despatched as
Governor of the Cape Colony and High Commissioner, with larger powers than any of his predecessors had possessed, and with a general instruction to
bring about confederation, and during the ensuing
session of the Imperial Parliament the South African
Confederation Act was passed. Of these three most
important measures, the last alone was fruitless. The
Act remains to this day a dead letter Of the effects
which flowed from the two appointments we have not
yet seen the end.

During the five turbulent years which followed the
London Conference neighbourly negotiations were impossible. History surged along, carrying with it the
wreckage of policy and purpose. Sir Bartle Frere
from the moment of his advent kept steadfastly in
view his ideal of confederation, but he found in
Capetown an uncongenial soil and an unsympathetic Ministry. Events in the Transvaal reacted in
the Cape Colony, and his dismissal of that Ministry,
necessitated by its usurpation of Imperial prerogatives, created a cleavage which was fatal to schemes
of unity. He never ceased, however, to propound
the policy he had been commissioned to promote. Wherever he went, he consulted the leaders
of opinion in regard to its development On arriving
in Natal in September 1878, the High Commissioner
at once invited discussion of the measure he had so

closely at heart, and the lines he sketched out for the framework of a union were guided by the strictest regard for the circumstances of each community.

Even when the Zulu war-cloud had burst in storm and disaster, the unflinching proconsul remained true to his mission Having swept away the standing menace to peace and native loyalty in Zululand, he sought by personal intervention to conciliate and harmonise the hostile elements in the Transvaal, and to harness the intractable Boer to the ark of Anglo-African unity. How lamentably he was sacrificed as a scapegoat by rabid partisanship and political folly need not be repeated here. Of all the chapters of Imperial statesmanship in the nineteenth century, that is the darkest and least creditable. It was my privilege and pleasure from first to last, in whatever humble way might be open to me, to uphold Sir Bartle Frere's policy and work in South Africa, and no prouder duty ever fell to my lot than that of bearing to Capetown in September 1880 the farewell address of sympathy and appreciation, signed by over 6000 of the men and women of Natal, on the eve of his departure for England. That address and his reply were published on the occasion in the *Times*, but they have been long forgotten, and may well be reproduced at this time.[1] Sir Bartle Frere's valediction may be said to have embodied the policy which he had striven to carry out during the troublous period

[1] See Appendix

of his administration. That his pathetic words in conclusion will prove to have been prophetic I do not and cannot doubt: "I hope that hereafter, when Natal is a branch of a great South African dominion, some one diving into the records of the past may light on the name of one who did not in his day escape bitter censure for doing what you and he believed to be his simple duty, but who, the historian may think, did some good service for the permanent peace and security of his fellow-subjects in this part of the great South African continent."

Twenty years have passed since these last words fell in accents of deepest feeling from the lips of the grave and dignified man, as he stood in the throne-room of Government House to receive from all parts of South Africa and all classes of its people touching testimonials of affection and regret. There were many tearful eyes amongst the throng of representative colonists who pressed around, but none of us then present dared imagine how completely the policy and the prescience of that great servant of his Queen and Empire would be vindicated, by events as tremendous as they are terrible, ere the century had quite run out.

The friendly attitude of Natal towards its republican neighbours was clearly indicated by a resolution of the Legislative Council unanimously passed on the eve of the struggle which terminated at Amajuba. It ran as follows: " In view of threatened hostilities between the Imperial Government and certain of its Transvaal sub-

jects, and in anticipation of Natal again becoming the
base of military operations, this House feels called upon
to place on record its opinion that the Colony ought
not in any way to be held responsible for the cost, or
any portion of the cost, of such offensive or defensive
measures as may be deemed necessary by her Majesty's
officers."

In a spirit very different from that manifested by the
British colony when Sir George Colley advanced to the
relief of the Imperial garrisons in the Transvaal, did
the republicans of that country act nineteen years later,
when they wantonly invaded, overran, and devastated
Natal. Could the colonists have foreseen what has
happened now, or had they realised the true intent and
scope of Boer ambitions, it may safely be said that that
resolution would never have been recorded. It suffices,
however, to show that the attitude of Natal towards
its republican neighbours has not been antagonistic or
distrustful. Even after the retrocession, which was regarded in the Colony as an unspeakable humiliation, its
representatives were ready to extend the olive branch.
In 1883 the Legislative Council expressed its readiness
to confer with the Free State on matters of mutual concern, and in 1884 a conference of delegates from both
Governments was held at Harrismith, when certain proposals were agreed to. It should be understood that
the Cape Government had declined to attend this meeting, without the express sanction of its Legislature,
"then, and since then, out of session." The Transvaal

Government also pleaded inability to be present. No definite conclusions were arrived at on the occasion, though resolutions generally in favour of joint action in regard to railway extension, defence, postal facilities, telegraphic communication, and tolls were adopted. It was also determined to submit to the Governments of the Free State and Natal, academic questions as to the right of a maritime state to charge a friendly neighbouring power with an arbitrary customs tariff, and whether an inland state could claim transit for its produce and goods through a maritime state without contributing a fair share towards the government of that state. These somewhat vague resolutions did not lead to much practical result. It was felt that they foreshadowed a policy of union between the republics and Natal, to the exclusion of the Cape Colony, and doubt was cherished in certain quarters as to the wisdom of such a coalition. It would have virtually amounted to the division of South Africa into two political groups—into South-western and South-eastern Africa. It would also, and this was esteemed its gravest aspect, have split up the British interest into two rival sections, each being dominated by a numerical Dutch majority. One well-known Cape Minister was not slow to point this out, but the scheme, though amicably conceived, was never heartily supported, and it came to nothing. No further definite step was taken in the direction of closer union until the Cape Conference in 1888, to which I have already referred.

Though the door was closed to any chance of early participation in the existing Customs Union by the action of Natal itself, efforts were made to get into closer touch with the republics by other methods, and especially by means of railway extension. Natal's independent initiative in carrying on its railway from Ladismith to Newcastle and then from Newcastle to Charlestown, was regarded by the Free State as inimical to its own interests and aspirations, in so far as such an extension would command the chief trade route to the interior. Before the outgrowth of Johannesburg, it had seemed probable that the ideal railway system of South Africa would be represented by a great trunk line passing from the Cape Colony through the Free State to Pretoria, and joined somewhere near Bloemfontein by a main line from Natal. This policy was upset by the suddenly announced intention of the Natal Government, while the Cape Conference was still in session, to extend its line from Ladismith to Newcastle, thereby opening up the coalfields of Dundee, and securing a direct route to the Transvaal. Whatever may have been the genesis of that proceeding, it had the twofold effect of quickening the construction of the Cape line to Bloemfontein, and of delaying any extension of the Natal line into the Free State.

It was not until 1889 that a step forward was made in the latter direction. In that year a Conference was held between representatives of the two countries, and an agreement was arrived at under

which Natal undertook to extend its line from Ladismith to Harrismith, and to work the Free State
section of it in connection with its own. As usual in
most negotiations between the colonies and the republics, the balance of advantage was largely on the
side of the latter; but Natal was so anxious to make a
beginning of railway communication with its neighbour
that it was content to bear some sacrifice in order to
attain that end. No guarantee was afforded of any
early continuation of the line so as to connect it with
the great central system at Bloemfontein or elsewhere,
and to this day it still stops short at Harrismith. Com-
plexities of republican politics, and differences as to the
choice of route, have prevented its completion, and in
so far have frustrated the hopes and aims of Natal
politicians.

The turning of the first sod, however, on the 7th
November 1889, was made the occasion of much
festive demonstration. The Governor of Natal, Sir
Charles Mitchell, performed the function. Messrs.
Fraser and Fischer represented the Republic, and there
was much effusion of fraternal sentiment. I was asked
in behalf of the local Legislature to invite the Governor
to turn the sod, and in doing so expressed a hope that
the line would bind together by a link of steel, in per-
petual amity, the two communities. The Governor said
that the occasion would, he believed, prove the prelude
of the day, so ardently desired by all true lovers of their
country, when South Africa would be one; when all the

states would be one politically, as they were in race, country, and religion. In that love of freedom which distinguished both they would join hands and say that they were brothers in all that was necessary to advance the country and make it take its place amongst the nations of the world. Mr. Fraser, in behalf of the Free State, reciprocated all these sentiments, and said that they all hoped to see South Africa take its place amongst the nations of the earth, and to that end he hoped, in future, all their efforts would tend. Differences were natural and inevitable, but he sincerely cherished the hope that all these differences would disappear, and they would all strive to help each other in bringing about the much-desired union of South Africa.

Similar ebullitions of friendly enthusiasm attended the extension of the northern line to the Transvaal. On April 7, 1891, a demonstration of unparalleled proportions signalised the opening of the line to Charlestown. Natal had then pushed on its line to the extreme border. It had done so in spite of much opposition on President Kruger's part in earlier stages of the enterprise. He was steadfastly adverse to the junction of any colonial railway with the Transvaal until his "own line" from Delagoa Bay had become a practically accomplished fact. It was only when that consummation was guaranteed that he relaxed his hostility towards competing projects. Mr. Rhodes's advances to the northward, and other developments of Cape policy, had not improved the relations of

S

the South African Republic with the Cape Government.

It seemed expedient to keep on good terms with the nearer Colony. The President, therefore, accepted the invitation of the Natal Government, and was received with almost sovereign honours as a guest of state at Charlestown. His journey to Durban was a triumphal progress. Not only at the border terminus, under the very shadow of Majuba—where cannon had not been heard since Colley's terrible reverse—but at Newcastle, at Maritzburg, and at Durban, the rugged but not undignified old President was fêted and flattered as though he had been the Colony's best benefactor. Marshalled school-children sang the Volkslied, addresses were presented and speeches delivered, all aflame with friendly ardour: cheers rent the air, and everywhere was shown the most anxious solicitude to soothe the visitor's republican sensibilities. He accepted—or rather submitted to—it all with a grim and grumpy sententiousness that left nothing to be inferred. His few and oracular utterances were followed with eager expectation in the hope that some hint might be dropped of early railway extension in the future. But in vain was the net spread. Not an indication of policy did the President vouchsafe. When he returned to Pretoria, gorged with assurances of goodwill, he left the colonists as much in the dark as ever as to the realisation of their desires. It is probable, however, that the manifestation had some

effect in persuading President Kruger of the cordial
temper of Natal, and in paving the way for the Convention which a few years later secured the final
connection of the Natal railway system with that of
the rest of South Africa

It fell to my lot on that occasion to represent the
Government of Natal. President Kruger was either
unable or disinclined to take part himself in the
celebration of the event, and the Governor therefore
did not visit the Republic The former deputed the
State Secretary, Dr. Leyds, to represent him, and once
again I was brought into direct association with one
who has played so potential a part in the affairs of
the Transvaal. A year before he had visited Natal as
the guest of the Governor, and been warmly received
there. The 10th of October was the day fixed for the
linking together of the two sections of the line, that
from Johannesburg and Pretoria constructed by the
Netherlands Railway, and the much larger section
from Charlestown, the execution of which had been
undertaken by the Natal Railway department, acting
as contractor for the Republic. Johannesburg at that
time was the centre of political agitation and unrest.
The intrigues and controversies, which culminated
within less than three months in the Jameson Raid,
were in full activity, and the great gold centre was very
scantily represented at the Heidelberg function The
people, or at any rate the Government of Natal knew
little if anything of what was going on at the Rand,

and I can truthfully say were not less astounded
and shocked than the world was by Dr. Jameson's
adventure

There was no presage of coming disorder in the air
when the special train conveying our party arrived at
Heidelberg A lovely crystalline morning had ended
in a fury of wind—such wind as the high veld of the
interior only knows—bringing with it such an onswoop
of dust as words fail to describe. It was no easy matter
to stand up against the tempest, when we emerged
from our saloon and found Dr Leyds and his colleagues
waiting for us in the yet disconnected line. Tall hats
and umbrellas were distinctly incompatible with the
weather, while it was difficult to speak or to listen
amidst the uproar and buffeting of the gale. But
we managed to get through with the ceremony Dr.
Leyds screwed in his bolt, and I screwed in mine, and
we both declared, he in Dutch and I in English, that
we thereby bound together the interests of our several
countries by a link of iron and a tie of common interest
Other friendly things were said, and champagne was
drunk, and cheers were given for the Queen and the
President, and we then got into the carriage and passed
over the line. A little later a collation was given,
under the presidency of Dr. Leyds, and speeches full of
friendly feeling were delivered all round, and in both
languages, the most important being interpreted for
the benefit of the other race. In the evening a ball
was held, and in the general hilarity no murmurings

of the coming storm were audible. I noticed at the time how few Boers, properly so called, took part. They were as conspicuous by their absence as were the Johannesburgers. It was essentially an official celebration, but as such it was an assurance that at that time neither distrust nor dissension marked the relations of the Republic and the Colony.

On the day following Dr Leyds accompanied me on my return to Natal. We were alone together throughout the whole journey until he joined his family at Howick, and we talked of many things and of many books. Cultivated in mind, gentle in manner, and attractive in appearance, Dr. Leyds is a most agreeable companion, and it is hard even now to realise that that suave and genial personality covered the most strenuous enmity to British dominancy in South Africa, and an inflexible resolve to establish Boer-Hollander ascendency in its place. Had the late State Secretary been a man of more repellent aspect and demeanour, he would no doubt have been much less dangerous than he has proved to be.

CHAPTER X

THOUGH the coast of Natal was first discovered by Vasco da Gama on Christmas Day 1497, he did not land there, and the records of his expedition contain no descriptive references either to the country or its people. Another Portuguese navigator, Perestrello, sent by King Sebastian in 1575 to explore coasts and countries in South Africa, was more inquisitive. Travelling southward from Mozambique, he went ashore at various points, and he speaks of Natal as being "populous and well stocked with animals." In 1683 an English ship, the *Johanna*, was lost somewhere about Delagoa Bay. Its crew journeyed overland to the Cape of Good Hope, being guided thereto by the natives of the intervening territories, of whom we are told that they showed the shipwrecked men "more civility and humanity than some nations who pretend much religion and politeness, for they accommodated their guests with whatever they wanted of the product of the country at very easy rates, and assisted what they could to save part of their damaged cargo, receiving very moderate rewards for their labour and pains. Their language was by signs, and for a few glass beads, knives, scissors, needles, thread, and small looking-glasses"—such are the chief staples of "Kafir truck" to-day—"they hired themselves to carry many things to a neighbouring country, and procured others, who also served them for guides towards the Cape of Good Hope, and provided eatables for their masters all the way while they were under their conduct." And this 'kindly service was continued all along the route, through an unknown country, the white strangers being passed on from tribe to tribe, "the sick being carried in hammocks, till they either recovered or died." The writers who tell this pleasant story say that the natural fertility of those countries made the natives lazy, indolent, docile, and simple.

A like description of them was given a few years later by the officers of the ship *Stavenisse*, which was wrecked, apparently on the present site of Durban, in 1687. These people were a year and a day at Natal, where they built a rude craft, and thus escaped to the southern settlements. They were long enough ashore to learn much about both the land and its people, and their report on both was not less favourable than that of their predecessors. "They found the country very fruitful and prosperous, and the natives friendly, compassionate, obliging, strong, ingenious, armed with only one assegai, obedient or submissive to their king or chief, living in communities, in huts made of branches, wrought through with rushes and long grass and roofed like haystacks in Holland. In manners

dress, and behaviour, they are much more orderly
than the Cape Hottentots. The women attend to
cultivation, the men herd and milk the cows; they
do not eat poultry because these feed on filth; still
less do they eat eggs, and it makes them sick to see
Europeans eat them. For a copper arm-ring or a
common neck-ring of the thickness of a tobacco pipe
they sell a fat cow or ox of 600 lbs. weight more or
less; for a similar ring they give as much corn as
will fill an ordinary meat-tub, from which corn they
make very well-tasted and nourishing bread and brew
beer, both small and strong, which is not unpleasant
to the taste, and which they keep in earthen vessels:
they eat beside, a certain bean, in size and taste not
unlike the European horse-bean, also some roots,
weker (sic), and worse flavoured than sweet potatoes.
They have tobacco and smoke it, by good management its quality might be improved; of fruit they
have only an unknown kind of prune."

It would be difficult to improve upon this artless
but truthful description of a primitive people. Other
writers of the same period add further details which
serve to complete the picture. "The natives of this
country," says Captain Rogers, "are but of middle sta-
ture, yet have very good limbs. The colour of their skin
is black, their hair crisped. They are oval visaged,
their noses neither flat nor high, but well proportioned.[1]
Their teeth are white, and their aspect altogether

---

[1] This is more than can be said nowadays.

graceful, they are amiable people, but very lazy, which probably is for want of commerce. Their chief employment is husbandry. They have a great many bulls and cows, which they carefully look after, for every man knows his own; though they run all promiscuously together in their savannahs, yet they have pens near their own houses where they make them gentle and bring them to the pail. . . . Here are no arts or trade, but every one makes for himself such necessaries as need or ornament requires, the men keeping to their employment and the women to theirs. They wear but a few clothes, and these extraordinary mean. The men go in a manner naked, their common garb being only a piece of cloth of silk grass as an apron. . . . They have caps made with beef-tallow nine or ten inches. They are a great while making these caps, for the tallow must be very pure. It would be ridiculous for a man to be seen without a cap,[1] but boys are not allowed to wear any. The women have only short petticoats which reach to the knee. When the men meet to make merry, they make themselves extraordinary fine, with feathers stuck in their caps very thick Besides this they wear a piece of cowhide, which hangs behind like a tail, and reaching to the ground. Every man may have as many wives as he pleases, and without buying none are to be had; neither is there any other commodity to be bought or sold but women. Young virgins are dis-

[1] As a matter of fact they are fixtures.

posed of by fathers and brothers, the price according
to beauty. They have no money in the country, but
give cows for wives, and therefore the richest man is
he that hath most daughters or sisters. They make
merry when they take their wives, but the bride cries
all her wedding day. They live together in small
villages, and the oldest man governs the rest, for all
that live together are of kin, and therefore they submit to his government. They are very civil and just
to strangers. This was experienced by two seamen
who were among them five years. Their ship was
cast away on the coast, and the rest of their consorts
marched to the river De la Goa, but they stayed
here until Captain Rogers accidentally came and took
them away. They had gained the language of the
country, and the natives freely gave them wives and
cows too. They were beloved by all the people, and
so much reverenced that their words were taken as
laws, and when they came away many of the boys cried
because they could not take them with them."

I repeat that it would be difficult to compress within
fewer words a more luminous or picturesque account
of the native races that inhabited Natal then, and
two centuries ago, and—let me add—that are to be
found there to-day. It is more particularly of the
natives of Natal that this may be said. The same
writers speak of the natives who were found two or
three hundred miles to the south and north in far
less favourable terms. They were too often treacher-

ous, deceitful, hostile, and bloodthirsty. It will be admitted, I think, that the impression left by the description is, with due regard to the condition of barbarism, agreeable and somewhat Arcadian It suggests the existence of a peaceable, friendly, homely people, heathen and uncivilised it may be, but marked by many admirable social and domestic qualities — a people who, according to European lights, were no doubt in certain ways callous in sensibility and indifferent to brute suffering—whose customs were those of uncouth and uncultured men—children of nature, upon whom the mollifying influences of a fair and fertile land, of a bland and healthful climate, had wrought with gracious and domesticating effect. Very different were they from the Bushmen and Hottentots of the desolate regions of the West, where the physical difficulties of existence had begotten fiercer and more repellent characteristics The Natal native was a home-bird, by virtue of his surroundings, and not a nomad by the stern necessities of life. This is a root condition of his being, which may be said to have largely shaped his history, and should ever be remembered in connection with his government and treatment. It places him on a plane distinctly higher than that of the ordinary savage, and helps, perhaps, to account for his loyalty and amenability as a subject

For with the exception of such changes as have been incidental to continued contact with civilisation, the native of Natal is very much to-day what he was three centuries ago, and what, for aught we know, he may have been for centuries before that. The ruins at Zimbabwe, so admirably explored and described by Mr Bent, are evidences that man, considerably advanced beyond the barbarian, lived and worked in South-eastern Africa in comparatively remote ages, and there is no ground for supposing that that part of the continent was not more or less populous at a date far beyond any of which we have written trace.

Such were the native inhabitants of Natal up to the beginning of the nineteenth century. There is no exact evidence as to their numbers, but they are always described by writers in those days as being very numerous, and the remains of stone kraals, or circular cattlefolds, in the upper districts prove that they were so These interesting vestiges of the past are thickly scattered about the country between Mooi River and Ladismith. They are rings of piled-up boulders, innocent of chisel or cement, but sufficiently substantial to have withstood the wear and tear of weather for centuries. No such structures have been erected by the natives of these times within the memories of white men. They show that whenever they were built the natives possessed cattle, and were fixtures on the soil. It has been reckoned that there must have been at least two hundred tribes or kingdoms within the present limits of Natal. It was upon the descendants of these people, peaceful, contented, and wealthy according to their own ideas, that the organised warriors of the newly com-

pacted Zulu nation fell during the earlier years of the
now expiring century. First Senzangakona, then Chaka,
and after him Dingaan, aflame with ambition and lust
of conquest, sated their passion for bloodshed and
dominion in the lives of these helpless and harmless
neighbours. It was the first of these chiefs who began
to weld together the Amazulu nation, originally but a
small and insignificant tribe. His successor was Chaka
or Tyaka, who has been justly styled the Attila or
Napoleon of South Africa. At the age of thirty he
began that career of conquest which made him the
terror and the tyrant of all the country between Inham-
bana, north of Delagoa Bay, and the Umzimvubu. He
was a good deal more than a butcher, however. His
policy, at any rate at first, was that of Rome, not so
much to destroy, as to subjugate and incorporate the
tribes around him. Having subdued and captured
them, he so distributed them amongst his own people,
that while contributing to the strength and magnitude
of his empire, he kept them in complete subordination.
Thus he went on, ever swelling the numbers of his
subjects and tributaries, and making his rule and
influence felt half-way to the Atlantic. "Many were
slain by his forces, many were taken captive, and many
others fled for a time from the land of their fathers
and took refuge in surrounding districts, while others
still hid themselves in seasons of danger among the
mountains, rocks, and ravines of their own land, and
there remained until the enemy had passed and re-

passed, and left them to rest for at least another
year." Large numbers of these fugitives fled before
the Zulu hosts far beyond the borders of Natal to
the frontier tribes of the Cape Colony, by whom they
were enslaved, or classified as Amafengu,—an inferior
race—now known as Fingoes—the always loyal, and
perhaps most civilised of all the native tribes

It has been estimated that at one time Chaka had
at his command no less than one hundred thousand
fighting men. One of his chief kraals is described as
having been three miles in circumference, and as containing thirteen hundred huts. Fifteen thousand warriors were always ready for any emergency or expedition.
The slaughter of men, and the rule of celibacy, led to a
decrease in population, but at the same time they
fostered the practice of polygamy on the part of the
older and emancipated men. Though he devastated
and depopulated Natal, his own more immediate territory swarmed with people who fed his vanity and
chanted his praises as the tiger, the lion, the elephant,
the huge mountain, the mighty black prince, the
Supreme Ruler, the King of Kings, the undying Only
One One of the chief psalms sung in his honour has
been rendered in these words —

"Thou hast finished, finished the nations!
Where will you go out to battle now?
    Hey? where will you go out to battle now?
Thou hast conquered kings!
Where are you going out to battle now?

Thou hast finished, finished the nations !
Where you going to battle now ?
Hurrah ! Hurrah ! Hurrah !
Where are you going to battle now ? "

Dingaan, who succeeded his brother, was far inferior in character and capacity, though even more cruel and bloodthirsty. Under him the depopulation of Natal was completed, and only such remnants of tribes as clustered round the few British settlers at Durban remained in the country. Most touching is the child-like confidence with which these survivors of the aboriginal tribes came forth from their lurking-places and attached themselves to the friendly white man, whenever he appeared upon the scene. I have in former times talked to grey-headed old men who had saved themselves from destruction by hiding in the bush that skirts the shore and living on fresh roots and herbs. One of them is reported to have said. "I remember the time well. I was then a young man. The Amatuli all collected upon a plain near the Umko-manzi. The Zulus came up in the afternoon. We gave them battle and drove them back to the Umzim-basi," a few miles northward, "leaving the dead in heaps on the way. With this right hand I slaughtered many." So they often made a stubborn fight for existence, if only to be overwhelmed in the end.

When Mr. H. F. Fynn, an old friend of mine, for many years a leading magistrate, and the oldest living resident of Durban, travelled as a young trader in 1824

and subsequent years between the Tongaat and Umzimvubu River—a distance of 250 miles—he did not find a
single tribe, with the exception of about thirty natives
residing near the Bluff, at Durban They belonged to
the tribe of Umnini, which, by reason of its unbroken
aboriginal tenancy, was specially rewarded a location of
its own on valuable coastland. This tract of country,
some 12,000 acres in extent, was vested in a special
trust, and can only be exchanged—as it may be, for
a larger area of ground elsewhere — with the direct
consent of the people

As soon as the English settled at Port Natal—
"Durban" had not been laid out in those days—
fragments of the scattered tribes gradually congregated
under their protection, and in a few years three or
four thousand were settled there This process of
accretion continued as time went on, and though peace
was always menaced as long as Chaka or Dingaan
reigned and was often broken, the desire of both those
chiefs to conciliate the English power, availed to draw
back to their ancient home stragglers from the dispersed
people. In 1827 or 1828 refugees from the Zulu
country began frequently to arrive, and on being
reported to Chaka were permitted by him to reside
at Natal. The inflow slowly increased until, when the
British Government finally took possession in 1843,
there may have been about seven or eight thousand;
no precise record exists of the number, but as there
were only three or four thousand when the Dutch

arrived in 1838, and as their policy was not to encourage any large settlement of native refugees, that
estimate is probably correct. These people were mostly
gathered round Durban, though some lived not far
from Maritzburg. They formed the nucleus of the
present native population of Natal, whose fidelity to
the British Government during more than half a
century bears such signal and happy testimony to the
claim and capacity of Anglo-Saxon men to rule wisely
and well subject aboriginal races.

The principles which have governed the administration of native affairs in Natal were practically embodied
in or foreshadowed by the noble Proclamation issued
by Sir George Napier when extending the Queen's
sovereignty over the infant Colony in 1843. A loftier
or more enkindling declaration of Imperial purpose
never proceeded from the pen of a British representative: "That her Majesty's said Commissioner
is instructed distinctly to declare that the three next
mentioned conditions — all of them so manifestly
righteous and expedient as to receive, it is to be hoped,
their cheerful recognition by the inhabitants of Natal—
are to be considered as absolutely indispensable to the
permission which it is proposed to give the emigrants
to occupy the territory in question and to enjoy therein
a settled government under British possession.

"1st, That there shall not be in the eye of the law
any distinction or disqualification whatever, founded
on mere distinction of colour, origin, language, or creed,

T

but that the protection of the law, in letter and in substance, shall be extended impartially to all alike

"2nd, That no aggression shall be sanctioned upon the natives residing beyond the limits of the Colony under any plea whatever, by any private person or any body of men, unless acting under the immediate authority and orders of the Government.

"3rd, That slavery in any shape or under any modification is absolutely unlawful, as in every other portion of her Majesty's dominions. . . ."

Thus was made known "the gracious desire of her Majesty to knit the hearts of all her subjects to her person and Government, as evinced by her willingness to concede to her people at Port Natal every just personal right and every reasonable political privilege; and that the natural resources of the country may be gradually developed under her Majesty's firm but fostering rule, stimulating the industry which can never prosper but beneath settled institutions, and securing the advantages which are enjoyed by every Colony of Great Britain."

Though actual experience may have necessitated some modification of policy in regard to the first of the three conditions thus laid down, the history of Natal is a full vindication of the purposes which inspired its founders.

It is not surprising that a government established on such principles, and guided by such rules of action, should attach to its authority a steadily swelling stream of population. Six years after the Colony was definitely recognised as a part of the Empire, the natives in Natal were officially computed and classified as follows: There were 41,452 belonging to aboriginal chiefs and tribes, who on the advent of peaceful and settled rule had flocked back to the home of their forefathers; there were 24,044 representing a mixed class of aborigines and refugees, who had abandoned the country for the time being, and established themselves elsewhere under the rule of neighbouring chiefs; and there were 35,608 who were refugees, in the strict sense of the term, from outside territories.

Less than two years after Mr. West took office as the first Lieutenant-Governor of Natal in 1845, a Commission was appointed to consider the best mode of providing for the internal management and defence of the native locations, and for the improvement and welfare of the natives generally. It consisted of the Surveyor-General, the Diplomatic Agent (Mr. Theophilus Shepstone), two American missionaries, and an officer of the Royal Engineers. The report submitted by this body, in March 1847, is a State document of the highest interest and importance It embodied a scheme of native policy which, had it been carried out, would have revolutionised the conditions of the native population. The chief points in this policy were: (1) the vesting of the location lands in the hands of trustees, the Government reserving to itself the right to convert these or any portion of them

into freehold grants to natives who had so improved
their land by industrial diligence as to have earned
a claim to special reward or recognition; (2) the
energetic control of each location by a European superintendent and assistants, supported by a native police
force, under a European officer — these functionaries
were to be men of high moral standing, sound judgment, and decision of character, whose education and
conduct would, apart from their office, command the
respect and confidence alike of native and European;
(3) in the administration of justice the native chiefs
or councillors were to assist as a sort of jury, and
deliver their opinions according to the merits of each
case — in all cases where white men were concerned
trial was to be under the established law of the district,
and all serious criminal cases were to be tried before
the Supreme Criminal Court of the district; (4) regis-
tration of natives, of cattle, of removals, and of contracts
was to be enforced; passes were to be issued and the
superintendents to be empowered to execute contracts
of service between master and servant; (5) marriage
and divorce laws were to be remodelled, and efforts
made to improve the status of women; (6) agriculture,
and especially the cultivation of perennials, was to be
encouraged so as to wean the people from dependence
upon stock-raising and to fix them upon the soil; (7)
firearms were to be registered, and trespassing upon
farms prevented; (8) weekly reports were to be submitted by each superintendent, and the head of the

native department was to periodically visit the location and act as a court of appeal; (9) missions and schools were to be encouraged and assisted, and model mechanical schools established; (10) roads through and to the locations were to be constructed, and each location properly surveyed and defined.

Such were the outlines of the policy which was thus, in the extreme infancy of Natal, proposed by a responsible and representative body of Commissioners, prepared and submitted for the effective control and guidance of the then sparse native population. These outlines have been at all times recognised by colonists as wise, far-seeing, and practical, but the suggestions fell on stony ground. The Home Government, while generally approving of them in spirit, declined to find the means of carrying them out. The creed of Manchester was then dominant, and no money was forthcoming for purposes outside Great Britain. At that time a sum of about £5000 would have sufficed to give the scheme a start, but no Minister was bold enough to support even that modest contribution towards the cult of Imperialistic heresy. The maintenance of a small garrison of 400 troops was all, by way of permanent responsibility, which the Empire could, or would, afford in behalf of the new dependency. So nothing was done and matters drifted, until after Governor Pine's arrival in 1850. He, as might be expected, took a large and true grasp of the situation, and was supported in so doing by one of the

ablest Ministers who has ever presided over the destinies of the Colonial Empire. Lord Grey's despatches
on Native policy, written in 1850–51 are monuments
of wisdom and foresight He clearly perceived the
necessity of firm and enlightened administration. He
strongly opposed any building-up or perpetuation of
the powers of chieftainship. He as strongly advocated
the discouragement and undermining of all savage
customs and institutions, and he favoured every
measure and means by which the native might be
raised in the scale of civilisation and citizenship. But
he too stopt short at the expenditure of Imperial
money in the pursuit of these high aims and ends.
As early as December 4, 1846, Earl Grey wrote: "It
is mainly for the benefit of the native inhabitants of
Africa that this Colony is to be maintained, and
therefore it is only just to require that no part of the
cost of supporting it for which they can be made to
provide, should be thrown upon this country. Nor do
I think it impossible that the Colony of Natal may
be so managed as to prevent it from bringing any
considerable or permanent charge upon the British
revenue." That was the keynote of Imperial policy
then and ever afterwards, and though it is true that
Natal never has imposed any such charge upon the
home taxpayer—apart from military expenditure—the
result was at the time the failure of every effort to
govern the natives on the lines of a large progressive
policy. In 1850–51 a forward step was taken in the

appointment of certain resident magistrates—three of whom were sent from England—but there action ended.

Meanwhile both the Europeans and the natives in the Colony increased in numbers, and mainly in each case from without. Refugees from Zululand flocked in, until in 1851 about 100,000 were estimated to be settled in the country. Byrne's immigration scheme between the years 1849 and 1852 planted from 4000 to 5000 British settlers on the soil. The Cape frontier war was raging through most of that period, and the white new-comers were naturally disposed to look with suspicion and some antagonism on the alien native people amongst whom their lot was cast. Their Dutch neighbours, moreover, encouraged them to regard the "Kafir" as the natural enemy of the white man, as a being who could only be kept in subjection and order by drastic and penal processes. In the Boer view the only way to govern the native was to keep him down, in the place which God had assigned to him. On this point some of the Dutch witnesses before the Native Commission held in 1852–3 spoke very clearly. At least five of the Commissioners were Boer farmers—or Voertrekkers—and they were among the first to give their testimony. Said Mr. F. C. Scheepers: "One of the reasons which led to the emigration from the Cape Colony was that black and white were subject to the same laws . . . I do not think that the same law will restrain a savage man which will restrain a white man. I think it would be just and good that if a Kafir refuses to work, the law should be that he is to leave the country. . . . I am of opinion that white and black cannot live together in peace in the same country unless the black man is in a state of subjection to the white. . . . In my opinion, if a line were drawn defining the country inhabited by whites, I would have all the blacks removed beyond that line except those who would remain as servants to the whites." Field Commandant Maritz said: "I think it would tend more to their advantage if the females were apprenticed as well as males. From my experience of Kafirs there is no mode of dealing with them except that of compulsion or severity." Mr. Caspar Labuschagne "entirely concurred with the evidence and opinions of his fellow-commissioner." So also did Mr. Spies, who also considered that "everybody should be at liberty to have as many Kafirs as he was inclined to." Mr. Pretorius was convinced that if the British Government "was to give up the country to the Boers, they would enjoy much more security than they did at present from the natives. He would make a law for the Kafirs that every man having a Kafir should be allowed to flog him when he misbehaved, of course in a moderate way. If this was known by the Kafirs it would be almost unnecessary to inflict the punishment. In the time of the Volksraad this was the law, and then the Kafirs were in good order." This statement he subsequently qualified by explaining that it was rather a rule than a law, and was merely the exercise of parental authority like that of a father over his children. He also disclaimed any present recommendation that such a law should be passed, but the original suggestion no doubt indicated the actual trend of his mind. He added: "The Kafirs are much more insolent now than when first we came. This has considerably increased since the English took possession of the country. Thefts have become more common. The cause is the unbounded humanity of the English Government towards them" Mr. Lotter very succinctly expressed his opinion that "the apprenticing of young Kafirs of both sexes, until they are of age, will be of great use both to civilisation and to their own interest," and also "that a separate law should be made for the Kafir—distinct from the white man and very severe, as I know from experience in the old Colony that mild laws are unsuited to them and to the prejudice of both."

In considering these frank avowals of opinion, made with obvious sincerity and in perfect good faith, it is but fair to remember that the witnesses in their early lives had been brought into contact with a distinctly lower type of native in the Cape Colony, and had, as we know, suffered acutely from treachery at the hands of Dingaan on their first arrival in Natal. Their memories also went back to days when slave-holding was a lawful and general practice, sanctioned by Scripture and familiarised by usage. It would have been strange had the British settlers not been to some extent influenced by the precepts and opinions of their more experienced fellow-colonists, and had their expressed sentiments not at times been tinged by prejudices which fuller experience has failed to justify. The mind of Mr. Shepstone, as head of the Native department, was so much impressed by the apparent outgrowth of unfriendly relations between the two races that in December 1851 he formally submitted a scheme for the removal of the native population to the unoccupied country south of the Umkomas, where they might be governed somewhat on the lines laid down by the Commission of 1847, but as a separate community. At that time—in 1852—the natives of the Colony were mostly distributed in six or seven locations, situated in different parts of the Colony. These tracts of country had in the first instance been occupied by the natives as they flocked in, because their broken and precipitous outlines repelled white settlers. Both Boer and British farmers preferred more open and accessible districts, while the natives were glad to isolate themselves in localities far removed from white neighbours, where they could live their lives of barbarism with small risk of oversight or interference. Natal offers many such districts—regions of picturesque beauty and grandeur, whose depths of craggy bushland and rockbound mountain and shadowy valley seem made to be the happy abiding-places of untutored savages. At

least two million acres of such lands were at that time
appropriated by and to the native inhabitants of Natal.
Mr. Shepstone's proposal practically amounted to the
substitution of one large location, for several smaller
locations, in the southern portion of the Colony, which
had not so far been occupied by white men. Lord
Grey strongly combated the scheme for reasons which
Mr. Shepstone admitted to be correct and statesmanlike, though hardly sustained by the change of circumstances. In consequence of the Secretary of State's
hostility, as well as of the opinions expressed at a
meeting of magistrates held in 1852, Mr. Shepstone
offered to remove with the native population entirely
beyond the boundary of the Colony, into the country
afterwards known as No Man's Land, "and there to undertake its control without interference from the British
Government, except in so far as to guarantee the
country to these people so long as they behaved in
good faith towards it and its subjects, and to acknow-
ledge his (Mr. Shepstone's) position over them."

This last proposal to settle the native difficulty by a
wholesale policy of migration met with no more approval than had its predecessor. Though Lord Grey
was no longer at the helm in Downing Street, Sir
George Grey had been appointed Governor and High
Commissioner at Capetown, and he criticised and
condemned the project in terms of almost scathing
severity. It would, he contended, amount to the setting up of a native sovereignty in the southern districts,

which would be all the more difficult to deal with because it was under the kingship of a white ruler. His essential objection, however, was the evil of segregation. Our policy, he said, should be rather to mix the natives up amongst the white population—to bring them into daily contact with civilisation and industry—than to isolate them from these improving influences. The scheme would, he urged, perpetuate and consolidate the evils of chieftainship and tribalism, and interpose between the two British colonies a compact barrier of protected barbarism. Thus opposed by the highest Imperial authorities in England and South Africa, the project collapsed, and was never again revived. Henceforward native administration in Natal took its normal course, amidst constant criticism and controversy, but without any violent attempts at revolutionary change. The Commission to which I have referred took a great deal of valuable evidence and adopted a very exhaustive and luminous Report, but little in the way of substantial result came of it. In 1856 the Royal Charter, establishing a representative Legislature, was promulgated. Mr. Shepstone's office became that of Secretary for Native Affairs, and the controversies to which I have referred in a previous chapter [1] engaged public attention between the years 1857 and 1862.

From time to time laws were passed to secure better control of the natives, or to modify such native customs as might be repugnant to or in conflict with the usages

[1] Chap. VI.

and interests of civilisation But on the whole what was
known as the "Shepstonian policy" prevailed, in despite
of the abuse and denunciations heaped upon it Mr.
Shepstone was a silent, stubborn man, whose power of
resistance was passive rather than aggressive. He was
found fault with less for what he did than for what
he failed to do. The charge commonly levelled against
him and his methods was that of *laissez faire* He
was accused of doing nothing—of standing still—instead
of moving on Ardent regenerators yearned to attack
the main citadels of barbarism—polygamy, wife-barter,
witchcraft, and idleness They would fain have passed
measures to abolish polygamy, to forbid the exchange
of cattle for wives, to punish witch-doctors and penalise
their practices to compel the natives to work for wages,
and with that end in view to increase the taxation
imposed upon them, to apprentice the children, above
a certain age, and to register the whole native population throughout the Colony. As a rule the missionaries
contended for these changes, or for most of them, with
the one notable exception of Bishop Colenso, who for
years protested against any forcible interference with
the existing marriage institutions of the natives I do
not pretend to reflect the heated controversies which in
those years centred around these questions. Volumes
might easily be filled with a review of them. Cut off
from frequent communication with the outer world—
with only a monthly mail-service, and no ocean cable
—colonists had more time for academical discussion

than they have now, and confined within the narrower
arena of their own topics and interests, they debated
vexed questions with a vehemency and persistency
which seldom mark their controversies in these busier
and fuller times. Supported as he usually was in his
attitude of passive resistance to sudden change by the
Governors and Secretaries of State of the day, Mr.
Shepstone went on his way doing as little as possible
in the direction of innovation or reform, and only yielding when he could hold out no longer.

Thus it has come to pass that after fifty years of
British rule the native population of Natal has swollen
in numbers from 100,000 to 500,000, and yet in its
general conditions and aspects it remains very much
the same people that were found in the Colony half
a century ago. Yet by no means altogether so, as I
shall shortly show. For Mr. Shepstone's inertia was
qualified by legislative activity, and though he was
slow to move, in the end he did advance, in the direction of a more vigorous and enlightened policy. The
conjunction of these two influences in the years
between 1860 and 1880, while it prevented actual
retrogression or absolute inaction, was eminently conservative and salutary in its effects. Whatever changes
might be introduced were carried out with care and
caution — were deliberate and tentative, not violent
or radical. Though I was usually on the side of a
progressive policy, looking back to those days in the
light of subsequent experience, it seems to me now

that the peace and order that have so conspicuously marked the history of Natal have been greatly due to this admixture of official conservatism with colonial progressiveness. While barbarism has been curbed, and while civilisation has made some headway, native animosities have not been aroused, nor native discontent fostered. Let me here state categorically some of the changes which have been peacefully effected by legislation since the Royal Charter first gave the colonists a share and a voice in their own government :—

1. The yearly hut-tax has been increased from 7s. to 14s a hut, and has at all times been paid without a murmur.

2. Marriages are conducted under strict legal supervision, and the fee or dowry payable by a bridegroom is limited to eight cows on each wife ; whose voluntary acquiescence is also required.

3. The location lands are all vested in a Board of Native Trust, consisting of the Governor and Executive Council of the Colony.

4. Chiefs have had their powers defined and limited, they receive small annual stipends, and their succession is most carefully regulated and dealt with by the Secretary for Native Affairs, according to recognised rules and usages, and subject, more or less, to the concurrence of the tribe.

5. An elaborate codification of native law has been

effected by experts. It is based upon established
native customs and canons, and though it embodies
usages that are distinctly at variance with many Anglo-
Saxon ideas, it has been purged from more revolting
associations.

6. A native High Court of three specially qualified
judges (one of them is a Dutch Africander) has been
created for the trial of more serious offences between
native and native.

7. A permanent Under Secretary for Native Affairs
is provided for under the Constitution Act of 1893,
to secure fixity of official representation in the eyes
of the natives.

8. An appropriation of £10,000 per annum is set
apart by the same Act for the improvement and
welfare of the natives.

9. All qualified mission schools—they number 188
—receive yearly grants in aid from the public exchequer.

10. Though witch-doctors are not absolutely done
away with, the practice of witchcraft is sternly discouraged and forbidden, and cases of violence due
thereto are severely punished whenever detected.

Though none of these measures can fairly be called
revolutionary, they make a distinct advance upon
aboriginal conditions, and they have been readily submitted to, or acquiesced in, by the natives themselves.
I can call to mind only one occasion upon which the

enforcement of law has been openly resisted, and that was the refusal of Langalibalele in 1873 to register the guns purchased by his people at the diamond-fields. I have already described this incident.[1] It recalls another cardinal point in our native administration. Though there has been a general disposition to leave the native in uncurbed enjoyment of his customary freedom and immunities, colonial policy has debarred him from three privileges, namely—

The right to acquire firearms

The right to buy or acquire liquor.

The right to vote.

All classes of the community have agreed that these disqualifications are necessitated in the interests of peace and order, and by a regard for the natives themselves. The native not unnaturally attaches an undue value to the possession of guns, as weapons both of offence and defence. Thus armed, he is apt to deem himself a match for the white man. He becomes truculent and warlike. This was clearly shown in the case of Langalibalele. Other instances could be cited outside Natal. Precisely the same influence operated upon the Boer mind in connection with the present war. The Dutch Africanders thought that, armed with Mauser rifles and Creusot cannon, they could drive the *rooinek* into the sea. The natives of Natal have no use whatever for guns, except to destroy monkeys, or other depredators of their crops, and

[1] Chap. V.

U

in cases of that sort special permits are sometimes
granted to deserving and trustworthy applicants. The
right to hold a gun, or fowling-piece, under such conditions is regarded as a special privilege, and is occasionally conceded as a reward for fidelity and good
service. Experience has clearly shown that the habit
of carrying lethal weapons is inimical to general
security, and this is especially the case in a community
of African natives divided by tribal feuds, jealousies,
and rivalries. As it is, the sticks and knobkerries
which are commonly borne by the native as he moves
about the country are far too often employed as
weapons of offence, in the frequent faction fights that
occur between tribe and tribe. The law deals strictly
with the offenders in these frays, in which heads are
often broken, and now and then life is lost. Fines
are imposed all round, and ringleaders are sometimes
imprisoned. The belligerents do not resent these
punishments They have had their fun and they are
prepared to pay for it. The frequency of such incidents, however, serves to show how little unity exists
among the native population, and how devoid the
natives are of a cementing common cause It also
proves how wise and necessary is the restriction which
keeps modern implements of destruction out of the
hands of a savage race Can we doubt that this policy
has largely to be thanked for the complete security
of person and life which has prevailed in Natal ever
since it became a British settlement? If the native

has been denied the use of firearms, the white man
has been under no compulsion to carry them. You
may travel, and men constantly do travel, from end
to end of Natal along the public roads, or by lonely
by-ways through remote locations, without any means
of defence other than a riding-switch.

Not less efficacious in preventing disorder has been
the prohibition of the sale of liquor The native dearly
loves intoxicants A glass of grog tempts him as
nothing else will. He sips it with a pious unction that
is almost comical in its ecstasy. Had he free access to
the seductive cup, his degeneracy would soon be sealed.
This is shown at Johannesburg, where for several years
the liquor trade was virtually uncurbed, and where
even now prohibitory regulations are systematically
evaded. It is a matter of common complaint that the
natives who flock to the gold mines, in quest of the
high wages ruling there, come back corrupted and
spoiled. For many years much trouble was caused by
the manufacture, in the coast districts, of "Shimyaan,"
a concoction of treacle and water allowed to ferment
in the sun. This beverage was maddening in its
effects, and the parent of much crime. The natives,
fortunately both for themselves and the community,
have realised how pernicious the mixture is, and we
hear much less of its production than of yore Considering that large quantities of rum are made at the
sugar plantations, it is surprising that drunkenness is
not more rife amongst the natives, though in the

season of beer-drinkings, when the natives gather at
their kraals to drink the fermented produce of the
newly harvested millet, there is much boozing and
excitement. Though the liquor laws are often evaded
at the back doors of roadside hostelries and country
stores, where rum is illicitly sold as "paraffin," their
value and efficacy are vindicated not less by what
they prevent than by their failures Cynical observers
have suggested that the easiest way to settle the
"native question" would be to abolish all restrictions
on the sale of liquor, and thus to leave the native free
to destroy himself as fast as he likes, but such a rule
of action (I will not call it a "principle") will never,
I venture to believe, defile the policy of Natal in its
treatment of the native races.

The exclusion of the natives from the franchise is so
obvious a necessity of circumstances that it hardly calls
for comment The electoral franchise is a privilege
which the natives would fail to understand, and would
only exercise, did they possess it, under the guidance,
if not the dictation, of some superior influence or
authority Were it certain that that guidance would
be shaped by strictly patriotic motives, and directed to
wise and benevolent ends, this might not in itself be
an unmixed evil But there is no sort of guarantee
that the natives would be so led On the contrary,
there is every reason to fear that they would be the
prey of party or interested agitators, and that their
votes would be cast on the side of perilous or mis-

chievous legislation. The natives, moreover, would be the great majority. Their representatives might make or unmake Ministries. Race cleavage would be the dominant factor in deciding elections Race bitterness and discord would rend and curse the country. Public opinion amongst the European electors of Natal is so united and so earnest on this question that in 1896 the first Responsible Ministry of Natal, with the cognisance of the Home Government, introduced a measure which excluded from the franchise persons "who (not being of European origin) are natives or descendants in the male line of natives of countries which have not hitherto possessed elective representative institutions founded on the Parliamentary franchise, unless they shall first obtain an order from the Governor in Council exempting them from the operation of this Act." This measure had first been submitted in a more restrictive and specific form, and at no stage met with opposition in the Colonial Parliament, but, in deference to representations from Mr Chamberlain, who shrunk from placing an apparent stigma upon any class of her Majesty's subjects, the law was finally modified, as will be seen, so as to exclude any direct application to race or colour, and power was given to the Governor in Council to admit to the franchise any specially qualified and approved applicants. I may add that the proposal had its origin primarily in the apparent probability that the electoral roll might be swamped at no distant date by illiterate and inexperienced Asiatic voters.

As regards the natives, no objection was raised from any quarter to a measure which only gave legislative expression and effect to a practice that had been in vogue ever since the Charter was first promulgated, Native electors have at all times been conspicuous by their absence from the voters' rolls of the Colony. In 1865 a law was passed under which the Governor was empowered, under certain very definite conditions, to admit to the franchise any native who had been exempted from the operation of native law, but as a matter of fact scarcely any appreciable use has been made of this privilege, possibly because of the restrictions attending it. The natives have neither missed nor craved for a privilege which only a very few amongst them, who have been civilised and educated, appreciate or understand.

That the question of native representation will bulk more and more largely in the future is as certain as that the natives—or some of them—will advance in civilisation and in culture, in wealth and property, as time goes on So far this question has remained quiescent, and it is to be hoped that it will remain so; at any rate until the federation of South Africa, and the establishment of a Federal Parliament, has provided the means whereby such questions can be dealt with from the standpoint of national interest and responsibility. At present it cannot be said that the native races have any direct or responsible representation in any South African legislature. Individual members who may happen to have been brought into close personal contact with the natives contribute out of their knowledge and experience to the information of their colleagues when native topics are under debate, but of any actual voicing of native views or aspirations there is none In New Zealand this has been effected by the introduction of Maori members into Parliament itself. In South Africa there would be much repugnance to such an innovation on the part of the white electors, and yet it is obviously desirable to get at the native mind in matters that affect native life and interests. How the problem presented by these conflicting requirements and prejudices is to be solved remains to be seen Meanwhile it is encouraging to know that in the Parliaments of both the British colonies, so far, there has been no violation of those principles of justice, humanity, and good faith that have been the glory of Anglo-Saxon policy in the treatment of subject races The ebullitions of race feeling which occasionally drop from the lips of Africander members when native questions are under discussion must be interpreted in the light of history They may at any rate claim to be sincere.

Year has followed year, decade has succeeded to decade, half a century has passed, and still the native population of Natal thrives and grows, and spreads and multiplies, without any material change in its domestic conditions The locations set apart for its occupation have been added to from time to time, but long ago all the spare land available for the purpose was appropriated, and such of the people as desire to do so have to find homes as tenants of private lands, or possibly, if rich enough to purchase, as landowners themselves. No law is in force which prohibits the ownership of land by either native or Asiatic. The proscription of "colour" as a disqualification for the possession of immovable property was a distinction confined to the late Dutch republics. A good many "farms" have been bought by native chiefs or native communities, and interesting questions are likely to arise as time goes on in connection with the tribal or communal administration of these estates. A large area of private land is occupied by native tenants, mostly on a yearly tenure, and at a rental ranging from £2 to £5 per hut. It is an easy mode of raising an income from land held by absent proprietors, but on economic grounds there is much to be said against it. Colonial feeling would much rather that these lands were occupied by European residents, whose improvement of the soil would contribute materially and manifestly to the advancement and betterment of the Colony.

For though the native is a loyal, peaceful, and law-abiding subject, though he seems contented with his condition and happy in his surroundings, he lives very much as his predecessors lived centuries ago. His hut may be bigger, so as to reduce the burden of rental and taxation, but his kraal is less shipshape and symmetrical as a village or hamlet than it was when the first delineators of the country limned and described it. In those days it was a circle of from six to a dozen huts, more or less, with an inner enclosure for cattle and an outer fence. Now it consists ordinarily of two or three huts planted promiscuously on the hill-side or hill-top, with the cattle-fold, less carefully constructed than of yore, in close proximity These huts are just the same perishable grass-built, bee-hive-like structures, innocent of door or window, that they have ever been, and the people who live in them —when at home—are no more clad than they used to be. Clothes are worn freely enough when in service, but in the seclusion of their own kraals the natives are still content to clothe their nakedness in the slender girdles or loin-cloths that satisfied their ancestors. Nor is their food much changed from what it was when the old navigators visited the country. The taste for salt or treacle has developed, and the native gladly eats bread when he can get it; but his culinary methods continue as crude and primitive as ever. The general conduct of his daily life—his work, his hunts, his feastings, his celebrations, his marriage ceremonies, his *indabas*—differ little from the vogue and usage of the past.

Yet it must not be supposed by any means that no progress has been made. Imperceptibly in many ways the native has levelled-up towards the higher life of his white neighbours. He works for wages far more

generally than he did. Though a few months' service
in most cases suffices to satisfy his needs, and leads
him to bend his footsteps homeward, he is glad to
seek employment either in the Colony or at Johannesburg in all sorts of capacities—in households, in stores,
on farms, in transport work, on public works, as "togt"
Kafirs, by the day or the job, or as ricksha-pullers.
Cheerful, apt, and ready, though often careless and
evasive, he plays a prominent and active part in the
industrial life of the community Though the colonists often deplore his unreliability and cupidity, they
would sorely miss his services were his existence to
be blotted out. Native girls, moreover, are more and
more disposed to enter domestic service. One of the
oddest contrasts of habit is the fondness of these girls
for dress and finery when in town or in service, and
their readiness on returning to their kraals to cast
off all the trappings of civilisation, and to revert to
the simple garb of Eden. This remark does not, of
course, apply to the denizens of mission stations, who
keep decently clad, both at home and abroad, all through
the year.

Then too, as an advance in civilisation, must be
credited to the natives their use of ploughs, their use
of picks instead of rude hoes, and their acquisition
of waggons for employment in road transport Just
as the hoe used to be the implement of the woman,
so is the plough the instrument of the man The
change signifies a much larger area of cultivation

and an improved status for women. On the latter
point, indeed, the difference worked by time, law, and
civilised intercourse is a marked gain to civilisation.
Women have ceased to be mere dumb chattels and
slaves, to be beaten, cowed, and misused. They have
had their status and their rights secured to them, and
they act accordingly The girl cannot be disposed of
against her will, or without power of protest, while the
woman has become a factor to be recognised and respected, with a voice which she knows well enough
how to use when occasion arises. In the draping of
her person the woman of the kraal has advanced even
less than the man She comes into town to visit her
male relatives with just as little costume on her as
suffices to meet the elementary requirements of the
law—that she be covered from neck to knee.

In respect of native education the policy of the
Colony has been neither vigorous nor comprehensive.
The reserved appropriation of £5000 per annum for
"Native Purposes" in the Royal Charter had the
effect of stifling any interest which the non-official
members of the Legislature might otherwise have
taken in the subject. The Crown having reserved to
itself the right of making provision for the higher
needs of the natives, elected members felt themselves
absolved from any responsibility in the matter. The
representatives of the Crown failed for some years
to include native education within the scope of their
energies In earlier years money was spent to little

purpose in the support of a central sugar-mill and
in the encouragement of cotton-planting, but without
appreciable result. Much has been said about industrial schools, but the only effort made in that direction under Government auspices was so stunted in its
shape that it soon collapsed. For many years past
the action of the Government has been confined to
the subsidising of all the mission schools of the Colony,
irrespective of nationality or creed. At the end of last
year 188 different schools received such aid. Twenty-
six of them were boarding-schools attended by 2087
children. They represented Protestant and Catholic
churches, conducted by mission bodies of all denomi-
nations, and they had a total school-roll of 10,725.

Whatever may have been the merits or demerits of
native administration in Natal, whether it has erred in
excess of toleration and indulgence, or failed in dis-
ciplinary grasp and progressive tendency, it has, at
any rate, produced a contented, loyal, and light-hearted
population. Visitors have not been twenty-four hours
in Durban before they notice the airy, cheerful, unconstrained demeanour of the natives around them. They
remark it at the water-side, on the very threshold of
the Colony, where the crowds of natives working on the
wharves, engaged in loading and unloading the vessels
that lie alongside, haul and carry, and lift and pass
their burdens, regardless of heat or rain, with a merry
abandonment and an apparent zest in labour that
bespeak perfect contentment with life and its burdens

They note it in the streets and roads, where the ricksha-
pullers bound and shout, and coax for fares, as though
their task were the most delightful pastime under the
sun. They see it everywhere; in the driving of laden
trollies and waggons, in the bearing of messengers and
errand-boys, of "kitchen-boys" and "store Kafirs," and
in the carriage-loads of crowding, chattering, happy
people (of both sexes) that enliven the railway trains.
If they go into the country, they have the same experience amongst the field hands of sugar plantations,
or the herd-boys that tend the cattle or the sheep in
outlying stock-farms. And if they wander yet farther
afield and observe the native at home in his kraal and
in his location lands, they find a race leading a life
of almost idyllic freedom and repose, with as much
absence of real cause for care, as much enjoyment of
the primal elements of existence, as any people unen-
cumbered by the obligations of civilisation could desire.
If crops fail or stock dies, food can always be purchased
with the wages that are the equivalent of work, and
work can always be secured at the cost of their white
neighbours. If it be scarce in their own neighbourhood, it can be found at distant centres to which the
railway now carries them at a trivial cost. Taxation
imposes little burden. The paternal Government which
provides them with security and justice, asks in return
a payment so small that the produce of a few fowls, or
the wages of a small boy, will suffice to meet it. In
former years a particular fowl, dubbed "Shepstone's

hen," would be set apart for the satisfaction, by the
sale of its eggs or chickens, of the yearly tax-gatherer
Natives who choose to live outside the locations on
private lands have, of course, heavier rent-charges to
pay, but where prices of produce rule so high, and where
the demand for labour is ever so pressing, they have
really little difficulty in satisfying their landlords.

The continued loyalty of the natives of Natal con-
clusively confutes the predictions of the old Dutch pioneers, who fifty years ago denounced English systems of
native control and management as certain to result in
discord and bloodshed. To this day the same men, or
their descendants, plead colonial methods of native treatment as a barrier to British rule or intercolonial union.
Yet the facts I have endeavoured to set forth, however briefly, in these pages are incontrovertible. The
loyalty of our natives has again and again withstood the
severest strain. Ties of racial sympathy have not been
strong enough to snap it. Shocks of calamity have not
availed to shake it. Langalibalele's rebellion drew within
its radius of disaffection but one neighbouring tribe.
Through the tremendous crisis of the Zulu war our
natives remained absolutely stanch and loyal. Though
they saw British troops overwhelmed and massacred,
though they knew that the Colony was for weeks at
the mercy of Cetywayo's hordes, they did not waver
in their allegiance, nor lift a hostile hand against their
white fellow-subjects. On the contrary they fought
gallantly by the side of our forces, only asking to be led

by men who knew their language and their ways, a splendid tribute to the confidence which the colonists had inspired. The bravery and fidelity shown in the field by the organised mission natives of Edendale were unreservedly recognised at the time by Sir Garnet Wolseley and Sir Evelyn Wood.

But not on such occasions only has native loyalty been tested. In 1893 and 1894 smallpox broke out in the Colony amongst the native kraals, and vigorous measures of suppression were resorted to. Although the restrictions and obligations imposed were repugnant to native prejudices and ideas they were willingly submitted to, and the pestilence was subdued; simply because the natives had faith in the humanity and wise intentions of their rulers. The plague of locusts then ravaged the country, destroying impartially the crops of white and black alike. Again the natives acquiesced without a murmur in the measures devised to combat the pest, and co-operated to the very utmost of their ability in whatever duties were required of them for the extirpation of the common plague. But a yet sorer strain upon their patience and submission was imposed by rinderpest. To the Zulu his cattle are his most cherished possession. They share with his wives and women the most ardent cravings of his nature. Every one of them is the fond object of his daily thoughts and observation. They represent to him riches, property, and preoccupation. As the dread murrain swept slowly but relentlessly southward its possible effects upon the native mind added greatly to the disquietude of local administrators. How the natives would act under the wholesale destruction of their stock was a most alarming factor in the prospect. In efforts to keep out the invader the most stringent measures had to be resorted to. Cattle in infected districts had to be destroyed without pity or exception. All the steps taken were futile. The plague pursued the ruthless tenor of its way. Natal and Zululand, like the neighbouring territories, were devastated. The herds of both white and black were mown down like grass under the scythe. Yet through it all the natives of both Natal and Zululand maintained an attitude of uncomplaining calm. They submitted to their losses with stoical equanimity. No protest against their white rulers passed their lips. They knew how strenuously those rulers had striven, first to repel, and then to battle with the plague; they knew that they suffered in common with every white stockholder, and they prepared, as their neighbours did, to repair their losses and to cope with misfortune.

And now the fiery ordeal of war has once again tried the temper and proved the genuineness of native loyalty. The splendid behaviour and self-restraint of the vast native population of South Africa during the present struggle must have been a revelation to the world of what British rule has been in and to South Africa to the coloured races within its influence. How anxiously the representatives of the Empire have awaited possibilities

only they can say. Not that they can have had any
doubt as to the side upon which native sympathies
would be cast. No student of South African affairs can
have been in doubt on that point. The natives know
by too long and too bitter experience what they might
expect were the Boer to become the dominant power,
and were the restraining hand and example of Great
Britain to be withdrawn from the scene. Anxiety concerning the natives during this crisis has been twofold:
(1) as regards the possible effect of complete or continual Boer successes upon the native mind, and (2) as
regards the ability of the British authorities to hold
back the natives from joining in the fray. That the
natives everywhere have longed to take part in the war
against their ancient enemy—to pay off old scores, and
to assist in his humiliation—has never been doubted.
At all points they have been straining in the leash. In
Natal they have yearned to be led into the field, to do
something to help in the war. In the upper districts
they have seen the Colony invaded by the enemy, its
northern towns abandoned or besieged, and colonial
authority superseded by that of the republics. Boer
forces have roamed through some of their locations, and
their crops, their herds, and their flocks have—to an
extent that is yet unknown—been at the mercy of the
invader. They have witnessed the victorious march of a
great Boer commando through country occupied by British
settlers, and the looting of the property of those settlers
by the raiders. They have seen a large British force

X

shut up for four months in Ladismith, and yet larger British forces vainly striving to fight their way to its relief through Boer intrenchments on the Tugela. They themselves before the war broke out were coaxed to join the Boers in their struggle for supremacy. Yet in spite of all they have never wavered in their allegiance nor have doubted the certainty of British victory in the end. Whenever an opportunity has occurred they have voluntarily given expression to their sympathy with the power that rules them. On two occasions chiefs have sent contributions of coin to the relief funds, saying that though they are debarred from fighting for the Queen as they fain would fight, they want to show in some other way their sympathy for her brave soldiers.

What has happened in Natal and Zululand—where for many years the natives have been governed by colonial ministers—has happened in Pondoland, in Kafirland, in Basutoland, and partially in Swaziland. British influence has been strong enough to curb the passionate longings of the natives to help in the conflict with the Boer, and to confine that conflict to a struggle between white men only. Whatever the vicissitudes of the war may have been, British men will be able to look back upon them with perfect clearness of conscience in so far as the action of their Government and countrymen on this point is concerned. Had the latter chosen to let loose the native-born dogs of war upon their foes the horrors of the campaign would have shocked mankind, but no such outrage upon humanity has at any moment been possible. And the Boers have to thank the operation of the much-despised policy of the Anglo-Saxon for their salvation from such a calamity.

I cannot more fitly close this chapter than by citing the impartial testimony voluntarily borne by the oldest missionary body in the country to the character of colonial rule over the native population. The American Zulu Mission of Natal had its representatives there before the British Government had actually taken possession For sixty years it has worked quietly but zealously, and at all times its relations with the Government and the colonists have been amicable and harmonious. In February last, its missionaries felt impelled to express their "sympathy with the suffering Colony," and they did so in generous and touching words: "We have been identified with the Colony since its foundation, and have shared, together with the colonists, its vicissitudes. But there has been no time like the present. A hostile army is firmly intrenched within its borders, fathers and sons are giving their lives in its defence, a multitude of homes are filled with anxiety, and some with anguish; a fair town is closely beleaguered, thousands of refugees are homeless among us, sad reverses have deferred hope, though they have stimulated determination. . . . Our missionaries from first to last have experienced great kindness from Government and people. . . . We are not a political body, and are bound to avoid political entanglements, but it is only just that as a Missionary Society, which has had the interests

of the native races at heart for so many years, we
should bear testimony to the truth we believe at such a
judgment-forming crisis We believe that, as far as the
great work in our hands is concerned—the enlighten-
ment and development of the native races—the British
are incomparably more humane and enlightened in
their native policy than any other political Power in
South Africa The task is a vast and difficult one for
any Government For to elect and perfect a policy
which shall be far-seeing, firm, and just for an overwhelming mass of people but one remove from savagery,
is sufficient to tax the statesmanship of the world. We
desire to declare here and over the sea, without prejudice to the neutrality of the American nation to
which we belong, without flattery or political bias, our
appreciation of the administration of law and order on
behalf of the black races under the ægis of freedom-
loving Britain."

Such is the tribute paid by the ministers and citizens
of the great Republic, to the work done by Great Britain
and her colonists amongst the native races of South
Africa—after the Government of the Colony, and the
administration of native affairs, had been for more than
six years in the hands of the settlers. The system of
Government has changed, but the principles laid down
by the statesmen who founded the Colony are as faithfully observed under the rule of the colonists as they
were under the rule of the Crown.

CHAPTER XI

THE WAR—ITS GENESIS AND ITS REVELATIONS

Speaking at the South African Dinner in London on the 18th of May last year, I used these words: "The three cardinal conditions upon which our hopes of peaceful development in South Africa appear to rest are those embodied in the time-honoured trinity—'Liberty, Equality, and Fraternity.' Freedom as self-governing communities under the British flag; equal rights of citizenship to all civilised men, brotherhood of feeling and action between States and races. Given these, and I see no reason why peace and progress should not go hand in hand in South Africa throughout a long and happy future." That was, I believe, the general conviction of all fair-minded colonists at the time. The aspirations thus expressed were in strict conformity with Sir Alfred Milner's demands and the Uitlanders' requirements. It seemed to me then, speaking after an absence from South Africa of more than two years, that they were capable of realisation. When asked in England last year as to the probabilities of war, I replied that, as far as I could see in the light of such information as I had, there was no warrant for a belief that war was inevitable, that there was nothing in the situation to justify despair of a peaceful issue. If the legitimate demands of the Imperial Government for the redress of Uitlander grievances were firmly but temperately pressed—as they were—I believed that President Kruger and his advisers would in the end comply with them.

I thought then, however, that the real question at issue was much less the concession of this or that privilege to the Uitlander than the supremacy of Great Britain as the paramount power in South Africa. The suzerainty rather than the franchise was the actual bone of contention. The course of diplomacy had clothed the grievances of British subjects in the Transvaal with an importance which properly pertained to a matter of far graver moment.

When a few weeks later I arrived in South Africa, it became evident that the controversy had narrowed and simplified. The Bloemfontein Conference had ended without result so far as its ostensible objects were concerned, but with a very definite result in another direction—namely, the disclosure of President Kruger's fixed resolve to be satisfied with nothing short of full independence " as an international sovereign state." Out of the mist of discussion, with its evasions, equivocations, and quibblings, that resolve stood revealed, and to that extent the Conference was by no means abortive.

Everything that happened subsequently, all that I heard and read, made more and more manifest the fact that British supremacy was the one thing hanging in the balance. Conversations with leading men on both sides deepened the conviction that the struggle was a contest for existence between Boerdom and the Empire, between British paramountcy or Republican domination. Even then, however, a doubt prevailed whether, in the last resort, when England's readiness to hold her own at any cost was clearly demonstrated and seen, President Kruger might not yield—at any rate to such a point as to make it difficult for the Empire to demand further guarantees. I had not been back in Natal a week before it became indubitable that nothing short of disarmament would suffice to secure the peace of South Africa, and to assert the supremacy of Great Britain. Mere paper promises or engagements would be worthless as safeguards or conditions as long as every Boer, old and young, was armed with a Mauser rifle and equipped with unlimited ammunition, as long as splendidly built forts, bristling with modern guns, frowned over Pretoria and Johannesburg, as long as trained bands of foreign and home-bred artillerymen stood ready to uphold Boer pretensions and exercise Boer domination. Even then, none of us had any adequate conception of what the Boer preparations and armaments consisted. How misled Imperial authorities were on that point imminent events were soon to reveal.

Englishmen are naturally optimistic where their own resources and capabilities are involved. Great Britain has been so long the dominant power in South Africa that it was hard to realise any serious menace to her

position Up to the issue of the Boer ultimatum no
apprehension of immediate danger was indicated anywhere. Whatever anxieties may have been felt by either
the Colonial or the Imperial Government were not
suffered to appear. That as early as May the Natal
Government had had reason to be "nervous" the Blue-
Book has told us, but their contentment with the
slender promise against attack made by the Imperial
authorities shows clearly enough how completely they,
like the rest of South Africa, failed to grasp the magnitude of the peril that threatened both the colonies and
the Empire.

At that time an addition of 2000 men to the Imperial
garrison in Natal was deemed sufficient by the local
authorities; while the despatch of an army corps, of say
35,000 men, was regarded in London as ample to meet
any emergency that might arise, or as an effective
demonstration of British supremacy.

These facts may surely be accepted as conclusive evidence that war was not regarded as a probable or an imminent contingency either in the mother country or the
colonies. Nor would war have broken out had President
Kruger and his Government chosen to recognise the
suzerainty of the Queen, and to deal honestly and fairly
with the Uitlanders. But they had other ends in view.
They did not at heart desire a peaceful solution of pending difficulties. They might have been content with
peace for a time, had England submitted to their pretensions and abated or abandoned her demands. But

it would have been only for a time. They were ready for war, they had prepared for war, and they were only awaiting their opportunity to try conclusions with the power they hoped to oust.

It would take volumes to describe at length the causes which led to a state of things so feebly realised on the spot by those most competent to grasp the situation. Other writers have ably undertaken this task, and there is no occasion to traverse the ground they have so usefully occupied. My purpose here is simply to set forth as succinctly as I can the incidents and the influences that seem to me to have brought about the present conflict. The experience of fifty years as a colonist, thirty-seven of which have been spent in public life, emboldens me to add these impressions to the common testimony.

The war, I submit, has its roots in the following causes :—

1. Boer dislike to and distrust of the Englishman.
2. Hollander influence.
3. The workings of the Africander Bond.
4. Boer delusions after Majuba.
5. The fruits of gold discovery.
6. The Jameson Raid.

I

Boer relations towards the English are not easily defined. They are mixed and not uniform. Collectively they are distrustful if not hostile. Individually

they are very much the product of immediate circumstances.   The Boers never forget that the Cape Colony,
from which they all spring, was a conquered country.
Their fathers were its first settlers.   The British followed   They forget that the conquest of the Cape of
Good Hope was subsequently acquiesced in by the
Government of Holland, and that England paid handsomely for whatever rights she acquired there.   In the
earlier years of British rule, administrative methods
were not as amiable as they became later on   The
hand of Government was felt.   British legislation was
not in harmony with the settlers' interests or with
Batavian methods.   The Dutch regarded all coloured
races as inferior people, as hewers of wood and drawers
of water.   Slavery was an established institution.   When
it was abolished they were wholly dissatisfied with
the compensation awarded to them.   They were still
more offended by the treatment of native affairs.   The
vacillations of Imperial policy puzzled and provoked
them.   Their own processes of dealing with the natives
were sharp, summary, and decisive.   British processes
were variable, indulgent, and to them incomprehensible.
The ways of philanthropy in their eyes were ways of
folly and madness, tending to disaster and destruction.
The black man was the natural enemy of the white
man, and must be ruled with a stern hand.   He was
the marauder of cattle and the despoiler of homes, and
life with him was only possible so long as he was kept
in a subject and servile condition.   The Bible told

them that God had given His people the heathen for their inheritance and the outermost parts of the earth for their possession. Then, as now, the Old Testament was the citadel of the Boer's faith in his own destiny and in his own exclusive rights. The attacks made by missionaries and emissaries of Exeter Hall upon the colonial treatment of the natives, embellished as they were by many calumnious exaggerations, and unjust as they were in their undiscriminating censures, embittered the minds of the settlers and intensified their discontent with existing conditions.

The famous and deplorable incident of "Slagter's Nek," revived by President Steyn and Mr. Reitz in their inflammatory manifestoes, arose out of the insolent refusal of a Dutch colonist to allow of any interference on the part of Justice between him and his Hottentot servants. "He told the Field-Cornet that he set at defiance both himself and the magistrate, and falling upon Booy," the Hottentot, "gave him a severe beating, and bade him go and tell the authorities that he would treat them, including the Governor, in the same manner if they should dare to come upon his ground to claim the property of a Hottentot." I refer to this story—which has been industriously served up, after the lapse of eighty-four years, in a wholly misleading and distorted form, in order to excite Africander passions—as an indication of the feeling which more and more estranged the Boer colonist from his British rulers and neighbours. Where the natives were concerned their two

points of view were irreconcilable. The Boer could not
brook the thought of any equality of law for the two
races. Estrangement and separation were the natural
outgrowth of so complete a variance of thought and
practice.

The impulses and cravings which led the Boers to
migrate beyond the Orange River have never ceased to
operate as a cause of cleavage. Though Great Britain
cannot be said at any time to have foregone her claim
to political supremacy in South Africa, she did distinctly, by solemn covenant, hand over to the settlers
of the Orange Free State and the Transvaal the right
to manage their own affairs. She thereby encouraged
them to aspire to a measure of independence which,
had her statesmen cared to think about it, was certain
sooner or later to be in conflict with her own claims to
sovereignty. Though the Convention of 1854, which
declared the inhabitants of the Free State to be "to all
intents and purposes a free and independent people,
and their Government to be treated and considered
thenceforth a free and independent Government," was
never formally confirmed and ratified by the special
instrument provided for, and though, therefore, they
have never been legally freed "from their allegiance to
the British Crown," the general spirit of the Convention
has been observed in so far as the internal administration of the country is concerned. And as events have
proved, the Boers themselves have construed all the
Conventions entered into with them in a spirit of com-

prehensiveness far in excess of the scope contemplated by Imperial statesmen   In other words, the existence of the two republics and the attitude of the British Government towards those communities have fostered the idea of republican independence in the Boer mind throughout South Africa, and have kept constantly under the eye of the Boer the embodiment of a political ideal in which Dutch influence, Dutch language, and Dutch modes of thought are dominating factors The necessary result has been the establishment of two opposing interests in South Africa—the British and colonial on one side, and the Dutch Africander and republican on the other That the sympathies of the Dutch-speaking settlers everywhere should gravitate to the latter was inevitable, and as the two are in a sense antagonistic, the natural effect has been the nourishment and spread of an anti-British spirit on the part of the Dutch population The republics became identified with *land en volk*, with country and race; Great Britain and her colonies were regarded as alien and usurpatory. Dutch Africanders forgot that the republics owed every jot of their freedom to the generosity of Great Britain, and that in the colonies they enjoyed perfect equality of right and privilege with their fellow-citizens of British descent   They only remembered that in the republics the Dutch were the dominant and ruling race, and that in the colonies the Queen of England was the sovereign power.

This feeling of prejudice or antipathy has been

fostered by home influences The Boer is essentially a
domestic being Living on isolated farms, he sees little
of other men, least of all of men of other races. His
women are more bitter in their race prejudices, as a
rule, than he is himself. His mother teaches him in
childhood to distrust and dislike the *roomek* His mind
is stored in infancy with the grim legends of the past.
He has little chance of knowing better or of learning
the truth. Much might be said, moreover, concerning
the hostile influence exercised by the Predikants, or
ministers of the Dutch Reformed Church, in this
respect. The Dutch parson is even a more powerful
personality in Boer households than are the Roman
priest or the Scottish minister in their own spheres.
There are no doubt exceptions, but as a rule it is
to be feared that the Predikant has been the most
active propagandist of anti-English prejudice or feeling
throughout recent years.

It may frankly be conceded that events have co-operated to strengthen these antipathies The absence of
fixity of purpose—of clearly defined and firmly pursued
principle—that has so notoriously marked Imperial
policy in the past has conduced to, if it has not absolutely created and justified, distrust and suspicion. Had
England from the first held on unflinchingly to her
great cause and mission there would have been no war
to-day. Had she been as resolute in holding the states
of the interior as she was, most fortunately, in clinging
to Natal, South Africa would years ago have been a

great dominion. She has had splendid representatives in South Africa, who have clearly perceived the outlines of Imperial duty, and who (each in his time) have not shrunk from indicating and urging them, but their voices have passed unheeded. Sir Benjamin Durban, Sir George Napier, Sir George Grey, and Sir Bartle Frere all saw the truth and boldly proclaimed it, but their appeals fell on deaf ears, their warnings were ignored, and their policy discredited. Had the Orange River sovereignty not been abandoned; had the Boers in the Transvaal, like the Boers in Natal, been kept under the firm restraints of British sovereignty; had South Africa been treated as India has been, with reference to the large interests of the future rather than in deference to the changing caprices of party expediency for the moment, history at the end of the century would have presented a very different retrospect. England, in the eyes of her Boer subjects, would then indeed have seemed the "Grave Mother of majestic works," not the fickle power blown about by the winds of transient impulse—of party warfare—snatching one year what she surrenders another, and drifting, under the direction of no settled policy, towards unseen and unshaped consequences.

It must not be supposed, however, that Dutch and English are incapable of harmonious admixture in the ordinary affairs of life. Under normal circumstances they get on well enough together. Rooted as they are deep down in very much the same soil of origin and race, there is no congenital antagonism between them. Both have more or less the same standards of thought as regards domestic life, religion, love of freedom, and attachment to home. They often intermarry, and they intermingle amicably enough in many relationships. The younger Dutch Africanders—and especially those who have been at school—speak English, and associate with their contemporaries of British birth on the friendliest footing. They compete with each other in class, in sports, and in business or duty. The differences which divide them are more artificial and political than physical or racial. Could the past be wiped away, and all start afresh in an atmosphere of perfect equality, with a common rallying centre of national regard, there is no apparent reason why the amity that prevails amongst the people of Great Britain, or Switzerland, or the United States, or Canada, should not also prevail amongst the white population of South Africa.

One of the chief instruments of social cleavage, in the Transvaal more especially, has been the question of language. Every effort has been made by the dominant clique at Pretoria to proscribe the use of English, and to prevent or to attenuate the teaching of it in the public schools. I believe that in the Free State a more enlightened policy has been pursued, owing perhaps to the fact that the head of the Education Department for many years was a gentleman of Scottish origin. The strenuous efforts made in the sister republic to stamp out English as a medium of instruction, however futile in the end, have necessarily encouraged a prejudice against the language in the mind of the younger generation, and to a certain extent thwarted the expansion of English culture, thought, and ideas. That the localised patois, or *taal*, which passes current for Dutch throughout South Africa will speedily disappear is by no means probable, no matter what shape the future government may take. Its homely and not inexpressive idioms impregnate the daily speech of that large class of coloured and half-coloured people, who may be said to form the "common folk" of the Cape Colony and the republics. They suit the conditions and requirements of those people far better than do more cultivated but less complex English forms of speech The older Boer, moreover, is passionately fond of his own tongue, no matter what its derivative perplexities may be, and in his own household and sphere he will continue to use it. But that English will prevail in South Africa, as it has elsewhere in all parts of the Empire, as the language of culture, of trade, of journalism, and of social usage, cannot be doubted, provided that it be freed from the fetters that have hitherto hampered it in the Transvaal The mere pressure of circumstances and of daily convenience will secure for it legitimate and unchallenged supremacy And in the general use of a common tongue the younger people of both races will find an effective bond of union.

Y

II

Hollander influence has of late years been a plant of rapid, if forced, growth, but its roots may be found deeply planted in the past.   Though in 1620 two commanders of British Indiamen took possession of Saldanha Bay in the name of Great Britain, no settlement was established there, and it practically fell to the lot of Holland to form the first European Colony on South African soil.   In 1652 Van Riebeek, so we are told by the official record, "duly commissioned by the Chamber of Seventeen" at Amsterdam, landed at Table Bay, accompanied by 100 persons, and took possession of what is now the site of Capetown on behalf of the Dutch East India Company.   Although the "burghers" of the infant Colony strove to escape from the arbitrary rule of that body by migrating into the interior, the Company followed these earlier " Voertrekkers " up, just as the British Government followed up their successors in later days, and maintained an effective administration over the country, until it was captured for the second time by a British force in 1806, and finally ceded in perpetuity to the British Crown, by the Powers of Europe, under the Peace of Amiens in 1814.   Nor should it be forgotten just now, that Great Britain not only holds South Africa by right of conquest, and by the solemnly expressed consent of Europe, but that she also paid not less a sum than six millions to Holland for the rights acquired by her.

For a century and a half therefore, roundly stated, Holland was regarded as the parent state of the Cape Colony. It is not strange that this fact has never been forgotten on both sides of the ocean. It helps to explain the attitude which Holland has always maintained towards the Dutch-speaking Africanders, and they have preserved towards that country. Though the Napoleonic wars left the Low Countries shorn and dwarfed, the old settlers beyond the sea were hardly conscious of the fact, and continued to look towards the little kingdom by the North Sea, not only as the home of their progenitors, but as an active and potential factor in the affairs of the world. When, therefore, the Voertrekkers were endeavouring to establish an independent republic at Natal, they eagerly turned to Holland for help and encouragement in the furtherance of their designs. What happened at that time (in 1842) is so well set forth by Judge Cloete (himself a Dutchman) in his admirable lectures, that I make no apology for introducing the narrative here :—

"There is no doubt that in this case the hostile attitude assumed by the emigrant farmers left the Governor of the Cape no alternative but either to admit or deny their independence, and the measure of sending a military force became the only one calculated to put that question at once to the test; but perhaps the result of that movement might have been quite different had it not been for an incident in the history of this district, which exerted an overwhelming influence on the minds of the inhabitants generally and of the members of the Volksraad in particular. The very next month after their solemn protest had been transmitted to Sir George Napier, a Dutch vessel, called the *Brazilia*, anchored in the Port of Natal, and the supercargo, Mr. Smellekamp, who afterwards resided in the Orange Free State (as it is now called), informed the emigrant farmers upon his first arrival that a number of merchants in Holland had taken a deep interest in their affairs, and had despatched this vessel for the express purpose of opening a direct trade with their country, and supplying them with 'notions' of Dutch produce and manufacture; this arrival, and the display of the Dutch flag, aroused in all the emigrant farmers the most extravagant affection for the country and people to which most of them traced their descent. Mr. Smellekamp was received at this place with triumphal honours; public dinners were given him; the Dutch flag became the ensign of the new republic, and Mr Smellekamp, led away by the enthusiasm with which his arrival had been greeted, gave the inhabitants of Natal the most exaggerated ideas of the power and influence of Holland in the council of nations; moreover, assuring them of the sympathy and support of the King of Holland, and finally entered into a formal treaty with the Volksraad, assuring them of the 'protection' of Holland, to which he affixed his signature in these terms :—

" 'Accepted in the name of the King of the Netherlands, subject to his Majesty's formal approval' !

"He further gave them the strongest assurances that they would soon be provided with ministers and schoolmasters for the improvment of their moral condition, and with arms and ammunition to repel any hostile attack with which they might be threatened.

" I cannot give a more striking illustration of the manner

in which the Volksraad were misled on that occasion, as to the support they expected from the King of Holland, than by relating the following anecdote. Some days after my arrival here in June 1843, I had an interview with several leading members of the Volksraad, in the course of which I happened to allude to some political measures going on in Europe, and to state that such a measure was under the consideration of the five great powers, whereupon I was at once asked by the spokesman, which were these five great powers to which I had alluded? I replied that those powers were England, France, Russia, Austria, and Prussia. The querist at once exclaimed, 'And is Holland not one of them?' This compelled me to enter at some length into the modern history of Europe, and to explain to them how Holland had, since the year 1830, by the rebellion and subsequent formation of Belgium into a separate kingdom, dwindled into a third-rate power of Europe, when the spokesman significantly and bitterly replied, 'We were never told that before, but the very reverse!'

"The emigrant farmers were, however, so fully convinced at the time that they had now obtained the countenance of a first-rate European power in support of their independence, that Mr. Smellekamp had all his travelling expenses paid to enable him to return to Holland direct (as the *Brazilia* was destined for a lengthened cruise to the eastward); and he was, moreover, made the bearer of a number of official and other letters to the Ministers of State of his Majesty the King of Holland, and to many influential persons in that country, claiming the interposition of those persons in support of the independence of Natal; this was the state of feeling which prevailed among all classes and both sexes of the community here, when arrangements were at length completed to enable Captain Smith to break up from the Umgazi camp, and to pursue his course overland to Natal."

The astute and subtle Mr Smellekamp was the natural antetype and forerunner of other countrymen of his who, thirty years later, began to find in the republics a favourable field for political exploitation I may say at once that I find no fault with these gentlemen, either for the conception of their schemes or for their activity in prosecuting them. They were under no allegiance or obligations to Great Britain. They found in the republics two States whose rulers and people—at that time—were mostly the descendants of old Dutch-speaking colonists whose "independence" had been voluntarily conceded by the British Crown They saw in these facts an opportunity for the extension of Dutch influence and for the building up, on the basis of Dutch dominancy, of a new power in whose development vanished dreams of Batavian greatness might have glorious realisation Though her East Indian possessions in Java and Sumatra had brought Holland wealth and trade, they had not proved the birthplace of a great and populous Dutch community in whose territorial magnitude and importance the Dutch race might find compensation for, and security against, all the political mischances of European politics. Though the Netherlands might disappear as a sovereign power from the map of Europe, a great Dutch-speaking Republic of South Africa might perpetuate the name and race and tongue of the fatherland in the southern world.

I do not say that these ambitions did actually stir

and sway the emissaries or emigrants from Holland who began about thirty years ago to play an active part in the affairs of the republics. No printed evidence of the fact is before me. I only desire to point out that all the drift of events points in that direction, and to say that from a Dutch point of view such aspirations were neither wrong nor outrageous, so long as the two republics remained independent, and so long as the pursuit of these designs did not menace the peace of South Africa or the supremacy of Great Britain.

It is highly probable that at first our friends from Holland did not contemplate any more formidable undertaking than the nourishment and consolidation of the Dutch language and of Dutch influence in the republics. Their first object was to control as far as possible the Dutch press and the schools in both States. The *Express* in Bloemfontein and the *Volksstem* in Pretoria have at no time made any attempt to veil their hostility to England and the English. So long as President Brand held the reins in the Free State there was little to fear in the way of active interference in school control, or indeed of any serious outgrowth of anti-British action or feeling in local administration. He was no friend to the intrusion of the Hollander, nor did he at any time during his long and honourable career say anything or do anything to justify an impression that he was hostile to the primacy of the Crown. He was a Cape Africander of the best type. Son of the first Speaker of the Cape House of Assembly, and for a short time a member of that body, he ever regarded with a filial eye the great Colony of his birth, and though his loyalty to the new State could never be impugned, he always recognised the claims of seniority and parentage. His political Mecca, if he had one, was centred in Cape Town rather than in Amsterdam. Conciliation and unity — not estrangement and division — were the ends of his action. Though he was largely instrumental in bringing about the retrocession of the Transvaal after Majuba, it is very doubtful whether he would have lent his powerful influence in that direction could he have foreseen the use to which his neighbours twenty years later would have put their liberty.

President Brand's successor was a man of wholly different calibre and tendency. As Chief-Justice of the Free State he had already disclosed his aspirations, but they can best be dealt with in the next section. With Mr. Reitz's advent to power the way was, relatively speaking, free to the propagation of Dutch-Africander republicanism and the cult of Holland. Leading Hollanders at Bloemfontein and Pretoria had an open field for their operations. Fomenting repugnance to English rule, English speech, English institutions, and English interests generally, they naturally fostered a corresponding preference for republican independence and for the Dutch language, Dutch ascendency, and Dutch associations. They and their co-workers in the press, in the pulpit, and in the school or class, found it an easy matter to inflame and to deepen prejudices already implanted, and to convert into an article of household faith the conviction that England and Englishmen were implacably antagonistic to the Boer.

In 1880, when recording his impressions of Dutch loyalty in the Cape Colony, Sir Bartle Frere wrote "Dutch disaffection of a dangerous kind is confined to a small clique of Hollanders and colonial Dutch republicans who have little influence except through a temporary alliance with English humanitarians and Radicals now in Opposition."

This was said a year before Sir George Colley's ill-fated expedition, whose results entirely changed the political outlook in South Africa. Hollander influence thenceforward became aggressive, audacious, and unresting. It openly identified itself with the cause of republicanism. After the conclusion of the London Convention of 1884 President Kruger and his colleagues visited Holland and Germany, and sought to establish there the relations which he has never ceased to cultivate. In Holland he was welcomed as the visible embodiment of Dutch republicanism in South Africa. Latent enthusiasms and ideas were revived by his presence. It was then that he enlisted the services as State Attorney of the young law-student Dr. Leyds, of all Hollanders in South Africa England's most strenuous and mischievous foe. It may be doubted whether he forecast, when starting for South Africa, the part he was destined to play. It is probable that it grew with

opportunity, for Dr. Leyds knows well how to take
occasion by the hand, and bend it to his will. I have
referred elsewhere to the charm of his personality, a
quality that has presumably contributed to his success.
He would have been less dangerous had he been less
attractive and insidious. Two men more unlike each
other in manner or aspect than he and his rugged old
chief could hardly be conceived, but both are probably
united by certain affinities of character and tempera-
ment—subtlety, reserve, silence, impassivity—as well as
by their pertinacity in pursuit of a common end, and
their copartnery in the tortuous policy of the past.

Before Dr. Leyds's arrival at Pretoria a considerable
infusion of Hollander influence had already taken place,
in the form of young Africanders who had been educated at Leyden or elsewhere, or of young Hollanders
attracted to the land of promise. As years went on
the stream rapidly increased in volume. The Bench
was recruited by young Dutch advocates who blossomed
into judges as soon as they had left their studies.
Public offices were filled by candidates from Holland.
The control of the State schools fell into the hands of
a youngish Dutch graduate, who made no secret of his
desire to obstruct, as far as he could with decency do
so, the teaching of English in all State-aided institutions.

A yet more effective agency for extending and establishing the influence of Holland was presented by the
Netherlands Railway Company, established under the

auspices of the State, and practically endowed with a monopoly of railway construction and administration. The history and vicissitudes of this great corporation would fill a volume ; indeed it does so already, in the shape of one of the handsomest tomes ever issued by the Dutch press.   I only name it here, however, in order to point out how powerfully it has operated to promote the ascendency of Holland in the Republic. Its officials, numbering many hundreds, were mostly im- ported from Holland, and, wherever the railway runs, there they were, each a propagandist in his way of Dutch, as opposed to English, influence.   It is only right to add, however, that in the working of the joint systems our railway authorities in Natal have always found it possible to work with the representatives of the Netherlands Company in perfect good faith and goodwill.   Mr. Middleburg, the late director of that company's operations, under whom the Natal junction was carried out, and now living in retirement in Holland, is always referred to by his colonial coadjutors in terms of almost affectionate appreciation.

Though I think that Hollander influence has been pernicious in so far as it has led President Kruger and his associates to pursue a policy of blind hostility to British interests and British supremacy, it has, never- theless, from the Dutch point of view, been inspired by a certain type of patriotism.   Hollanders had been led by the drift of events to regard the Transvaal as a Dutch preserve, where many good things awaited the astute

exploiter, and where circumstances had secured the
preference to their race. If the burghers were the
chosen people as regards the land and its government,
the Hollanders were their natural allies in the apportion-
ment of the gifts of both England had again and
again, and yet again, allowed these territories and the
opportunities pertaining to their possession to slip from
her grasp. She could not fairly, therefore, find fault
with the old inhabitants for making the most of their
chances, or with their fellow-Dutchmen from Holland
for joining in the same effort.

The Hollander began his career in the republics by
making himself useful, he continued it by making
himself necessary: he crowned it all by making himself an integral element in the social structure of the
communities He knew that, with the advent of the
Uitlander to political power, his value as a factor in
affairs would diminish, and his predominance would
soon pass away The downfall of monopolies and concessions would mean his downfall. When his influence
came to be shared on equal terms by others, its poten-
tiality would decline, and its effects would disappear.
He played a high game, and he played it with all his
might

III

The workings of the Africander Bond have been
often described and denounced, but their real scope
and significance are only now being fully understood.

Though its operations have been marked by mystery, as they have been fruitful in untold mischief, it cannot be said that the Bond was either conceived, or born or developed in secret. Its objects were openly proclaimed to the world in the columns of the Dutch press, but somehow they failed to seize hold of the imagination, or to arouse the active anxieties of the loyal colonists. At the time of its birth British patriotism in South Africa was still stricken by the collapse which followed Majuba. Loyalists of all classes were smarting under a sense of desertion. They knew not what further surprise of Imperial policy might be in store for them. The recall and humiliation of Sir Bartle Frere, the retrocession of the Transvaal; the apparent desire to scuttle out of Imperial responsibilities, the favour shown to Boerdom, the obloquy heaped on the colonists after the Zulu war—all tended to depression and hopelessness. The wild and seditious shriekings of the republican press passed unheeded by people who felt that the ears of England's statesmen were deaf alike to protest and appeal.

The Bond was the direct offspring of the Boer war. For some time it was regarded by the British colonists as little more than an endeavour to promote and consolidate the interests of the Dutch farmers as distinguished from those of colonial townsmen and British citizens. We are indebted to the Grahamstown *Journal* for the publication, in suitable form, of a translation of a Dutch pamphlet, issued in 1882, entitled " *De Trans-*

vaalse Oorlog" (The Transvaal War). This pamphlet consisted of a series of leading articles culled from *De Patriot*, at that time the recognised organ of the Bond. This newspaper was, and is still, issued at the Paarl, near Capetown, and has at all times been regarded as an organ of distinctively Dutch sentiment. That its seditious utterances should have passed at the time, unnoticed and untranslated, can only be explained, as I have said, by the sense of despair that had settled down upon all colonial loyalists.

There is no occasion to go further than the limits of this pamphlet for a full comprehension of the real objects and operations of the Bond. The aims set forth in these pages, without any pretence at disguise or concealment, have been faithfully and steadfastly pursued from that day to this, and the results have been witnessed by a staggered world.

One merit at any rate must be conceded to the Boer propagandists,—that of consistency and persistency. What they said in 1881 they say in 1899 and 1900. The *Patriot's* adjurations are almost identical with the fulminations of Presidents Kruger and Steyn, of Messrs. Reitz and Viljoen nineteen years later. The *Patriot* started with a pious ascription of praise to God for the deliverance and victory of their brethren. "God's hand has been visible in the history of our people as it never has been since the days of Israel." Might could not prevail against Right. England had thieved and murdered. God, not England, was almighty.

England had been repeatedly humbled and beaten. "The little respect which an Africander still had for British troops and cannon is utterly done away." The Transvaalers had now got what they wanted, the restoration of the South African Republic. " England must now keep her claws off from the Transvaal long enough for us Africanders to recover strength a little and pull things to rights." Africanders, and especially the young ones, had come to hate England and the English language. English sovereignty over South Africa had gone back at least half a century. Africanders had seen that they could govern themselves in war as well as peace, they had revealed a feeling of nationality, they had discovered able generals, "Piet and Franz Joubert, Cronje and Smit, Henning Pretorius and Greyling."

The *Patriot* then proceeded to invoke a practical issue from all these disclosures and sentiments, and to urge the establishment of a Bond. I learn from other sources that it had been deemed desirable that this movement should have its chief birthplace on republican soil, and to the Bloemfontein *Express*, therefore, belongs the distinction of having first put forward the concrete embodiment of Boer aspirations in the form of a Draft Constitution, which was substantially adopted by the leaders of the party, and has been acted upon ever since. At that time the Chief-Justice of the Free State was Mr. Reitz, afterwards its President, and now State Secretary of the Transvaal. He never made any

secret of his cherished objective, which was a united
South Africa, governed on republican principles, under
the naval protection of Great Britain. The Empire was
to be absolved from all responsibility for control or
sovereignty on land, but was to be graciously permitted
to guard the South African seaboard from foreign invasion. That was the ideal of Mr. Reitz in the eighties.
Since then he appears to have lifted his aspirations to
the yet higher level of complete "international sovereignty," and therefore, I presume, he proposes to dispense altogether with Imperial protection, even on the
seaboard.

The constitution of the Bond as thus defined by its
Boer-Hollander authors at Bloemfontein can best be set
forth in their own words —

"The Bond knows no nationality whatever other than
simply that of Africanders, regarding as such all from whatever origin who promise, under the limits of this Constitution,
to work for the good and welfare of South Africa.

"The object of the Africander Bond is the establishment of
a South African Nationality through the cultivation of a true
love of this our fatherland.

"This object must be attained both by the promotion and
defence of the national language (*Volkstaal*), and by Africanders both politically and socially making their power to be
felt as a nation.

"*Politically* through the establishment of the Bond in all
States and Colonies of South Africa, and maintaining it by an
organisation which embraces them all, and *Socially* by the
promotion of a worthy and fitting instruction in the spirit of
Article I., and by watching over the Press,"

The organisation thus provided for was minute and far-reaching It consisted of Central, Provincial, District, and Ward bodies, which were to meet yearly, half-yearly, quarterly, or monthly, as the case might be, reporting the one to the other, and all keeping closely within touch The whole country, therefore, was to be covered by a network of Bond workers and organisers The Ward Committees were to circulate books, encourage the subscribing to Bond newspapers, and to promote the establishment of Bond schools The Central Governing Body was to consist of five members—two from the Cape Colony and one each from the Transvaal, Natal, and the Free State. This Junta of Five was to have supreme control of finances and policy, and to prepare an annual report for publication " defining the course of action during the coming years."

A few extracts from the pages which follow will best serve to illustrate the sinister purposes for which the Bond was established —

"The Bond must be our preparation for the future confederation of all the States and Colonies of South Africa. The English Government keeps talking of a Confederation under the British Flag. That will never happen We can assure them of that. We have often said it. There is just one hindrance to Confederation, and that is the English flag. Let them take that away, and within a year the Confederation, under the free Africander flag, would be established.

"Away with the English flag. But so long as the English flag remains here, the Africander Bond must be one Confederation And the British will after a while realise that

Froude's advice is the best for them. They must just have Simon's Bay as a naval and military station on the road to India, and give over all the rest of South Africa to the Africanders.

"Africanders must be on the top 'Let us calculate it is we on top or they on top; they must be under or we under.'"

These words are so pertinent and pithy that I might confidently stop here. They completely account for all that has happened since, for all that is happening now. The struggle for paramountcy was thus openly forecast nineteen years ago by the Boer leaders. It is instructive, however, to glance at the practical methods of action by which it was proposed that the Bond should pursue its crusade. The pamphlet proceeds to classify the English—that is, the enemy—under three heads: the Soakers (or drunkards), the Robbers (or traders), and the Reds (or soldiers). The first of these forces it proposes to ignore. The Boers do not drink, and cannot therefore be harmed by "canteens, hotels, and the contents of broken bottles." The "Robbers," or tradesmen, are more difficult to deal with. They "let the farmers buy and buy till they are half ruined. These robbers buy our produce cheap and sell their English rubbish to us at the dearest rates." And with the proceeds they start English newspapers, establish English schools, and promote English legislation. "These, then, are the most dangerous sort. These are the chief agents towards the Transvaal annexation."

The steps by which the wiles of English storekeepers are to be circumvented are clearly stated :—

"Buy nothing from any Englishman, nor from any Anglicised Africander, nor even from any one who advertises in an English newspaper.

"We must form trading associations with Europe and the United States of America

"It will be easy to establish the desired trade connections. Nor should we be surprised if many Dutch and German firms send out their first consignments at half price, so as to obtain a footing The Amsterdam *Handelsblad* (Journal of Trade) remarks 'The future of England lies in India, and the future of Holland in South Africa. When our capitalists vigorously develop this trade, and, for example, form a syndicate to buy Delagoa Bay from Portugal, then a railway from Capetown to Bloemfontein, Potschefstroom, Pretoria, Delagoa Bay will be a lucrative investment And when in course of time the Dutch language shall universally prevail in South Africa, this most extensive territory will become a North America for Holland, and enable us to balance the Anglo-Saxon race.'"

The Boer stores which were thus to be established "must be Dutch or Africander through and through, not any English. No English signboard, no English advertisements in English newspapers, no English book-keepers."

The establishment of National Banks, with branches in all towns and villages, was a natural corollary of this policy. How far it has been successful the bank returns of South Africa sufficiently reveal. The next advice is more germane to the moment :—

"Let every Africander in this Colony for the sake of security take care that he has a good rifle and box of cartridges,

and that he knows how to use them   But the two republics
must study the matter further.   As independent States they
must think of self-preservation, and two things are wanted—
(1) to make their own ammunition, and (2) to be well supplied
with cannon, and provide a regiment of artillery to work with
them. . . . When once the Transvaal gets its independence
back, the Government of the Republic will have learned from
the recent war a lesson as to what they must do for the
future."

History has told us how faithfully the republics
carried out this part of the Bond programme.   All the
complications and troubles that have occurred in connection with gunpowder and dynamite concessions are
no doubt traceable to the solemn injunction placed on
the republics in 1882 by the founders of the Bond:
make your own ammunition; establish your own gunpowder factory; be independent for your means of
defence "of the favour, friendship, or hostility of the
enemy."   Out of this small seed of advice sprang the
policy which has converted the Transvaal into a huge
arsenal, and has enabled the Boers to struggle for
mastery with the greatest empire of the world.

The closing passages of this luminous pamphlet read
like an anti-climax   After insisting upon the absolute
exclusion of the English language in every relation of
life—in parliament, in law courts, in public offices, in
railway stations, in telegraph departments, in schools,
in churches, in household life, in private correspondence
—the writers proceed to warn their readers against
one class in particular, politely named by them "the

Bluffers," that is, "the English and Anglified school-masters and schoolmistresses who teach our children from early youth." The vehemence with which the innocent tutors and governesses who are—or used to be—freely engaged by Boer farmers for the tuition of their children is so ludicrous in its intensity and malig-nity that it is a revelation in itself. These inoffensive and mostly quite estimable persons are indicted because they teach—

"(a) That the English language is the finest and best, whereas it is only a miscellaneous gib-berish, without proper grammar or dictionary.

"(b) That English history is the most interesting and glorious, whereas it is nothing more than a concatenation of lies and misrepresentations.

"(c) That they must give the chief place to English geography, whereas all England is nothing more than an island in the North Sea.

"(d) That they are educated as soon as they can gabble English, whereas they simply make themselves ridiculous by it in the eyes of every judicious person.

"(e) That English books and periodicals are the finest and best to read, though really they are the greatest mass of nonsense (with some ex-ceptions) that you can find anywhere, and finally in one word

"(f) That it is an honour for every one to ape the

English in everything, and in fact to become
English, whereas it is the greatest shame and
disgrace for any people to belie their own
God-given nationality."

With this "declaration of war against the English
language" the pamphlet closes The Bond leaders
rightly felt that in that language, with its mighty resources of learning, precept, and example, their crusade
had its chief opponent. The fact at once explains the
tenacity with which the Transvaal authorities have
striven to prohibit the use of English as a medium of
public, or official, or formal speech How vain the
effort has been young Transvaalers themselves are
living and daily evidences. President Kruger's own
grandchildren speak as freely and correctly in English
as though to the language born, at any rate that was
the case with regard to two of his granddaughters with
whom as a fellow-passenger I travelled to South Africa
a year ago, and I believe the same may be said of the
younger masculine members of his family. And therein,
let me add, consists one of our strongest hopes for the
future of South Africa under a better dispensation.

The Africander Bond has had a powerful ally in the
Church—in that branch of it which is associated so
closely with the Dutch population. The pamphlet does
not say much on this point, but what it does say is
clear enough· "The Church has hitherto been our
Laing's Nek against the English language. But see

how many Anglified preachers try now in every way
to smuggle into our Church the English language.
Therefore war against the English speech in our Church.
It is the Dutch Reformed Church   What has English
to do with it ? "   Dutch Predikants appear to have
taken this advice to heart, as in later years the ministers
of the Dutch Reformed Church have been the most
active propagators of the national or Africander spirit,
which is little more than avowed hostility to British
rule and British ascendency.   The organisation of the
Bond has naturally lent itself to this influence.   Planted
as they have been in every township or village, in the
districts where Dutchmen most do congregate, with
tentacles that touch every outlying farm or homestead,
the Bond and the Church together have formed an
alliance against which the elements of loyalism have
had no counteracting forces to operate.   An informant
who has seen much of the inner working of the Bond
has described to me the subtle manner in which politics
and religion have combined to further the cause of
Africander republicanism.   Young Men's Debating
Societies connected with the Church have become
nurseries of agitation and anti-English sentiment.
Periodical wapenschaws, or rifle-shootings, have become
training-schools for military organisation—the nuclei of
Boer commandoes.   Even in Natal, where the Bond as
such has not openly flaunted itself, the meetings of the
local Boeren Vereeniging, or farmers' unions, have been
practically allied branches of the same organisation.

It fell to my lot some years ago to attend one of these meetings by invitation, and I was much impressed by the strong religious character which marked the proceedings. Hymns were sung, long extempore prayers delivered; passages of Scripture were read. I might have been present at a Dutch prayer-meeting rather than at a gathering of a semi-political character. There cannot be a doubt that the Bond owes its spread (and the Boers owe much of their success) to the devout if not impassioned earnestness which devotional habit has inspired and cultivated in its adherents. In all ages religious fervour has been the most powerful incentive to action, just as religious differences have been and are the bitterest forms of contention. Could the pastors be enlisted on the side of unity, loyalty, and order, under the British flag, the problem of the future would soon be solved

IV

The years which followed the Retrocession were marked by a rapid development of Africander hostility and Hollander ambition on the one side, and by a fatal shrinkage of Imperial activity on the other. The Bond was born and started on its sinister course Hollanders waxed stronger in numbers and in influence. Other foreign agencies operated at Pretoria. The railway from Delagoa Bay gradually grew into a fact On the east and on the west Boer "filibusters" sought to extend the boundaries of the Transvaal.

President Kruger's vision of an independent seaport took shape and substance. But the British Government sat with folded hands and saw its inheritance slipping from its grasp. Just in time it roused from its torpor, and Sir Charles Warren's expedition in 1884 saved Bechuanaland and the interior to the Empire. Then came the agreement under which England, Germany, France, and Portugal marked out and severally recognised their own spheres of influence in Africa and Madagascar. East of the Transvaal, however, the emissaries of the Republic, and with England's acquiescence, got possession of a large part of Zululand. The wonder is that they did not get the whole.

There still remained the undefined country (still called "No Man's Land" by the Republic) lying between Zululand and Delagoa Bay, and it was therein that President Kruger hoped to secure a footing on the seaboard. He was nearly doing so in 1890 when the High Commissioner, with the concurrence of the Cape Government, offered him a strip of land stretching from Kosi Bay to the Transvaal, with the right to make a harbour and build a railway. How inimical this proposal was to the interests of Natal need hardly be pointed out, but Natal had chosen to stand aloof from the Customs Union, and our Cape friends would not have been sorry to punish the little Colony for its waywardness. The project offered a bait to both sides. The Transvaal would get its own port, but only on one condition, namely, that it joined the Customs Union within three years from the date of the agreement. The Cape would, in that event, secure to itself, as it hoped to do, the greater share of the trade of the Transvaal, and the political copartnery of the fast-growing Republic. President Kruger, however, had no desire nor intention to part with any fraction of his country's independence. He was already bound to Portugal for a term of years by an unexpired treaty. He wished to retain a perfectly free hand to regulate his customs tariff as he liked. Above all he sought for no restraint upon his power to import from Europe whatever munitions of war he might seek to introduce. As a member of the Customs Union he would have been under conditions and obligations that were quite in conflict with his aspirations for independence and sovereignty. Time went on, therefore, and the Convention lapsed by effluxion of time. It was never submitted again. President Kruger lost his access to the sea, but he pressed on the completion of his own line from Delagoa Bay, trusting to the chances and changes of political events to open for him a way seaward.

V

Meanwhile the *Gold Discoveries* at Witwatersrand completely changed the aspect of affairs. Up to 1886 the Transvaal had been regarded as Boer land only—as the land of possibility rather than of realisation—

where, apart from a few struggling and sequestered townships, the only evidences of the white man's presence were the humble homesteads of Boer farmers sprinkled at wide distances from each other over a vast territory, mere specks of rudimentary civilisation in the void wilderness around

At that time Pretoria stood alone, an oasis of rustic urban life in the veldt. Heidelberg, some sixty miles distant, was the nearest village. Whispers of gold deposits were in the air, and men in quest of riches poked and tapped about rocky outcrops on the plains to the southward. Traces of the precious metal were sometimes found; owners of farms now and then fancied that Pactolus was within their reach, but disappointment supervened; prospecting was but languidly pursued; capital was lacking, and confidence was variable. The search for gold in quantity had gone on for nearly twenty years, with results that were quite incommensurate with the hopes that had been cherished and the interest displayed. Game still sported over the summer pastures, and the winds of winter swept unregarded across the silent plains.

Then all at once the discovery came. Geologists were confounded and experience was at fault. Gold was found in a new formation and under conditions that had no counterpart elsewhere. In the face of doubt, disbelief, and denial, the reefs of Witwatersrand were not only found to be gold-bearing but to be capable of enormous and highly lucrative develop-

ment. A new Golconda, surpassing all others in poten-
tialities of wealth, was found to exist. The richest
capitalists of the world hastened to participate in the
gains which stubborn colonial energy and enterprise
had opened up to view, and in a few years Johannesburg became the most active centre of mining energy
that mankind had witnessed. More than that, it became the busiest spot in South Africa; Capetown,
Kimberley, Durban, were all cast into the shade by
the hive of human industry and life that had sprung
up in the heart of the inland Boer Republic. In five
years the new city had become the chief objective of
colonial trade and statecraft, the goal of every South
African railway, the dominating interest of every class,
the supreme factor in legislation and policy. Its
markets were the first preoccupation of the commercial
mind, its share lists were the daily food of devouring
newspaper readers.

Nor was this circle of interest confined to South
Africa. It extended to every mart and exchange in
the world. In London, in Paris, in Berlin, in New
York, in Chicago, and in Melbourne — wherever men
speculated in stock, wherever money-making was a
pursuit—Johannesburg was a familiar name, and the
"Rand" a household word.

It is not my purpose here to describe the growth
and importance of Johannesburg. Many able pens
have dealt exhaustively with that theme. My aim
is simply to point out how great a revolution in South

African life and history was wrought by the development of Johannesburg as a centre of wealth and activity in the Boer Republic.

In the short space of twelve years the gold-fields of Witwatersrand passed from the condition of a virgin and barren wilderness to that of a throbbing and swarming community, with a European population of 60,000, a yearly gold output of 15 millions sterling, a trade of 12 millions irrespective of gold output, and an aspect which in architectural effect would vie with that of the larger cities of older lands. Up to the end of last year the total output of gold from the Rand mines amounted to the enormous aggregate of about 80 millions sterling.

This sudden outpouring of wealth revolutionised the situation. It altered the whole conditions of life not only in the Transvaal but in South Africa. For in the first place it set up a new standard of thought and effort. Wealth, rapidly acquired, became the absorbing idea and interest. To a certain, but only a limited, extent this tendency had already been generated by the diamond discoveries at Kimberley. Circumstances there, however, and especially the monopoly-creating policy pursued by Mr. Rhodes, had placed bounds upon the spread of speculation, and the feverish activities that prevailed prior to the consolidation of De Beer's, had largely subsided as the field of operation restricted itself. In the case of gold-mining, however, no such restraints or limitations existed. The opportunities of

the share market were open to the humblest operator.
Men and youths, women and maidens, all could have
a "flutter" : the merchant and the clerk, the employer
and the working-man, all could try their luck ; and
most of them did, until sad experience and burnt
fingers taught them the danger of the pastime. The
spirit of speculation, which is another name for the
lust of gold, seized hold of the community, and made
Johannesburg the Mecca to which, with but a few
exceptions, eyes and hearts were daily turned. It was
not a healthy nor an improving process, but it made
the Transvaal what it is now, the focus of interest and
anxiety to every South African. The completion of
railway communication only served to concentrate the
attention of the colonists and of visitors upon the
Republic. Cheap railway fares enabled folks from the
remotest centres to visit the place where fortunes
were made and lost, and to listen with their own ears
to the roar of the machines that were rifling from the
rocks their stored-up treasures.

Gold-mining revolutionised the public conditions of
society in South Africa not less effectively than it
influenced domestic and personal life. It produced an
immense expansion of trade. Imports sprang up from
a value of $8\frac{1}{2}$ millions in 1887 to 24 millions in 1897–98.
Exports bounded forward in the same period from $10\frac{1}{2}$
millions to 21 millions. The combined revenues of the
two colonies advanced from $4\frac{3}{4}$ millions to $9\frac{1}{2}$ millions.
I have already shown how completely the fiscal policy

of the whole country has been dominated by the requirements of the gold-fields trade.

If such were the effects produced upon the two British colonies by the eruption of wealth at Witwatersrand, the effects upon the Republic itself have been, as they were bound to be, not less startling and revolutionary. A community of impoverished and illiterate yeomen suddenly found itself placed in command of resources far in excess of anything which the wealthiest amongst them could have conceived or desired. In 1877, when Sir Theophilus Shepstone hoisted the British flag at Pretoria, the infant Republic was virtually penniless and bankrupt, without means to pay its officials or to discharge its debts, without credit and without friends. In 1887 the restored Republican Government still had difficulty in paying its way. In 1897 the revenue of the Republic had mounted to £4,480,218, and two years later it was estimated to have reached a considerably higher figure; almost as much as that of the whole Cape Colony.

How this great revenue had been contributed is far too wide a question for me to enter upon here. The inquiry may be said to cover the whole field of those grievances which were, until the war broke out, the main grounds of controversy. It is enough to point out that the revenue of the Republic has been almost entirely contributed by the gold industry, and by the people connected with it. Before gold was discovered the Government had little to tax, except the property of absentee holders, who at that time were more disposed to part with than to keep possessions that were productive only in burdens. The Boers themselves, with their meagre requirements, contributed next to nothing in the shape of customs duties, while such charges as they were subject to in the shape of quit-rents or railway tax were systematically evaded. With the production of gold and the acquisition of wealth by the Uitlanders, the state of poverty was all at once exchanged for a condition of revenue-earning abundance. Inspired by the astute advisers at their elbows, President Kruger and his associates found themselves possessed of unbounded opportunities for the amassment of national and private wealth. Taxation became easy where Value had acquired such abnormal proportions. Concessions and monopolies bringing grist to the State exchequer, and perquisites to intermediary pockets, were the proper outcome of a patriotic policy. A pious regard for the interests of "land and people" demanded that the riches pouring into the purses and safes of foreign harpies should pay toll to both. The precious metal had obviously been placed by Providence under the soil for the benefit of its possessors not less than of the Uitlanders to whose efforts any knowledge of its existence was due, and by whose skill and energy alone it had been extracted and brought to the surface. In the eyes of the religious-minded pastoralists, whose fathers had wandered into the Transvaal to find ampler grazing-ground and more abundant elbow-room, nothing seemed more righteous than that they should share in the profits of gold for which they had not delved, and of property in the way of whose development they had placed every sort of obstruction or difficulty.   It was through no fault or action of the Boers that the gold-fields became a power either for good or evil   Had President Kruger had his way in the first instance, the precious metal would have remained for all time buried in the rocks which formed its matrix.   There is reason to believe that he foresaw the evils that gold discovery would bring upon his country.   He dreaded the inrush of foreign population which the magnet would draw across his borders.   But when the consequences came—when the inevitable happened—he had no hesitation in turning to account the unsought advantages of the position.

Gold discoveries supplied Boer-Hollander aspirations with just the stimulus that had been lacking.   They transmuted vague and nebulous cravings into concrete and definite designs   If money is the root of all evil, it is also the source of all power.   Mr. Rhodes had already found it to be so, and President Kruger was not less fortunate.   Gold-mining and gold speculations meant profit to the State as well as individuals.   They meant unheard-of possibilities of revenue.   They meant stores of wealth far exceeding the modest dreams of Boer avarice.   They meant, under ingenious manipulation, a national income so large that undertakings,

2 A

otherwise chimerical and impracticable, were brought
within reach of realisation They enabled the Republic
to equip itself with the costliest armaments that
European skill and science could produce. They permitted the establishment on the spot of dynamite and
other factories which would make the inland State
independent if need be of the outer world for the
supply of coercive commodities. Explosives are necessary not only for purposes of defence or attack, but
for the very existence of mining operations.

Gold discoveries therefore worked mightily in two
directions on the destinies of the Transvaal. They
brought to the Republic wealth, population, capital,
credit, foreign activities, and the world's regard; but
they brought also to the Government of the Republic
temptations to corruption and extortion, to nepotism
and abuse, and an unlimited capacity to do anything,
to purchase anything, to pursue any policy or to gratify
any ambition, which unscrupulous counsels or deep-laid
designs might suggest. They provided the motive-
power by which the press might be suborned, opponents "squared," political influence extended, European
opinion controlled and guided, forts erected and equipped,
cannon and rifles imported, local forces organised, the
resources of intrigue and diplomacy employed without
regard to cost or limit. The long purse in these days
means both the long arm and the strong arm, and
in the case of a people ready at a day's notice to
take the field on the call of their Government—an

unpaid army of natural marksmen — nothing more was needed to make war a feasible and a promising adventure.

VI

The *Jameson Raid* was an incident of which the world has heard so much that it is only necessary to name it as the last factor in the course of events that have led up to the present war. Most of my readers, if not all, are acquainted with the story of an episode which is never mentioned without regret. Though much has been said and written on the subject, much has been left untold. It is probable that the whole story never will be told, and for this reason, that no one has known, or can know, the full truth of the matter. My belief is that the chief agents in the deplorable business hardly know, or ever knew, how events came to happen as they did. Things went wrong—the happenings were not what were intended. Whatever blame we may impute for what actually occurred — on whatever shoulders we place that blame—accident as well as design must be held culpable also.

In any case, however, taking events as they are on record, two conclusions appear to me beyond dispute. From the British point of view the Raid was alike deplorable and inexcusable, while from the Boer standpoint it was a stroke of fortune. And it was the one because it was the other.

Should any one be really responsible for the Raid,

he may take credit for having played into President
Kruger's hands as completely as that astute personage
could have desired.

If the Raid was a deliberately planned scheme, devised
to upset, or to assist in upsetting, by a sudden and secret
movement, the Government of the Republic, then it was
a gross political offence, and the more so because it was a
blunder. My conviction on this point is so strong that
I still find it impossible to believe that the British-born
Prime Minister of a great British colony could take the
leading part in such a plot, unknown to his colleagues
in the Ministry, unknown to the Queen's representative
in that Colony, unknown to the Queen's Government
at home

If the magnitude of an offence is to be measured by
its consequences, responsibility for the Raid cannot
easily be defined or meted out. It gave President
Kruger just the grievance and provocation he needed
as an incitement to his Volksraad and his burghers,
and as an excuse for wholesale measures of armament
and other precautionary preparations against future
incursions or attacks. It fanned the flame of republican hostility and defiance. Above all, it lowered the
good name of the British Crown and Government in
the eyes of the Africander population, and shattered
the better faith in both that was gradually arising in
the Boer mind. It undid the slow work of many years
—work that had borne fruit in Railway Conventions,
and fiscal agreements, in other arrangements for mutual

benefit between the republics and the colonies. This outgrowth of better feeling might not, perhaps, amount to more than an appearance on the part of the ruling clique, but that it did exist amongst the less hostile and self-seeking class of Boers was apparent in many ways Amidst the passions excited by the Raid and its results all these hopes of improved relations vanished

It is because these results were so manifestly inevitable that I cannot believe the Raid to have been a seriously planned or approved adventure on the part of any sane responsible statesman. It was a miserable business at the best, and filled with dismay all thinking and earnest colonists who had the interests of British rule in South Africa sincerely at heart Wherever responsibility for it may lie, the episode is best forgotten.

The champions of Republicanism and Boerdom are fond of attributing the Raid, the war, and all the other sufferings of South Africa to the combined influence of "Capitalism" and "Jingoism." These are parrot-words which must be taken just for what they are worth. By capitalism nothing more can be meant than is represented by the amazing developments of gold-mining industry at Witwatersrand and the contingent movements of speculation and finance It has been a new experience to Africanders to find their country the field and focus of speculative enterprise, and they may be excused if they exaggerate its character and effects. It is right, however, to point out that the forces of capitalism, in so far as this war is concerned, are by no means as extensive or influential as the spokesmen of the republics would have us believe. Many, if not the bulk, of the men who have most strenuously supported the policy of the Imperial Government in regard to the war have little to do with either gold speculation or gold-mining. I may be allowed, perhaps, to state that, speaking for myself, I have not, nor ever have had, the smallest interest in any mining stock or mining property, or speculative investment whatsoever. I know that my case is that of many others who share the views which I venture to express in these pages.

How far this may be the experience of those who denounce capitalism as the fountain and origin of evil in South Africa I must leave them to say. That gold developments have introduced into South African life an element of sordid interest which did not exist to that degree before, I have already admitted, but it has been the natural outworking of cause and effect, and the same influences were probably being exercised under other aspects and through other agencies. It does not rest with the Transvaal Republic to complain of an influence which it has so effectively utilised for its own ends and in its own interests.

Though the Boers of the Transvaal may not have worked mines, or raised companies, or operated in the share-market, they have sold or leased their farms, disposed of mining rights, found a lucrative sale for their produce, profitable employment for their waggons,

remunerative occupation for their sons; they have in
many cases participated in the spoils of the conces-
sionaire, and have not hesitated to benefit as fully
as opportunity might allow, or their own aptitudes
suggest, from the fruits of speculation or capitalism.
Their Government and leaders have squeezed the
sponge of occasion with a deftness that could not be
surpassed. The Treasury returns of the Republic
show how large a harvest has been reaped by both
from the field which the Uitlander has cultivated.
If capitalism be the curse that is so eloquently denounced and described by the stern champions of
republican virtue, it has at any rate filled to over-
flowing the coffers of the State, and literally supplied
the sinews of war to the militant organisers of invasion. Without the gold from which capitalism
springs there could have been no wholesale armament and fortification—no attempt to surprise and
sweep away British authority from British soil. Apart
from that gold the hope of European intervention,
which has been a corner-stone of Boer diplomacy,
would never have been cherished, as the attention of
Europe would have failed to notice in any appreciable
degree the obscure interests of a feeble pastoral State.

It will be seen that I have made little direct allusion to the grievances of the *Uitlanders* as a factor
in the South African situation. A year ago it would
have been impossible to write or to speak upon that
subject without regard or reference to the experiences

of Johannesburg. To-day any such obligation has ceased to exist, except by way of illustration The action of the republics in declaring war and in invading, occupying, and despoiling British territory has torn aside any necessity to vindicate the righteousness of the British cause. If a man suddenly knocks you down, you do not pause to ask him why he has done so, before you resort to self-defence. The grievances of the Uitlander are only of importance now in so far as they show how unfit the Republican Government has been to rule, and how impossible it is in the future for independent republicanism and British supremacy to exist side by side.

Before the war broke out there were many loyal and reasonable men in South Africa who believed it would be possible to leave the republics intact in their internal freedom, without danger to the comity of South Africa. They knew that so far as the Free State was concerned there was no cause of friction, grievance, or hostility; on the contrary, the relations of that State with the neighbouring colonies were marked by nothing but amity and good-will. They believed that in the Transvaal the Government would gradually, but in the end, make such concessions as would remove the just grievances of the Uitlander, and bring the Republic within the circle of a common South African policy and interest. They did not believe war to be possible, because they did not realise how inflated were the pretensions of the Boer leaders, how deep-rooted and intense their hostility to British ascendency.

The ultimatum of the two Presidents blew to the winds these optimistic illusions, and unmasked the true features of Africander policy. It was a timely though appalling revelation. Had it come a few weeks earlier, Natal would have been swept from the Drakenberg to Durban by the invader, and no one can say what the ultimate issue might have been. As it was, the action of the Natal Government in urging the introduction of more troops, the promptitude with which the Colonial Volunteers were sent to the front, and the speedy arrival of the Indian contingent, were instrumental in checking the invasion. Their experiences at Dundee and Elandslaagte shook the confidence of the invaders at the outset of operations, while the heroic defence of Ladismith kept the foe at bay during the critical period which ensued.

As soon as the first armed Boer crossed our border the whole situation was changed. Questions of franchise, language, police, taxation, sunk out of sight. The struggle for supremacy or mastery between Boer and Briton began. Shall the Empire or the Republic prevail in the future control of South African destinies? Shall the Anglo-African or the Dutch-Africander mould the life of the coming nationality? Shall a century of civilising effort and labour go for nought as a title to just dominion? Shall the mighty mission of Great Britain as the mother of free, tolerant, justly ruled and wisely ordered confederacies throughout the world be wrecked by the folly and blind prejudices of a few misguided men ? These are the issues for which the forces and citizens of a whole empire have been fighting in South Africa. The misrule of the few, the happiness of the many? That is the alternative. There is not a Boer in Natal or the Cape Colony— there is not one acquainted with the truth in either of the republics—who does not know and feel that British rule as now exercised in both colonies is free, is generous, is just: that under the British flag the Dutch colonist enjoys just as fully and as freely the rights of citizenship as he does under the Vierkleur. But he shares them with others. He does not keep them to himself. He is not governed by an oligarchy. He is not the member of a privileged caste. There lies the difference, it is vital, and because it is so the two races are at war

CHAPTER XII

THE OUTLOOK

Any forecast of the future in South Africa must be contingent upon the outcome of the war. That is the obvious and absolute condition-precedent of all calculations or predictions. Unless the supremacy of the British Empire be established throughout South Africa, and the two republics be incorporated as parts of that Empire, any forecast worth consideration is impossible. A settlement that should fall short of such a result would have neither stability nor permanence. A peace which should leave the republics intact as independent States would be nothing more than a truce, lasting just as long as circumstances might delay the operations of intrigue, or the opportunity of renewed explosion. But before British supremacy can be deemed established, before republicanism has disappeared, the war has to be pressed on to a victorious conclusion. Not only has British territory to be freed from the invader's presence; not only has the British flag to be hoisted at Pretoria, but the republics have to be absorbed, pacified, and controlled. Those are the primary and pressing obligations of the moment. Until they are fulfilled, it seems to me that serious talk about

terms and settlements is presumptuous and premature.

My aim in the foregoing pages has been to show, perhaps too briefly and suggestively, that Great Britain's
claim to supremacy in South Africa rests upon her conquests in peace not less than upon her conquests in war
and her rights of cession. I have striven to show that
the British colonists who hold the seaboard and occupy
all the seaports, and who, in Natal, have spread themselves over the whole country, have even a stronger
claim to be regarded as sons of the soil, as dwellers
in the land, than have the Boers or Dutch-Africander
settlers, by reason of their superior energy and success
in utilising the resources of that soil, and in turning the
gifts of nature to account. I have indicated what their
early struggles and sacrifices as pioneers have been,
how they have fought against, and striven with the
savage for mastery of the land; how patiently they have
built up a free government and worked out a fabric of
just and equal law; how they have stamped the impress
of their life, their race, and their character upon the
conditions of the country. I have reviewed the efforts
made by the colonists to establish friendly and cordial
relations with their neighbours, and to spread the bless-
ings and agencies of civilisation into the far interior.
And I have proved by demonstrated facts how merciful,
indulgent, and acceptable has been Anglo-Colonial rule
over the native races both within and beyond the
Colony My only regret is that limitations of time

and strength have interfered with the fuller and more satisfactory accomplishment of this purpose.

The righteousness of Great Britain's claim to control the destinies of South Africa is based, therefore, upon these grounds :—

Right of conquest a century ago.

Payment to Holland for rights ceded in 1814.

Refusal at any time to relinquish supremacy.

Successive wars waged to suppress rebellion, to repel invasion, and to maintain authority.

Steadfast maintenance of just government, of un-corrupt administration, of security for person, property, law, and order.

Concession, stage by stage, of free, self-governing institutions.

Absolute equality of citizenship to all men of European origin.

Active industrial occupation of the soil; commercial expansion, and complete freedom of enterprise, unclogged by legal barriers and restrictions.

Development of social life in all its branches.

Cheerful acceptance by, and submission of, all the aboriginal inhabitants.

Railway extension, harbour improvement, and road construction, at the cost, almost exclusively, of colonial tax-payers.

An indebtedness to foreign creditors of thirty-three millions.

These are the title-deeds by which the Empire holds sovereignty in South Africa, and in defence of which it is now spending sixty millions of money and thousands of lives in the war that has, when I write, yet to terminate.

Such a war can have but one ending, if the British Empire is to remain a concrete fact and not a humbling memory. Taking that postulate for granted, what is the outlook to be? The answer must depend, of course, upon the wisdom of the course that may be followed, upon the character of the counsels that shall prevail. If the policy pursued be wise and temperate, if the measures adopted be far-reaching and curative, we may face the future with reasonable confidence and hope. The danger is that momentary impulses or hasty action may bear fruit in renewed collapse and ultimate disaster.

To some extent, no doubt, the war may have affected the relations of the belligerent races and modified the conditions of the past: but, generally speaking, the needs of South Africa remain very much what they were before a shot was fired, and while the grievances of the Uitlander formed the ostensible cause of contention. I see no reason to modify the view held by me after the Raid, and publicly expressed, to the effect that the future of South Africa seemed then to be governed by a threefold condition, namely, that no one man should be dominant in South Africa; that no one State should be dominant in South Africa, and that there should be no subordination of the destinies of South Africa to speculative or sordid interests. Above all was it imperative that South Africa should remain under the ægis of the freest and greatest Empire that the world had ever seen. Should that ægis be withdrawn, South Africa will become the battle-ground of revolutionaries and rivalries, and bloodshed and misery will be the lot of the inhabitants.

If these conditions were indispensable then, they are not less so now. It is rather the fashion in certain quarters to speak of monocracy as a salutary system of rule. Benevolent despots, it is true, have at times figured as the saviours of society. In most cases, however, they are the offspring of anarchic and revolutionary conditions. These do not really exist in South Africa. The present commotions are of external or adventitious origin. Their occurrence is due to the existence of the two republics and to the hostile foreign influences operating therein. We want no tyrannic or masterful personalities to mould our destinies, or to refashion our system of government. Both Mr. Rhodes and President Kruger have, each in his own sphere, exercised a dominating force; but it cannot be said that the results commend the experience. If such an influence be exercised at all, it should be in conjunction with the recognised co-operation of others as a responsible constitutional factor openly directed. South Africa needs a Washington rather than a Cromwell at the head of affairs; but, more than all, she needs a central, supreme, and representative authority, and that can best and, as I believe, can only be supplied by the creation of a Federal Government, under the shield of the Empire.

Before the war broke out I expressed my conviction that there could be no guarantee of permanent peace in the future unless the Transvaal were brought under control as member of a South African Confederation, subject as regards the obligations of defence, and general principles of rule, to the obligations and restraints that would bind all the constituent States. In other words the Transvaal must be placed under terms to the rest of South Africa, for the preservation of peace and order, and for the abolition of all inequalities of citizenship.

Any one State fortified and armed as the Transvaal has been, and governed as the Republic was by an oligarchy and a caste, must be an intolerable menace to its neighbours. Its existence would be a chronic peril to the rest of South Africa, a continuous threat to British supremacy, and a fatal bar to union. Were any other State to acquire a similar position of predominancy, whether it be Cape Colony, Natal, the Free State, or Rhodesia, its existence would be equally pernicious.

Union undoubtedly is the only true solvent of South African difficulties, but it must be union based upon equality—equality of citizenship, equality of representation, equality of influence, interests, and law, on the part of every component community.

This equality can, I believe, be only secured, in exist-

ing circumstances, under the British flag It may be,
as time goes on, that that flag may come to be distinguished and individualised as an Anglo-African flag,
just as in the order of events the flags of Canada,
and Australia, will bear some token of national existence—just as the flags of Great Britain, whether Royal
Standard, or Union Jack, or British Ensign, symbolise
the union of the three kingdoms. It may be that when
the federalisation of Greater Britain is completed, when
the Commonwealth of Australia and the Confederation
of South Africa take their place as actual entities by
the side of the Dominion of Canada, a new Imperial
standard will be devised and accepted, one that shall
not only comprehend the self-governing colonies of the
Empire, but the great Indian Empire as well. This
last suggestion may, I submit, be among the possibilities
of the future For myself I am quite content with the
old flag as it is, but then I am British-born, and generations that are already born and to be born, on distant
continents, may rightly yearn to see their own lands
betokened on the flag of a common Empire—an Empire
in whose traditions they proudly share, and to whose
greatness they would fain contribute.

Union therefore appears to be the only effective and
abiding safeguard against future trouble. How is it to
be brought about? Is union possible after so terrible
a clash of races? Is there any reasonable hope of racial
amalgamation after so furious an outburst of lethal
antagonism? Is it possible that two races that have

2 B

been clutching each other's throats in deadly earnest through so many months of battle can forget their strivings, can control their animosities sufficiently, to work together all at once as subjects of the same government, as citizens of the same country? The answer to these questions must depend upon the steps taken to bring about reconciliation, and the manner in which these measures are carried out.

I am told by those who know him best that the Boer is by instinct and belief very much a fatalist in his philosophy and impulses. He sees the working of God in all things, and it is this disposition that has nerved him to so stubborn a resistance in the field. Past events have strengthened him in the habit. Imperial vacillations and failures have contributed to the conviction that the Almighty is on his side. His own successes in the war served to fan the faith that has been so sedulously fostered by the fulminations and the assurances of his rulers and his advisers.

When the fortunes of war go disastrously against him, when the two republics have gradually been subjugated and pacified; when victory is conspicuously and signally on the other side; when, in a word, he is beaten and his country conquered, my informants feel confident that his attitude will change—his hostility collapse, his opposition disappear. Providence having forsaken him, he will yield to the inevitable, and submit, sullenly perhaps, but silently to whatever order of things may be established.

I speak, of course, of the Boer proper—the Dutch Republican Africander, the descendant of the Voertrekkers or his kinsmen—not of the many mixed allies, the foreign adherents or recreant colonists, who have ranged themselves under the Boer flag, and fought in the Boer ranks. They will instinctively fall in, as far as they are allowed to do, with the winning side, with the dominant power, and may at no distant date be found amongst the most eager upholders of British supremacy and Anglo-African rule. Their part as factors in the future need not trouble us

The Boer himself, however, is the man we have mostly to consider in the outlook. As to the colonists, the men of British birth or extraction, they are all of one mind and purpose. Whatever may best promise to consolidate and promote British supremacy and Anglo-African unity will be supported by them. That, too, I believe will be the attitude and desire of the German, American, and Scandinavian elements in the community. They have learnt by experience in the two colonies how liberal and just is the Government of the Empire, under colonial conditions. If they are birds of passage they know that under that Empire they have the fullest security for their commercial, financial, or industrial operations If they desire to root themselves to the soil, and aspire to become citizens of the community, they know that they can do so under the British flag as easily and as freely as though they were British-born, by the simple and almost nominal process of naturalisation.

The Africander, on the other hand, is not only a fixture on the soil and the offspring of it; he is also, and must for many years continue to be, a conspicuous if not a controlling figure in its population. If the whole European population of South Africa be counted together, his race is numerically preponderant. That proportion will diminish as time goes on, and as immigrants flow in from other lands, under the benignant influences of a strong and stable government, but for the present the balance of heads is on the side of the Africander, except in the larger towns, in Natal, on the Rand, and in Rhodesia. Of that majority a very large number are landholders, the owners and the occupants of farms which in point of acreage would be regarded elsewhere as considerable estates. Such a community can in no sense be disregarded or ignored. It cannot be dealt with as a proscribed and disinherited race. It cannot as a whole be disqualified from civil rights by any sweeping or summary process of disfranchisement. Individuals, of course, may and ought to suffer special disabilities. All who have been proved to have been in open rebellion ought to be deprived, for a time at least, of their electoral privileges. Convicted leaders of rebellion, or secret fomentors of sedition and strife, will have to bear the proper penalties of their crimes. If their culpability be measured by the mischief they have wrought, it would be difficult to overestimate their blameworthiness. But most of the offenders have been duped, misled, betrayed, or intimidated. They have yielded to persuasion or pressure. They have been blinded and led astray by false shepherds. They are victims, probably, in part of inherited prejudices, but most certainly of ignorance and misrepresentation—in many cases of coercion. Nor must we ever forget the atmosphere of race feeling and traditional antipathy in which these people have been brought up. It would be fatal permanently to estrange and alienate them. They have to be conciliated and incorporated into the future body politic by a wise and far-sighted policy, dictated far more by the interests of the future than by the impulses and passions of the moment.

If we survey history we shall find that only by such a policy have popular gashes been healed, great nationalities built up, and wars made fruitful in happier and enduring dispensations The story of the United Kingdom is one long record of such a process. Saxons and Normans, Yorkites and Lancastrians, Royalists and Roundheads, Jacobites and Loyalists, Highlanders and Lowlanders, all show us that in the end contending factions find it possible to coalesce and join hands in the support of a common sovereignty, and the unification of a common race The experiences of Germany, of Italy, of Spain, of Switzerland all tell the same tale Our Indian Empire is a grand example of such a policy and purpose. Most significant and instructive of all, however, is the lesson which the great American War of Secession teaches us, that a long war, a desperate war, a war costing hundreds of thousands of lives, many

millions of treasure, and untold sacrifices and sufferings
on both sides, may be followed a few years later by the
spectacle of a united and compacted people, free from
any traces of fermenting discord or revolt.

Not less suggestive and admonitory is the evidence
that the more decisive and complete the success of
the victor and the overthrow of the vanquished, the
fuller is the assurance of future peace and concord
Wars that are inconclusive, in which "honours are
divided," seldom close the game. What South Africa
wants, now, is finality, and that can only be secured
by the present triumph of British arms, by the undis-
puted establishment of British supremacy, and by the
early confederation of South Africa as a self-governing
community under the British flag.

Lord Roberts may be trusted to fulfil the first of
these conditions; the Imperial Government will not fail
to provide for the second, and the co-operation of South
African intelligence with Imperial statesmanship must
avail to secure the third.

I lay great stress upon the last of these requirements,
inasmuch as without it any prospect of a truly abiding
settlement seems dark indeed. The chief mainstay of
the British Empire in South Africa must be found in
the acceptance and attachment of the people. To rely
on force only would be to rely on a pliant reed. Were
British supremacy to be attacked again in South Africa
it would not be, as now, at a time when the whole forces
of a united Empire could be directed to these shores.

It would be at a moment when the Empire might be menaced or assailed by foreign powers; when the mother country would need all her land forces to protect her own coasts from invasion; when the other colonies would be called upon to hold their own at home; when the services of the navy would be urgently required in many far-divided seas. Anglo-Africa would have largely to trust to its own resources for the protection of its loyal inhabitants from any perils of insurrection or disturbance.

It is only through the medium of a common government that those resources can be properly organised and directed. No doubt it would be possible for each territory to maintain its own defensive organisation, but the result would be fragmentary and disjointed. We have seen what splendid results can be achieved by a relatively small body of men, when acting in concert in support of a common cause, and as parts of a common, homogeneous system. We have to reproduce the same results on a larger scale, and under a not less inspiring impulse. What the Boers have done for republicanism, we have to do for Anglo-Africa. We have to effect a change of centres; to give the Africander a new centre of gravity, to enlist his sympathies, not less than his assistance, in the cause of law and order, of freedom and of Imperial unity.

It is obvious that to do this we must give the Africander a government that he not only fears and obeys, but loves, trusts, cherishes, and is proud of—

a government which represents to him no sense of grievance or deprivation—a government that is large enough and free enough to satisfy his national and patriotic aspirations, and yet strong enough to make its authority felt and respected.

Such a government the mother country has; such an one, too, has Canada and Australia; such an one had the Cape Colony and Natal before the virus of hostile republicanism poisoned the minds of some, at any rate, of the Dutch inhabitants. Even now we hear in Natal a Dutch colonist, a descendant of the Voertrekkers, declaring vehemently again and again, at a Farmers' Conference, that there is not a disloyal Dutchman in his own county, always regarded, hitherto, as a hotbed of covert Boer disaffection Believe him or not as we may, his voluntary outburst means neither more nor less than his consciousness that the lot of a British colonist in Natal is preferable to any other.

That is the feeling we have to foster and to spread. Self-interest is proverbially one of the strongest motives in controlling human action. The Boer must be made more and more to feel that he has all to lose and nothing worth getting to gain by hostility to British supremacy. He must be taught to consider his lot as a citizen of the Empire the surest guarantee of his personal security and political liberty. As a matter of fact both Mr. Froude and President Brand recognised this truth when the one insisted upon the retention of the Cape peninsula as a necessary condition of his

policy of withdrawal, and when the other made the
protection of the seaboard by Great Britain a cardinal
condition in any scheme of a United South Africa
Before he became intoxicated by the thirst of power
President Kruger himself professed his belief in British
supremacy. For a century that supremacy has been
exercised, and it is a familiar idea to every Africander,
or rather a fact to which he has been accustomed from
his earliest days. Its existence is a lesson which he
has not to be taught anew.

If the war has been waged in order to maintain that
supremacy, the Boer knows that the challenge to uphold
it came from his own leaders. They prepared for the
war, they began it, they continued it. They invaded
and appropriated British territory, and shot down
British soldiers on British soil simply because they
stood in their way, and fought to protect British homes
and British territory from invasion, spoliation, and
outrage. This action on the part of the Boers has
placed them out of court as pleaders of provocation
and wrong, but it has given British representatives a
weapon of overwhelming power as the agents of a
policy of generosity, forbearance, and moderation in
the treatment of conquered foes.

Whatever may be said to the contrary by Boer
leaders or Boer sympathisers, it is out of their power
to fasten upon either the Empire or the colonies the
blame of blood-guiltiness. That might have been possible had war followed upon the heels of the Raid, and

it cannot be doubted that the fact weighed mightily
with all Imperial and colonial statesmen who were
responsible for the conduct of affairs through that
critical period. No such possibility exists now. The
Home Government and its representatives carried forbearance throughout subsequent negotiations to the
point of peril, and in the end were found disastrously
unprepared for the contingency of war. The two
Colonial Governments have all through shown the
greatest anxiety that peace should remain unbroken.
The hope and effort of all have been centred in a
bloodless settlement of outstanding grievances, in an
amicable adjustment of the claims of the Uitlander, in
the peaceful recognition of British supremacy.

The republics, with their allies in the colonies, have
to thank the infatuation and folly of their own leaders
for the issue they invoked, with all its consequences.
They rushed to the ordeal of battle, and they must
abide by the results. They unmasked their arms and
revealed their forces. They not only challenged the
Empire to a trial of strength, but they began the
struggle without a pause. Some of their forces were
across the border even before the time named in the
ultimatum had passed. And they knew what in that
event to expect.

In 1896 the Prime Minister of Natal said to a deputation of three leading Dutch colonists, who waited
upon him in connection with public affairs, that whatever views might be held by the Colonial Government

concerning the Raid and its causes, nothing was more
certain than that any invasion of the colonial frontier
by so much as half or a quarter of a mile would be
resisted by that Government with every resource at
its command. What was done therefore in 1899 by
another Ministry, when the volunteers of the Colony
went to the front on a day's notice, was the effective
fulfilment of the pledge given three years earlier
Whatever may have been the case as regards the
Cape Colony, the Boers have had no reason to suppose
that any actual invasion of Natal territory would not
be strenuously resisted by both the Empire and the
colonists.

The chasm opened by the war between the two races
was the work of republican intrigue and hostility. It
has now to be bridged and closed by the strenuous
co-operation of Imperial and South African representatives in striving for a common end—the fusion of the
races and the unification of the country. That must be
the objective of all. I fail to see what hope there can
be for South Africa as a place of abode for peace-loving
and order-seeking men on any other basis. It may
at this moment seem a difficult if not impracticable
undertaking. While the reek of war is in the air, and
passions bred by deadly strife are still seething, it may
seem folly to talk of racial amity and political union.
But peace must come in time, and it will be peace
based upon righteous victory, upon the overthrow of
a spurious and militant republicanism, and the estab-

lishment of constitutional freedom under the British flag.

This is neither the place nor the time to discuss the methods by which such a settlement is to be secured. When the war is over and resistance is at an end, terms and conditions can be considered. The task, moreover, is not to be performed by individuals. It must be undertaken by duly qualified representatives acting in concert under Imperial guidance. It must be entered upon in a calmer atmosphere than can be looked for as long as active hostilities are proceeding. All that is proper now is to suggest such principles of action as appear to be elementary and unavoidable. I venture to name the following :—

1. British, or Imperial, supremacy throughout the whole of South Africa, apart from German and Portuguese possessions.

2. South African autonomy on the basis of South African confederation.

3. The early establishment of a Central Government, in which each constituent province of the Confederation shall be proportionately represented.

4. Such a readjustment of provincial boundaries as shall leave the least chance of jar or friction between neighbouring communities.

5. The establishment of a common franchise open to all who have been used to exercise an elective franchise in the past, or who may not have been specially disqualified.

6. The absolute control by the Central Government of all measures connected with defence.

7. The effective punishment or disqualification of proved and prominent leaders or abettors of rebellion, and the exercise of a judicious and generous clemency towards all who have not been found guilty of pillage and outrage.

Other questions may confidently be left to the decision and discretion of statesmen and representatives. The framework of a suitable constitution may already be found outlined in the Dominion Act, the Commonwealth Act, and the South Africa Act, and if further examples be needed they can be found in the constitutions of Switzerland, Italy, and the United States. No lack of material need hamper the efforts of constitutional draftsmen. When once the main lines to be followed are agreed upon, all else will follow in due course. Solidity, permanence, and acceptability are the three conditions of success. Temporary or provisional expedients will only postpone an effort which will get more difficult as time goes on. Confederation has been talked about in South Africa for more than forty years. Sir George Grey proposed it in 1859. Had it been agreed to then there would have been no war to-day. Had Sir Bartle Frere's policy been suffered to proceed unthwarted twenty years later, South Africa would have been at rest years ago. In no part of the Empire are delays more dangerous than in South Africa. Again and again they have made shipwreck of possibilities

and hopes. The supreme opportunity for action has
now arrived. The Empire has asserted itself by a
majestic demonstration of its might and its resources.
Let it now establish itself immovably by a not less
imposing and impressive manifestation of purpose and
policy—of a visible resolve to hold South Africa as a
part of the Anglo-Saxon heritage, as a member of that
family of freemen whose rights are the envy of the
human race.

Peace, order, and unity—let these prevail, and no one
can limit the possibilities of expansion in this land of
struggle and misfortune. South Africa in the past may
have been a region of disappointment and regret, but
under those happier auspices she will have abounding
sources of hope for the future. Her endowments are
mighty and manifold. She has a commanding position
in the southern seas, as the dividing continent between
east and west. Her climate is pure, healthful, and in
the main exhilarating. Her vast plains, though arid
now, only need irrigation, as experience has proved, to
become generously fruitful. The garden lands of the
eastern seaboard are naturally fertile. Her pastoral
resources are capable of enormous development. In
mineral resources her wealth is incalculable and un-
surpassed. Diamonds and gold, iron and coal, to say
nothing of copper and other baser metals, are all parts
of the splendid inheritance which nature has blessed her
with. These are the roots of her material prosperity,
but she has other riches as well. The patriotic spirit

of her sons, no matter how misapplied on one side, has been proved by service and sacrifice in the field Her people, whether British or Dutch in origin, whether white or black, love their country, and are ready to fight in its defence They are industrious, domestic, religious-minded—in varying degree, perhaps, as in all communities, but sufficiently so to promise a worthy type of national character in the future. Above all they have been tried in the fire, and have learnt through affliction and adversity the futility of mad ambitions, the value of settled peace. I may be wrong in my forecast, and too confident in my hopes, but even at this moment, while the tragic drama is still in course of enactment, and the end of it yet out of view, I am fain to believe that with the dawning century we can welcome the near approach of a better time.

APPENDIX

THE RETURN OF SIR BARTLE FRERE

(From the "Times," October 6, 1880.)

CAPE TOWN, *Sept.* 15.

EVER since the tidings of his recall spread over South Africa, there has been a widespread and spontaneous outburst of feeling on the part of colonists against the injustice done to Sir Bartle Frere and the injury inflicted upon the country by his removal. There is not a town or district of any importance that has not borne testimony to his devoted and sagacious administration of affairs throughout a period of unprecedented trouble and difficulty. Cape Town and Port Elizabeth, Graham's Town and East London, Graaf Reinet and King William's Town, Kimberley, Pietermaritzburg, and Durban, Natal, besides a host of minor places, have all expressed the indignation and sorrow excited by the treatment he has received, and the valedictory addresses, some sixty-five in number, which have poured in upon him form such a tribute of popular sympathy as has rarely been received by any Governor.

On Monday Sir Bartle Frere held an informal *levée*, which was attended by all the leading citizens. In the afternoon a reception was held by the Misses Frere on behalf of Lady Frere, who unfortunately was prevented from being present owing to serious indisposition. Never was Government House so crowded, between 500 and 600 persons being present. In the course of the afternoon the Hon. Mr.

2 C

Robinson, M.L.C., from Natal, presented an address from that colony signed by 5000 of its inhabitants. In presenting it, Mr. Robinson said that he did so as the representative of the whole community moved by one impulse and bound by one purpose. He said that the reason of this unanimity was to be found in the fact that his Excellency recognised in all its fulness and intensity the dangers of the position into which Natal had drifted, not by its own action, not by its own will—for it had neither free action nor free will in the matter—but by reason of political measures and processes over which the colonists had had no control any more than Sir Bartle Frere. While in Natal they looked to union chiefly as the means of achieving an end which would be on broad grounds immensely to the advantage of South Africa at large, so they looked to participating in free, self-governing institutions as the only means by which they could allow themselves to enter upon any plan of political copartnership. Sir Bartle Frere had sustained the parent colony in its laudable aspiration to become a great self-governing State. He had stimulated Natal into claiming for itself the control of its own affairs. He had assisted in the task of bringing Griqualand West within the pale of self-government. He had urged upon the people of the Transvaal the importance of qualifying themselves for the restoration of constitutional privileges. But he had done more than that, he had taught them to look on South Africa as a whole, he had sought to widen their political vision and to raise their political contemplations. He had shown them that, whether they lived in the shadow of Table Mountain or under the frown of the distant Drakensberg, they were linked together by ties as strong and high and continuous and enduring as is the mighty mountain chain which binds these points together. Abiding peace and abiding safety had been the watchwords of Sir Bartle Frere's policy. His Excellency had been with them through the dark days of the Zulu War, and when he left them—though the immediate danger was past, though reinforcements were already pouring in—there was a feeling that they had lost the presence of one whose firm and calm judgment was of as much use as an element of confidence as regiments of infantry or squadrons of cavalry. Mr. Robinson concluded a powerful speech by saying that he presented the address together with a very handsome casket for its safe custody, in the name of the colonists of Natal, whose present safety his Excellency had purchased at a cost regardless of himself; and in the names of the loyal natives of Natal, who, when they looked towards Zululand, saw no longer there a power which once they deemed superior to our own. He said he spoke with certain knowledge when he said her Majesty's 400,000 native subjects in Natal regarded Sir Bartle Frere as their benefactor and their friend; and he entreated his Excellency to remember that wherever his lot might be cast, or whatever position of high Imperial usefulness he might be called upon to occupy, there would ever be among the scattered homesteads and the far separated townships in the distant Colony of Natal a tender cherishing of his name, and a prayerful hope that to him and his might come in God's abounding time all that their reverend love and dutiful gratitude could seek or could crave for him.

His Excellency replied as follows :—

" I thank you very sincerely for the kind terms in which you have been good enough to speak in presenting this address from the inhabitants of Natal. I have already, in my reply by telegraph to the first notice of the meeting at which the address was voted, stated how deeply I felt this testimony of their good opinion. I believe it is from no mere feeling of gratified vanity that I value the opinions to which you have given expression. There were none in South Africa who could estimate as the inhabitants of Natal could the reality of the facts which were before us when I took a step likely to be of very momentous consequences,

not only to myself personally and to all parts of South
Africa, but more especially to the Colony of Natal. We
acted then, as I need not remind you, in the presence of
what we believed to be a great and imminent danger. Our
action has been challenged since then on the broad ground
that no such danger existed. You, however, in Natal, with
all the facts before you and the means of estimating them
at their right value, believed that the danger existed, and
that no other steps were possible for the security of life
and property in the Colony than those which were then
taken. As to what was in the mind of the King of the
Zulus at that time, and as to the real motives which actu-
ated me in the course we then took, it is hardly possible
that more should be known with any certainty in this life;
but there were patent facts—facts which made the action
we took either a great service or a great crime—of which
most people in Natal who had their eyes and ears open to
what went on around them, and who were acquainted with
the history of the Colony, could not but be competent judges;
and I, therefore, greatly value your verdict on the occasion.
I hope that what was done during those terrible days of
the early part of 1879 have made life and property more
secure throughout your Colony and, indeed, in regions far
beyond it. I do not envy the Englishman who can visit
the valley of the Tugela and the scenes of the massacres
which took place in Weenen County, in the Bluekrantz and
Bushman's River valleys, within living memory, and who
could then turn aside and be at rest while it was possible
that such scenes might be repeated. I trust they can never
now recur, and that in days to come the subjects of her
Majesty, of every race and colour, may enjoy the fruits of
their own industry in those beautiful valleys, and may sleep
in perfect peace and security, such as they certainly did not
feel when I first set foot in Natal. For Zululand, also, I
trust what has been done has not been without good results.
It never was any part of my wish nor my duty to dictate

to the Zulus regarding their own form of government, further than was essential to the safety of our British fellow-subjects, their near neighbours in Natal and the Transvaal It is no part of my duty now, or in this place, to pass opinions on things as they are now in Zululand. I can only speak of things as I found them, when the crisis which had been long preparing arrived It seems to me a simple perversion of fact to speak of things as they then existed in Zululand as tolerable under any form of government. Whatever may be the shortcomings of the present system, it is certainly a vast improvement to have taken place in less than two years; and, what is more, it is a state of things which admits of yet further indefinite improvement, till every man in Zululand is able to enjoy life and the property which he may acquire with the same security as in Natal itself. It is a great question whether the Zulus will be happier left to their own devices, to their own superstitions and customs, ruled as they are now, with at least the power of acquiring the knowledge which has produced such marvellous results on the people of our own country. I myself have never felt any doubt as to which form of life the Zulus themselves would in the long run prefer , but the great struggle between barbarism and civilisation has now come in Zululand to this point, that it is at least possible for any Zulu to choose for himself with some degree of freedom, under which form of existence he would live. I hope the gentlemen who signed this address will be assured of the earnestness with which I return their good wishes for the future. For the Colony at large, I can wish you no better than that degree of self-government which has been for some years conceded to this Colony, and for which I feel assured, from what I saw of Natal and its inhabitants, your Colony is perfectly prepared and well fitted. I trust that your own brief stay among us will have given you the same impression that my longer stay here has given to me, that there can be no doubt as to the entire adaptation of the political institutions we have here to the country in which we are living. Imperfect those institutions may be, like all human inventions, but they have the great virtue of self-governing institutions, that they are capable of expansion and perfection to any extent desired by those who live under them, provided they seek such expansion and improvement by reasonable and legitimate means. In one respect I have found the institutions of the country as regards our native fellow-subjects in advance of any with which I am acquainted elsewhere. It is in the power of any native in the Cape Colony to rise politically and socially to any eminence for which his education and intellectual and moral qualities may fit him. Obstacles, formidable obstacles, there will always be of race and colour, but they are not insuperable. Which of us here present belongs to a nation so favoured that he may not at some time of his life have found when he leaves his own home that his race or nationality, of which he is justly proud, has been to him a disadvantage among associates of other races. Even Englishmen, who are so favoured by fortune in these respects, well know that there is no special charm to secure a man either political or social eminence, irrespective of his own intrinsic merits, and when this is once recognised, when we feel that it is not by hedging a people round with exceptional privileges (always carrying as they do some exceptional disabilities), it is not by petting or by patronising this or that race that we can raise them to a higher level—when we practically recognise the truth that the only process is to afford to other races the same advantages which we ourselves have enjoyed for so many ages, perfect equality before the law, equal political rights, to all who will labour for and earn them a fair field and no favour; when these truths are practically recognised and acted on, we shall have made a great step towards obliterating all invidious distinctions of race or class, so far as to enable any man of every race or colour to rise as high as his own personal merits may deserve.

I trust you will carry back with you to Natal not only my own assurance, but a conviction of your own, that one great element of progress in these colonies is to be found in a closer union of each State with its fellows. It is only thus that you can realise the full advantages of your position, and free the mother country from the responsibilities of parental management, the necessity for which you have, I believe, so far outgrown. I feel certain that among the inhabitants of Natal this conviction will not be coupled with any insensibility to the great honour and privilege of forming a part of one of the foremost empires of the world. It is because you and your fellow-colonists here are offshoots from the great self-governed natives of Northern Europe that you desire to be self governed here, and that you would not willingly have serfs or slaves for your fellow-subjects. It is because of this feeling identical with our name, and crystallised and enshrined in the idea of the British Crown and Empire, that the nation of which your Colony is one of the offshoots is among the foremost nations of the world. For myself personally I would ask you to return my warm and hearty thanks to those who concurred in the address for their good wishes. It is not in the nature of things that I should be spared to see very much of what is in store for your rising Colony, but my best wishes will ever be given for your prosperity, and I hope that hereafter, when Natal is a branch of a great South African dominion, some one diving into the records of the past may light on the name of one who did not in his day escape bitter censure for doing what he and you believed was his simple duty, but who, the historian may think, did some good service for the permanent peace and security of his fellow-subjects in this part of the great South African continent."

INDEX OF NAMES

THE END

Printed by BALLANTYNE, HANSON & Co
Edinburgh & London